Freytag's Technique of the Drama: An Exposition of Dramatic Composition and Art

Gustav Freytag, Translated by Elias J. MacEwan

BIBLIOBAZAAR

FREYTAG'S

ECHNIQUE OF THE DRAM.

AN EXPOSITION OF DRAMATIC
COMPOSITION AND ART

BY

DR. GUSTAV FREYTAG

AN AUTHORIZED TRANSLATION FROM THE SIXTH GERMAN EDITION

BY

ELIAS J. MACEWAN, M.A.

SECOND EDITION.

CHICAGO
S. C. GRIGGS & COMPANY
1896

CONTENTS.

BIOGRAPHICAL NOTE. - - - - - vii–ix

INTRODUCTION.—Technique of the drama not absolute. Certain craftsman's skill of earlier times. Condition of present time. Aristotle's Poetics. Lessing. The great dramatic works as models. - - - - - 1–8

CHAPTER I.—DRAMATIC ACTION.

1. THE IDEA.—How the drama originates in the mind of the poet. Development of the idea. Material and its transformation. The historian and the poet. The range of material. Transformation of the real, according to Aristotle. - - - - - - - 9–18

2. WHAT IS DRAMATIC?—Explanation. Effects. Characters. The action. The dramatic life of the characters. Entrance of the dramatic into the life of men. Rareness of dramatic power. - - - - - - - 19–27

3. UNITY.—The Law. Among the Greeks. How it is produced. How the unity of historical material is not secured. False unity. Where dramatic material is to be found. The character in the modern drama. Counter-play and its danger. Episodes. - - - - - 27–49

4. PROBABILITY.—What is probable. Social effects of the drama. The strange. The marvellous. Mephistopheles. The irrational. Shakespeare and Schiller. - 49–61

5. IMPORTANCE AND MAGNITUDE.—Weakness of characters. Distinguished heroes. Private persons. Degrading the art. - - - - - - - 61–66

6. MOVEMENT AND ASCENT.—Public actions. Inward struggles. Poet dramas. Nothing important to be omitted. *Prince of Homburg. Antony and Cleopatra.* Messenger scenes. Concealment and effect through reflex action. Effects by means of the action itself. Necessity of ascent. Contrasts. Parallel scenes. - - - - 66–84

7. WHAT IS TRAGIC?—How far the poet may not concern himself about it. The purging. Effects of ancient tragedy. Contrast with German tragedy. The tragic force (moment). The revolution and recognition. - - - 84–103

CHAPTER II.—THE CONSTRUCTION OF THE DRAMA.

1. PLAY AND COUNTER-PLAY.—Two halves. Rise and fall. Two kinds of structure. Drama in which the chief hero leads. Drama of counter-play. Examples. Spectacle-play and tragedy. - - - - - - 104–114

2. FIVE PARTS AND THREE CRISES.—The introduction. The exciting force (moment). The ascent. The tragic force or incident. Falling action. The force or motive of last suspense. The catastrophe. Necessary qualifications of the poet. - - - - - - 114–140

3. CONSTRUCTION OF THE DRAMA IN SOPHOCLES.—Origin of tragedy. Pathos scenes. Messenger scenes. Dialogues. Representation. The three actors. Scope of their work compared with modern actors. Same actor used to strengthen effects. Cast of parts. Ideas of preserved tragedies. Construction of the action. The characters. Ajax as an example. Peculiarity of Sophocles. His relation to the myth. The parts of the tragedy. *Antigone. King Œdipus. Œdipus at Colonos. The Trachinian Women. Ajax. Philoctetes.* - - - 140–181

4. GERMANIC DRAMA.—Stage of Shakespeare. Its influence on the structure of the pieces. Shakespeare's peculiarities. Its falling action and its weaknesses. Construction of *Hamlet.* - - - - - - 181–19[illegible]

5. THE FIVE ACTS.—Influence of the curtain on the modern stage. Development of the act. The five parts. Their technical peculiarities. First act. Second. Third. Fourth. Fifth. Examples. Construction of the double drama, *Wallenstein*. - - - - - - 192–209

CHAPTER III.—CONSTRUCTION OF SCENES.

1. MEMBERS.—Entrances. Scenes. Units of the poet. Their combination into scenes. Structure of the scene. Intervals. Change of scenery. Chief scenes and subordinate scenes. - - - - - - 210–216

2. THE SCENES ACCORDING TO THE NUMBER OF PERSONS.—Conduct of action through the scenes. Monologues. Messenger scenes. Dialogue scenes. Different structure. Love scenes. Three persons. *Ensemble* scenes. Their laws. The galley scene in *Antony and Cleopatra*. Banquet scene in *Piccolomini*. Rütli scene. Parliament in *Demetrius*. Mass scenes. Distributed voices. Battles. 216–245

CHAPTER IV.—THE CHARACTERS.

1. PEOPLES AND POETS.—Assumptions of dramatic characterization, creation, and after-creation. Variety of peoples and characters. Germans and Latins. Difference according to poets. Shakespeare's characters. Lessing, Goethe, Schiller. - - - - - - 246–266

2. CHARACTERS IN THE MATERIAL AND IN THE PLAY.—The character dependent on the action. Example of *Wallenstein*. Characters with portraiture. Historical characters. Poets and history. Opposition between characters and action. The epic hero intrinsically undramatic. Euripides. The Germans and their legends. Older German history. Nature of historical heroes. Inner poverty. Mingling of opposites. Lack of unity. Influence of Christendom. Henry IV. Attitude of the poet toward the appearances of reality. Opposition between poet and actor. - 266–303

3. MINOR RULES.—The characters must have dramatic unity. The drama must have but one chief hero. Double heroes.

Lovers. The action must be based on characteristics of the persons. Easily understood. Mingling of good and evil. Humor. Accident. The characters in the different acts. Demands of the actor. The conception of the stage arrangement must be vivid in the poet's mind. The province of the spectacle play. What is it to write effectively? - - - - - 303-322

CHAPTER V.—VERSE AND COLOR.

1. PROSE AND VERSE.—Iambic pentameter. Tetrameter. Trimeter. Alexandrine. Verse of the *Nibelungen Lied.* Dramatic element of verse. Color. - - 323-340

CHAPTER VI.—THE POET AND HIS WORK.

1. POET OF MODERN TIMES.—Material. Work. Fitting for the stage. Cutting out. Length of the piece. Acquaintance with the stage. - - - - 341-366

BIOGRAPHICAL NOTE.

Gustav Freytag, scholar, poet, novelist, critic, playwright, editor, soldier, publicist, was born in Kreuzburg, Silesia, in 1816. Still living in quiet retirement in Wiesbaden, he is one of the best known of modern German writers. His preliminary education was acquired at the Gymnasium of Oels, which he entered in 1829, at the age of thirteen. In 1835, he began the study of German philology under Hoffmann, at the University of Breslau. Later he continued this line of study with Lachmann, at the University of Berlin, where, in 1838-9, he was given the degree of Doctor of Philosophy, on the presentation of a thesis on *De initiis scenicæ poeseos apud Germanos*. Between this time and 1846, he was connected with the University of Breslau, as an instructor in the German language and literature. Having gained some notice, as the author of a comedy, *The Bridal Journey* (1844), and a volume of short popular poems, *In Breslau* (1845), he now (1847), in connection with Julian Schmidt, undertook the management of the political and literary newspaper, *Die Grenzboten*, in Leipzig. He continued his literary work, and entered in earnest upon what has proved the long and honorable career of a man of letters.

In 1847, *Valentine* appeared, followed the next year by *Count Waldemir*, both society plays, evincing the author's dramatic power, and with his inclination toward the spirit, the dialectics, and the sketchy manner of the younger writers, showing his delicate feeling for clearness and purity of style, his skill in the conduct of the action, in dialogue, and his genial fresh humor. His next play, *The Scholar*, is rather a psychological study in a single act, than a drama. In 1854, his greatest piece, *The Journalists*, was first acted; and it is still one of the most popular modern society dramas represented on the German stage. Perfectly natural and healthful in tone, it abounds in striking situations, depicts with fidelity many important types of German character, amusingly exhibits social rivalries and political machinations, and affords abundant opportunity for the author's effective satire. Another play, *The Fabii*, appeared in 1859.

Freytag's first great novel, *Soll und Haben* (1858), translated into English under the title of *Debit and Credit* (1859), has become a classic. In this, his view of human life is broader and his insight into the springs of human action deeper than in his plays. Its purpose is to show the value and dignity of a life of labor. It attempts to show that the active, vigorous life of a great German merchant is purer, nobler, more beneficent than the life of a haughty aristocrat, relying only on the traditional merits of his family; and, in this attempt, the author weaves a web of glory about the life of the ordinary citizen. A second novel, *The Lost Manuscript* (1864), in like manner shows the superiority of the scholar over the nobleman.

The Technique of the Drama was written in 1863, and dedicated to the author's friend—Wolf, Count of Baudissin. The book has passed through six editions, and attained the rank of a first-class authority on the matters of which it treats, though now for the first time translated into English.

In 1862, Freytag began his famous series of connected historic tales, in *New Pictures from the Life of the German People*, continued the next year in *Pictures from the German Past*, and still further in 1876 and later, in *The Ancestors*, including *Ingo and Ingraban; The Nest of the Hedge-sparrows; The Brothers of the German House; Marcus King; The Brothers and Sisters; From a Little City*, etc. These are all descriptions of German life, based on accurate research, and including periods from the fourth to the nineteenth century. Devoted to the glory of the German people, this, the author's most extensive work, makes an entertaining exposition of some of the noblest traits of German character. In 1870, he published a striking biography of his intimate friend, entitled *Karl Mathy; Story of His Life*.

Freytag continued to edit *Die Grenzboten* for twenty-three years, when he went over to a new journal called *Im Neuen Reich*. His political writings having introduced him to public life, he became in 1867, a representative of the Liberal party in the North-German Parliament. On the breaking out of the Franco-Prussian war in 1870, he entered the imperial army as an officer on the staff of the Crown Prince, remaining in military service till after the Battle of Sedan. He gave up public life in 1879.

INTRODUCTION.

That the technique of the drama is nothing absolute and unchangeable scarcely need be stated. Since Aristotle established a few of the highest laws of dramatic effect, the culture of the human race has grown more than two thousand years older. Not only have the artistic forms, the stage and method of representation undergone a great change, but what is more important, the spiritual and moral nature of men, the relation of the individual to the race and to the highest forces of earthly life, the idea of freedom, the conception of the being of Divinity, have experienced great revolutions. A wide field of dramatic material has been lost; a new and greater range has been won. With the moral and political principles which control our life, our notion of the beautiful and the artistically effective has developed. Between the highest art effects of the Greek festivals, the *autos sacramentales*, and the drama of the time of Goethe and Iffland, the difference is not less great than between the

Hellenic choral theater, the structure for the mystery play, and the complete inclosed room of the modern stage. It may be considered certain that some of the fundamental laws of dramatic production will remain in force for all time; in general, however, not only the vital requisites of the drama have been found in continuous development, but also the artistic means of producing its effects. Let no one think that the technique of poetry has been advanced through the creations of the greatest poets only; we may say without self-exaltation that we at present have clearer ideas upon the highest art effects in the drama and upon the use of technical equipment, than had Lessing, Schiller and Goethe.

The poet of the present is inclined to look with amazement upon a method of work in which the structure of scenes, the treatment of characters, and the sequence of effects were governed by a transmitted code of fixed technical rules. Such a limitation easily seems to us the death of free artistic creation. Never was a greater error. Even an elaborate system of specific rules, a certain limitation founded in popular custom, as to choice of material and structure of the piece, have been at different periods the best aid to creative power. Indeed, they are, it seems, necessary prerequisites of that rich harvest of many past periods, which has seemed to us so enigmatical and incomprehensible. We recognize still that Greek tragedy possessed such a technique, and that the greatest poets worked according to craftsman's rules which were in part common, and in part might be the property of distinct families and guilds. Many of these were well known to Attic criticism, which judged the worth of a piece according to them — whether the revolution scene were in the right place and the pathos scene aroused the desired degree of sympathy. That the Spanish cloak-and-dagger drama artistically wove the threads of its intrigue likewise according to fixed rules, no poetics of a Castilian informs us; but we are able to recognize very well many of these rules in the uniform construction of the plays, and in the ever recurring characters; and it would not be very difficult to formulate a code of peculiar rules from the plays themselves. These rules, of course, even to contemporaries, to whom they were useful, were not invariable; through the genius and shrewd invention of individuals, these gradually learned how to improve and remodel, until the rules became lifeless; and after a period of spiritless application, together with the creative power of the poets, they were lost.

It is true, an elaborate technique which determines not only the form, but also many æsthetic effects, marks out for the dramatic poetry of a period a limit and boundary within which the greatest success is attained, and to transgress which is not allowed even to the greatest genius. In later times such a limitation is considered a hindrance to a versatile development. But even we Germans might be well content with the unappreciative judgment of posterity if we only possessed now the aid of a generally useful technique. We suffer from the opposite of narrow limitations, the lack of proper restraint, lack of form, a popular style, a definite range of dramatic material, firmness of grasp; our work has become in all directions casual and uncertain. Even to-day, eighty years after Schiller, the young poet finds it difficult to move upon the stage with confidence and ease.

If, however, we must deny ourselves the advantage of composing according to the craftsman's traditions which were peculiar to the dramatic art as well as to the plastic arts of former centuries, yet we should not scorn to seek, and intelligently to use, the technical rules of ancient and modern times, which facilitate artistic effects on our stage. To be sure, these rules are not to be prescribed at the dictation of a single person, not established through the influence of one great thinker or poet; but drawn from the noblest effects of the stage, they must include what is essential — they must serve criticism and creative power not as dictator, but as honest helper; and under them a transformation and improvement according to the needs of the time is not to be excluded.

It is remarkable that the technical rules of a former time, in accordance with which the playwright must construct the artistic framework of his piece, have been so seldom transmitted in writing to later generations. Two thousand two hundred years have passed since Aristotle formulated a part of these laws for the Hellenes. Unfortunately his *Poetics* has come down to us incomplete. Only an outline has been received, which unskilled hands have made — a corrupt text with gaps, apparently disconnected chapters, hastily thrown together. In spite of this condition, what we have received is of highest value to us. To this our science of the past is indebted for a glance into the remains of the Hellenes' theater world. In our text-books on æsthetics, this still affords the foundation for the theory of our dramatic art, and to the growing poet, some chapters of the little work are instructive; for besides a theory of dramatic effects, as the greatest thinker of antiquity explained them to his contemporaries, and besides many principles of a popular system of criticism, as the cultured Athenian brought it into use in considering a new production, the work contains many fine appliances from the workshops of antiquity, which we can use to great advantage in our labors. In the following pages, so far as the practical purpose of the book will allow, these will be the subject of our discussion.

It is a hundred and twenty years since Lessing undertook to decipher for the Germans this stenography of the ancients. His *Hamburgische Dramaturgie* was the avenue to a popular comprehension of the dramatically beautiful. The victorious battle which he waged in this book, against the tyranny of French taste, will secure to him forever the respect and affection of the German people. For our time, the polemic past is of most importance. Where Lessing elucidates Aristotle, his understanding of the Greek does not seem entirely sufficient for our present time, which has at hand a more abundant means of explanation; where he exposes the laws of dramatic creation, his judgment is restricted by the narrow conception of the beautiful and effective, which he himself accepted.

Indeed, the best source of technical rules is the plays of great poets, which still to-day, exercise their charm alike on reader and spectator, especially the Greek tragedies. Whoever accustoms himself to look aside from the peculiarities of the old models, will notice with real joy that the skilful tragic poet of the Athenians, Sophocles, used the fundamental laws of dramatic construction, with enviable certainty and shrewdness. For development, climax, and return of the action, he presents us a model seldom reached.

About two thousand years after *Œdipus at Colonos*, Shakespeare, the second mighty genius which gave immortal expression to dramatic art, wrote the tragedy, *Romeo and Juliet*. He created the drama of the Germanic races. His treatment of the tragic, his regulation of the action, his manner of developing character, and his representation of soul experiences, have established for the introduction of the drama, and for the first half to the climax, many technical laws which still guide us.

The Germans came in a roundabout way to a recognition of the greatness and significance of his service. The great German poets, easily the next models after which we have to fashion, lived in a time of a spirited beginning of experiments with the inheritance of the old past. There was lacking, therefore, to the technique which they inherited, something of certainty and consistency in effects; and directly because the beautiful which they discovered has been infused into our blood, we are bound, in our work, to reject many things which with them rested upon an incomplete or insecure foundation.

The examples brought forward in the following discussion are taken from Sophocles, Shakespeare, Lessing, Goethe, and Schiller, for it has seemed desirable to limit examples to universally known works.

CHAPTER I.

THE DRAMATIC ACTION.

I.

THE IDEA.

In the soul of the poet, the drama gradually takes shape out of the crude material furnished by the account of some striking event. First appear single movements; internal conflicts and personal resolution, a deed fraught with consequence, the collision of two characters, the opposition of a hero to his surroundings, rise so prominently above their connection with other incidents, that they become the occasion for the transformation of other material. This transformation goes on to such an extent that the main element, vividly perceived, and comprehended in its entrancing, soul-stirring or terrifying significance, is separated from all that casually accompanies it, and with single supplementary, invented elements, is brought into a unifying relation of cause and effect. The new unit which thus arises is the *Idea* of the Drama. This is the center toward which further independent inventions are directed, like rays. This idea works with a power similar to the secret power of crystallization. Through this are unity of action, significance of characters, and at last, the whole structure of the drama produced.

How ordinary material becomes a poetic idea through inspiration, the following example will show. A young poet of the last century reads the following notice in a newspaper: "Stuttgart, Jan. 11.—In the dwelling of the musician, Kritz, were found, yesterday, his oldest daughter, Louise, and Duke Blasius von Böller, major of dragoons, lying dead upon the floor. The accepted facts in the case, and the medical examination indicated that both had come to their deaths by drinking poison. There is a rumor of an attachment between the pair, which the major's father, the well-known President von Böller, had sought to break off. The sad fate of the young woman, universally esteemed on account of her modest demeanor, awakens the sympathy of all people of sensibility."

From the material thus afforded, the fancy of the poet, aroused by sympathy, fashions the character of an ardent and passionate youth, and of an innocent and susceptible maiden. The contrast between the court atmosphere, from which the lover has emerged, and the narrow circle of a little village household, is vividly felt. The hostile father becomes a heartless, intriguing courtier. An unavoidable necessity arises, of explaining the frightful resolution of a vigorous youth, a resolution apparently growing out of such a situation. The creative poet finds this inner connection in an illusion which the father has produced in the soul of the son, in a suspicion that his beloved is unfaithful. In this manner the poet makes the account intelligible to himself and to others; while freely inventing, he introduces an internal consistency. These inventions are, in appearance, little supplementary additions, but they make an entirely original production which stands over against the original occurrence as something new, and has something like the following contents: In the breast of a young nobleman, jealousy toward his beloved, a girl of the middle class, has been so excited by his father, that he destroys both her and himself by poison. Through this remodeling, an occurrence in real life becomes a dramatic idea. From this time forward, the real occurrence is unessential to the poet. The place, and family name are lost sight of; indeed, whether the event happened as reported, or what was the character of the victims, and of their parents, or their rank, no longer matters at all; quick perception and the first activity of creative power have given to the occurrence a universally intelligible meaning and an intrinsic truth. The controlling forces of the piece are no longer accidental, and to be found in a single occurrence; they could enter into a hundred cases, and with the accepted characters and the assumed connection, the outcome would always be the same.

When the poet has once thus infused his own soul into the material, then he adopts from the real account some things which suit his purpose—the title of the father and of the son, the name of the bride, the business of her parents, perhaps single traits of character which he may turn to account. Alongside this goes further creative work; the chief characters are developed, to their distinct individualities; accessory figures are created,—a quarrelsome accomplice of the father, another woman, the opposite of the beloved, personality of the parents; new impulses are given to the action, and all these inventions are determined and ruled by the idea of the piece.

This idea, the first invention of the poet, the silent soul through which he gives life to the material coming to him from external sources, does not easily place itself before him as a clearly defined thought; it has not the colorless clearness of an abstract conception. On the contrary, the peculiarity in such work of the poet's mind is, that the chief parts of the action, the nature of the chief characters, indeed something of the color of the piece, glow in the soul at the same time with the idea, bound into an inseparable unity, and that they continually work like a human being producing and expanding in every direction. It is possible, of course, that the poet's idea, however securely he bears it in his soul, may never, during the process of composition, come to perfection in words, and that later, through reflection, but without having formulated it even for himself, he sets the possession of his soul into the stamped coin of speech, and comprehends it as the fundamental thought of his drama. It is possible, indeed, that he has perceived the idea more justly according to the rules of his art, than he has given the central thought of his work verbal expression.

If, however, it is inconvenient and often difficult for him to cast the idea of a growing play into a formula, to express it in words, yet the poet will do well, even in the beginning of his work, to temper the ardor of his soul, and sharply discriminating, judge the idea according to the essential requisites of the drama. It is instructive for a stranger to a piece to seek the hidden soul in the complete production, and however imperfect this may possibly be, give the thought formal expression. Much may be recognized in this way that is characteristic of single poets. For example, let the foundation of *Mary Stuart* be,—"The excited jealousy of a queen incites to the killing of her imprisoned rival;" and again of *Love and Intrigue*, "The excited jealousy of a young nobleman incites to the killing of his humble beloved." These bare formulas will be taken from the fulness of many-colored life which in the mind of the creative poet is connected with the idea; yet something peculiar will become distinct in the construction of both pieces, in addition; for example, that the poet using such a frame work was placed under the necessity of composing in advance the first part of the action, which explains the origin of the jealousy, and that the impelling force in the chief characters becomes operative just in the middle of the piece, and that the first acts contain preferably the endeavours of the accessory characters, to excite the fatal activity of one of the chief characters. It will be further noticed how similar in ultimate principle is the construction and motive of these two plays of Schiller, and how both have a surprising similarity in idea and plan, to the more powerful *Othello*.

The material which is transformed through the dramatic idea, is either invented by the poet specially for his drama, or is an incident related from the life which surrounds him, or an account which history offers, or the contents of a tradition, or novel, or narrative poem. In all of these cases, where the poet makes use of what is at hand, it has already been humanized by the impress of an idea. Even in the above supposed newspaper notice, the incipient remodeling is recognizable. In the last sentence, "There is a rumor of an attachment," etc., the reporter makes the first attempt to transform the mere fact into a consistent story, to explain the tragic occurrence, to bring to the lovers a greater degree of interest, so that a more attractive meaning is given to their condition. The practice of transformation, through which consistency and a meaning corresponding to the demands of the thinking person are given to real events, is no prerogative of the poet. Inclination toward this, and capability for it, are active in all persons, and at all times. For thousands of years the human race has thus transposed for itself life in heaven and on earth; it has abundantly endowed its representations of the divine with human attributes. All heroic tradition has sprung from such a transformation of impressions from religious life, history, or natural objects, into poetic ideas. Even now, since historic culture prevails, and respect for the real relations of the great events of the world has risen so high, this tendency to explain occurrences shows itself in the greatest as well as in the least matters. In every anecdote, even in the disagreeable gossip of society, its activity is manifest, endeavoring, even if what is real remains unchanged, to present vividly and with spirit some trait of narrow life, or from the necessity of the *raconteur*, to make himself in contrast with others more surely and better observed.

Historical material is already brought into order through some idea, before the poet takes possession of it. The ideas of the historian are not at all poetical; but they have a specific and shaping influence on every part of the work which is brought through them into being. Whoever describes the life of a man, whoever makes an exposition of a section of past time, must set in order his mass of material from an established point of view, must sift out the unessential, must make prominent the most essential. Still more, he must seek to comprehend the contents of a human life or a period of time; he must take pains to discover ultimate characteristics and intimate connection of events. He must also know the connection of his material with much that is external, and much that his work does not present. In certain cases, indeed, he must supplement what has been delivered to him, and so explain the unintelligible, that its probable and possible meaning is evident. He is finally directed in the arrangement of his work, by the laws of creation, which have many things in common with the laws of poetic composition. Through his knowledge and his art, he may from crude material create a picture exciting wonder, and produce upon the soul of the reader the most powerful effect. But he is distinguished from the poet by this, that he seeks conscientiously to understand what has actually occurred, exactly as it was presented to view, and that the inner connection which he seeks is produced by the laws of nature which we revere as divine, eternal, incomprehensible. To the historian, the event itself, with its significance for the human mind, seems of most importance. To the poet, the highest value lies in his own invention; and out of fondness for this, he, at his convenience, changes the actual incident. To the poet, therefore, every work of an historical writer, however animated it may be through the historical idea recognized in its contents, is still only raw material, like a daily occurrence; and the most artistic treatment by the historian is useful to the poet, only so far as it facilitates his comprehension of what has really happened. If the poet has, in history, found his interest awakened in the person of the martial prince, Wallenstein; if he perceives vividly in his reading a certain connection between the deeds and the fate of the man; if he is touched or shocked by single characteristics of his real life,

—then there begins in his mind the process of reconstruction, so that he brings the deeds and fall of the hero into perfectly intelligible and striking connection, and he even so transforms the character of the hero as is desirable for a touching and thrilling effect of the action. That which in the historical character is only a subordinate trait, now becomes the fundamental characteristic of his being; the gloomy, fierce commander receives something of the poet's own nature; he becomes a high minded, dreaming, reflecting man. Conformably with this character, all incidents are remodeled, all other characters determined, and guilt and calamities regulated. Through such idealization arose Schiller's Wallenstein, a figure whose enchanting features have but little in common with the countenance of the historical Wallenstein. Indeed, the poet will have to be on his guard lest, in his invention, there be made to appear what to his contemporaries may seem the opposite of historical truth. How much the later poet may be limited by such a consideration, will be discussed later.

It will depend on the personality of the poet, whether the first rapture of his poetic activity is derived from the enchanting characteristics of mankind, or from what is striking in real destiny, or from the really interesting in the color of the time, which he finds in the historical record. But from the moment when the enjoyment and ardor necessary to his production begin, he proceeds, indeed, with unfettered freedom, however faithfully he seems to himself to adhere to historical material. He transforms all available material into dramatic forces.[1] (See Notes, commencing page 383.)

Moreover, when the poet adopts material which has already been put in order more or less perfectly according to the laws of epic construction, as heroic poem, saga, artistically finished narrative, what is prepared for another species of poetry, is for him only material. Let it not be thought that an event with the persons involved, which has already been ennobled through an art so nearly allied, has for that reason a better preparation for the drama. On the contrary, there is between the great creations of the epic which shadow forth occurrences and heroes as they stand near each other, and dramatic art which represents actions and characters as they are developed through each other, a profound opposition which it is difficult for the creative artist to manage. Even the poetic charm which these created images exercise upon his soul, may render it the more difficult for him to transform them according to the vital requisites of his art. The Greek drama struggled as severely with its material, which was taken from the epic, as the historic poet of our time must, with the transformation of historical ideas into dramatic.

To transform material artistically, according to a unifying idea, means to idealize it. The characters of the poet, in contrast with the images from reality used as material, and according to a convenient craftsman's expression, are called ideals.

II.

WHAT IS DRAMATIC?

The dramatic includes those emotions of the soul which steel themselves to will, and to do, and those emotions of the soul which are aroused by a deed or course of action ; also the inner processes which man experiences from the first glow of perception to passionate desire and action, as well as the influences which one's own and others' deeds exert upon the soul ; also the rushing forth of will power from the depths of man's soul toward the external world, and the influx of fashioning influences from the outer world into man's inmost being ; also the coming into being of a deed, and its consequences on the human soul.

An action, in itself, is not dramatic. Passionate feeling, in itself, is not dramatic. Not the presentation of a passion for itself, but of a passion which leads to action is the business of dramatic art ; not the presentation of an event for itself, but for its effect on a human soul is the dramatist's mission. The exposition of passionate emotions as such, is in the province of the lyric poet ; the depicting of thrilling events is the task of the epic poet.

The two ways in which the dramatic expresses itself are, of course, not fundamentally different. Even while a man is under stress, and laboring to turn his inmost soul toward the external, his surroundings exert a stimulating or repressing influence on his passionate emotions. And, again, while what has been done exerts a reflex influence upon him, he does not remain merely receptive, but gains new impulses and transformations. Yet, there is a difference in these closely connected processes. The first, the inward struggle of man toward a deed, has always the highest charm. The second stimulates to more external emotion, a more violent co-operation of different forces; almost all that satisfies curiosity belongs to this; and yet, however indispensable it is to the drama, it is principally a satisfying of excited suspense; and the impatience of the hearer, if he has creative power, easily runs in advance, seeking a new vehement agitation in the soul of the hero. What is occurring chains the attention most, not what, as a thing of the past, has excited wonder.

Since the dramatic art presents men as their inmost being exerts an influence on the external, or as they are affected by external influences, it must logically use the means by which it can make intelligible to the auditor these processes of man's nature. These means are speech, tone, gesture. It must bring forward its characters as speaking, singing, gesticulating. Poetry uses also as accessories in her representations, music and scenic art.

In close fellowship with her sister arts, with vigorous, united effort she sends her images into the receptive souls of those who are at the same time auditors and spectators. The impressions which she produces are called effects. These dramatic effects have a very peculiar character; they differ not only from the effects of the plastic arts through the force of emphasis and the progressive and regular gradation of the chosen movement, but also from the powerful effects of music, in this, that they flow in at the same time through two senses, and excite with rapture not only emotional, but also intellectual activity.

From what has already been said, it is clear that the characters, presented according to the demands of dramatic art, must have something unusual in their nature which may distinguish them not only from the innumerable, more manifold, and more complicated beings whose images real life impresses on the soul, but also from the poetic images which are rendered effective through other forms of art, the epic, the romance, the lyric. The *dramatis persona* must represent human nature, not as it is aroused and mirrored in its surroundings, active and full of feeling, but as a grand and passionately excited inner power striving to embody itself in a deed, transforming and guiding the being and conduct of others. Man, in the drama, must appear under powerful restraint, excitement, transformation. Specially must there be represented in him in full activity those peculiarities which come effectively into conflict with other men, force of sentiment, violence of will, achievement hindered through passionate desire, just those peculiarities which make character and are intelligible through character. It thus happens, not without reason, that in the terms of art, the people of a drama are called characters. But the characters which are brought forward by poetry and her accessory arts, can evince their inner life only as participants in an event or occurrence, the course and internal connection of which becomes apparent to the spectator through the dramatic processes in the soul of the poet. This course of events, when it is arranged according to the demands of dramatic art, is called the *action.*[2]

Each participant in the dramatic action has a definite appointment with reference to the whole; for each, an exact, circumscribed personality is necessary, which must be so constituted that so much of it as has a purpose may be conveniently perceived by the auditor, and what is common to man and what is peculiar to this character may be effectively represented by the actor by means of his art.

Those spiritual processes which have been indicated above as dramatic, are, of course, not perfectly apparent in every person represented, specially on the later stage, which is fond of bringing forward a greater number of characters as participants in the action. But the chief characters must abound in them; only when these, in an appropriate manner, exhibit their real nature with power and fulness, even to the inmost recesses of their hearts, can the drama produce great effects. If this last dramatic element is not apparent in the leading characters, is not forced upon the hearer, the drama is lifeless; it is an artificial, empty form, without corresponding contents; and the pretentious co-operation of several combined arts makes this hollowness the more painful.

Along with the chief characters, the subordinate persons participate in this dramatic life, each according to the space occupied in the piece. It does not entirely disappear, even in the least rôle, in those figures which with a few words can show their participation; the attendant or the messenger, owes it as a duty, at least to the actor's art, by costume, manner of speech, deportment, gesture, posture at entering, to represent in a manner suitable to the piece what he personates, so far as externals wiil do it, even if meagerly and modestly.

But since the representation of these mental processes, which are the prerogative and requisite of the drama, requires time, and since the poet's time for the producing of effects is limited according to the custom of his people, it follows that the event represented must bring the chief characters much more boldly into prominence than is necessary in an actual occurrence which is brought about through the general activity of many persons.

The capability of producing dramatic effects is not accorded to the human race in every period of its existence. Dramatic poetry appears later than epic and lyric; its blossoming among any people depends on the fortunate conjunction of many impelling forces, but specially on this, that in the actual life of the contemporary public, the corresponding mental processes are frequently and fully seen. This is first possible when the people have reached a certain degree of development, when men have become accustomed to observe themselves and others critically under the impulse to a deed, when speech has acquired a high degree of flexibility and a clever dialect; when the individual is no longer bound by the interdict of tradition and external force, ancient formula and popular custom, but is able more freely to fashion his own life. We distinguish two periods in which the dramatic has come to the human race. This intensification of the human soul appeared for the first time in the ancient world, about 500 years before Christ, when the youthful consciousness of the free Hellenic community awoke with the bloom of commerce, with freedom of speech, and with the participation of the citizen in affairs of state. The dramatic spirit appeared the second time, in the newer family of European peoples, after the Reformation, at the same time with the deepening of mind and spirit, which was produced through the sixteenth century, not only among the Germans, but also among the Latin races, but by different methods. Centuries before the inception of this mighty effort of the human spirit, not only the Hellenes, but the various branches of migrating nations, had already been developing the rudiments of a speech and art of pantomime which was seeking the dramatic. There, as here, great festivals in honor of the gods had occasioned the song in ceremonial costume, and the playing of popular masques. But the entrance of dramatic power into these lyric or epic exhibitions, was in both cases a wonderfully rapid, almost sudden one. Both times, the dramatic was developed, from the moment it became alive, with a marvellous power to a beauty which, through the later centuries, it has not easily reached. Immediately after the Persian wars, came Æschylus, Sophocles, and Euripides in close succession. Shortly after the Reformation, there appeared among the European nations, first in England and Spain, and later in France, last of all among the Germans, left behind through helpless weakness, the highest popular florescence of this rare art.

But there is this difference between the beginning of the dramatic in the old world and in the new: the drama of antiquity originated in the lyric choral song; that of the newer world rests on the epic enjoyment in the exhibition of important events. In the former, from the beginning, the passionate excitement of feeling was the charm; in the latter, the witnessing of thrilling incident. This difference of origin has powerfully influenced the form and meaning of the drama in its artistic development; and however eminent the contributions of art were in both periods, they retained something essentially different.

But even after dramatic life had arisen among the people, the highest effects of poetry remained the prerogative of a few, and since that time dramatic power has not been accorded to every poet; indeed, it does not pervade with sufficient power every work even of the greatest poets. We may conclude that even in Aristotle's time, those stately plays with a simple action, with no characteristic desires on the part of the leading persons, with loosely connected choruses, had, possibly, lyric, but not dramatic beauty. And among the historic plays which, year after year, are written in Germany, the greater part contains little more than mangled history thrown into dialogue, some epic material thrown into scenic form, at all events nothing of dramatic character. Indeed, single poems of the greater poets suffer from the same lack. Only two celebrated dramas need here be named. The *Hecuba* of Euripides shows, until toward the end, only a little progress, and that entirely unsatisfactory, from the excited disposition, toward a deed; first in the final conflict against Polymnestor does Hecuba exhibit a passion that becomes a determination; here the dramatic suspense first begins; up to this point there was evoked from the briefly sketched and pathetic circumstances of the chief characters, only lyric complaints. And again, in Shakespeare's *Henry V.*, in which the poet wished to compose a patriotic piece according to the old epic customs of his stage, with military parades, fights, little episodes, there is apparent neither in the chief characters, nor in their accessories, any deeply laid foundation for their deeds, in a dramatically presentable motive. In short waves, wish and demand ripple along; the actions themselves are the chief thing. Patriotism must excite a lively interest, as in Shakespeare's time, and among his people, it always did abundantly. For us, the play is less presentable than the parts of *Henry VI.* On the contrary, to name only a few of one poet's pieces, *Macbeth*, as far as the banquet scene, the whole of *Coriolanus*, *Othello*, *Romeo and Juliet*, *Julius Cæsar*, *Lear*, up to the hovel scene, and *Richard III.*, contain the most powerful dramatic elements that have ever been created by a Teuton or a Saxon.

From the inner struggles of the leading characters, the judgment of contemporaries, as a rule, or at least that of the immediately following time, rates the significance of a piece. Where this life is wanting, no skill in treatment, no attractive material, is able to keep the work alive. Where this dramatic life is present, even later times regard with great respect a poetical composition and gladly overlook its shortcomings.

III.

UNITY OF ACTION.

By *action* is meant, an event or occurrence, arranged according to a controlling idea, and having its meaning made apparent by the characters. It is composed of many elements, and consists in a number of dramatic efficients (*momente*), which become effective one after the other, according to a regular arrangement. The action of the serious drama must possess the following qualities:

It must present complete unity.

This celebrated law has undergone a very different application with the Greeks and Romans, with the Spanish and French, with Shakespeare and the Germans, which has been occasioned partly by those learned in art, partly by the character of the stage. The restriction of its claims through the French classics, and the strife of the Germans with the three unities, of place, of time, and of action, have for us only a literary-historical interest.[a]

No dramatic material, however perfectly its connections with other events have been severed, is independent of something presupposed. These indispensable presupposed circumstances must be so far presented to the hearer, in the opening scenes, that he may first survey the groundwork of the piece, not in detail, indeed, lest the field of the action itself, be limited; then immediately, time, people, place, establishment of suitable relations between the chief persons who appear, and the unavoidable threads which come together in these, from whatever has been left outside the action. When, for instance, in *Love and Intrigue*, an already existing love affair forms the groundwork, the hearer must be given a sharp informing glance into this relation of the two leading characters, and into the family life from which the tragedy is to be developed. Moreover, in the case of historical material, which is furnished by the vast and interminable connections of the great events of the world, this exposition of what has gone before is no easy undertaking; and the poet must take heed that he simplify it as much as possible.

From this indispensable introduction, the beginning of the impassioned action must arise, like the first notes of a melody from the introductory chords. This first stir of excitement, this stimulating impulse, is of great importance for the effect of the drama, and will be discussed later. The end of the action must, also, appear as the intelligible and inevitable result of the entire course of the action, the conjunction of forces; and right here, the inherent necessity must be keenly felt; the close must, however, represent the complete termination of the strife and excited conflicts.

Within these limits, the action must move forward with uniform consistency. This internal consistency is produced by representing an event which follows another, as an effect of which that other is the evident cause; let that which occasions, be the logical cause of occurrences, and the new scenes and events be conceived as probable, and generally understood results of previous actions; or let that which is to produce an effect, be a generally comprehensible peculiarity of a character already made known. If it is unavoidable that, during the course of events, new incidents appear, unexpected to the auditor, or very surprising, these must be explained imperceptibly, but perfectly, through what has preceded. This laying the foundation of the drama is called, assigning the motive (*motiviren*). Through the motives, the elements of the action are bound into an artistic, connected whole. This binding together of incidents by the free creation of a causative connection, is the distinguishing characteristic of this species of art. Through this linking together of incidents, dramatic idealization is effected.

Let the remodeling of a narrative into a dramatic action serve as an example. There lived in Verona two noble families, in enmity and feuds of long standing. As chance would have it, the son of one family, together with his companions, play the presumptuous trick of thrusting themselves disguised into a masked ball, given by the chief of the other house. At this ball the intruder beholds the daughter of his enemy, and in both arises a reckless passion. They determine upon a clandestine marriage and are wedded by the father confessor of the maiden. Then fate directs that the new bridegroom is betrayed into a conflict with the cousin of his bride, and because he has slain him in the duel, is banished from his country by the prince of the land, under penalty of death. Meantime a distinguished suitor has visited the parents to sue for the hand of the newly married wife. The father disregards the despairing entreaties of his daughter, and appoints the day for the marriage. In these fearful circumstances, the young woman receives from her priest, a sleep-potion which shall give her the appearance of death; the priest undertakes to remove her privately from the coffin and communicate her embarrassing situation to her distant husband. But again an unfortunate chance directs that the husband, in a foreign land, is informed of the death of his wife, before the messenger of the priest arrives. He hastens, in secret, back to his native city, and forces his way into the vault, where lies the body of his wife. Unfortunately, he meets there the man destined by her parents to be her bridegroom, kills him, and upon the coffin of his beloved, drinks the fatal poison. The loved one awakes, sees her dying husband, and stabs herself with his dagger.[4]

This narrative is a simple account of a striking occurrence. The fact, that all this so happened, is told; how and why it so came about, does not matter. The sequence of narrated incidents possesses no close connection. Chance, the caprice of fate, an unaccountable conjunction of unfortunate forces, occasions the progress of events and the catastrophe. Indeed, just this striking sport of chance is what gives enjoyment. Such a material appears specially unfavorable for the drama; and yet a great poet has made from it one of his most beautiful plays.

The facts have remained, on the whole, unchanged; only their connection has become different. The task of the poet was not to present the facts to us, on the stage, but to make them perceptible in the feeling, desire, and action of his persons, to make them more evident, to develop them in accordance with probability and reason. He had, in the first place, to set forth what was naturally prerequisite to the action; the brawls in an Italian city, in a time when swords were carried, and combativeness quickly laid hand to weapon, the leaders of both parties, the ruling power which had trouble to restrain the restless within proper limits; then the determination of the Capulets to give a banquet. Then he must represent the merry conceit which brought Romeo and his attendants into the Capulets' house. This exciting impulse, the beginning of the action, must not appear an accident; it must be accounted for from the characters. Therefore it was necessary to introduce the companions of Romeo, fresh, in uncontrolled, youthful spirits, playing with life. To this necessity for establishing motives, Mercutio owes his existence. In contrast with his mad companions, the poet had fashioned the dejected Romeo, whose nature, even before his entrance into the excited action, must express its amorous passion. Hence his vagaries about Rosalind. This availed to make probable the awakening passion of the lovers. For this, the masque-scene and the balcony-scene were constructed. Every enchantment of poetry is here used to the greatest purpose, to make apparent, conceivable and as a matter of course, that henceforward the sweet passion of the lovers determines their lives.

The accessory figures, which enter into the piece from this point, must forward the complication, and aid in giving motive toward the tragic outcome. For the narrative, it was sufficient that a priest performed the marriage rites, and gave direction to the unfortunate intrigue; such aids have always been at hand; as soon, however, as he himself has stepped upon the stage, and by his words has entered the action, he must receive a personality which accounts for all that follows;—he must be good-hearted and sympathetic, and through his goodness of heart, merit full confidence; he must be unpracticed, and inclined to quiet artifices as frequently the better priests of the Italian church are, in order to venture later, the doubtful play of death for his penitent. Thus originated Laurence.

After the wedding, the unfortunate affair with Tybalt comes into the story. Here the dramatic poet had special motive in taking from the character entering so suddenly, all that was merely casual. It could not suffice for him to introduce Tybalt as a hot-headed brawler; without letting the spectator see his purpose, he must lay the foundation in what had gone before, for the peculiar hatred toward Romeo and his companions. Hence the little side scene at the masked ball, in which Tybalt's anger flames up at the intrusion of Romeo. And in this scene itself, the poet had to bring to bear the strongest motive, to compel Romeo to engage in the duel. Mercutio must first be slain for this reason, and for the further purpose of heightening the tragic power of the scene, and accounting for the wrath of the prince.

To send Romeo immediately into banishment, as is done in the narrative, would be impossible in the drama. To show the spectator that the loving pair were bound inseparably to each other, there was the most pressing necessity to give to their excited passion the deepest intensity. How the poet succeeded in this is known to all. The scene on the marriage eve is the climax of the action; and by poetic elaboration, which need not be explained here, it arises to the highest beauty. But this scene was necessary on other grounds. Juliet's character renders necessary a rising into what is noble. It must be shown that the lovely heroine is capable of magnificent emotion, of mighty passion in order that her later, despairing determination may be found consistent with her nature. Her marvellous inward conflict over Tybalt's death and Romeo's banishment must precede the wedding night, to impart to her nuptial longing the beautifully pathetic element which increases the interest in this always delicate scene. But even the possibility of this scene must be made clear. Its accessory persons, Friar Laurence and the nurse, are again significant. The character of the nurse, one of Shakespeare's unsurpassable inventions, is, likewise, not fashioned accidentally; just as she is, she is a suitable accomplice; and she makes explicable Juliet's inward withdrawal from her and the catastrophe.

Immediately after her wedding night, the command is given to Juliet to be married to Paris. That the beautiful daughter of the wealthy Capulet would find a distinguished suitor, and that her father,—for whose hot-headedness a sufficient ground has already been laid,—would exercise harsh compulsion in the matter, would be conceded by the hearer without further preparation, as probable and a matter of course. But it is a matter of much consequence to the dramatist, to lay beforehand the foundation for this important event. Already, before the marriage of Juliet, he has Paris receive her father's promise; he would throw this dark shadow upon the great love scene; and he would account right distinctly, and to the common understanding for the approaching calamity.

Now the fate of the loving pair has been put into the weak hands of Friar Laurence. Up to this point, the drama has carefully excluded every intrusion of any chance. Even to the most minute accessory fact, all is accounted for by the kind of characters. Now a tremendous destiny is weighing down upon two unfortunates: spilled blood, deadly family hate, a clandestine marriage, banishment, a new wooing,—all this is pressing upon the hearer's sensibility with a certain compulsion. The introduction of little explanatory motives is no longer effective, and no longer necessary. Now the stratagem of the stupid visionary priest can be thwarted by an accident; for the feeling that it was desperate and presumptuous in the highest degree, to expose a living person to the incalculable chances of a sleep-potion and burial, has become so strong in the hearer's mind, that he already considers an unhappy result as probable.

Thus the catastrophe is introduced and given a foundation. But that the hope of a happy outcome may entirely vanish from the mind of the spectator, and that the inherent necessity of ruin may yet at the last moment overtop the foreboding of unavoidable fatalities in the burial vault, Romeo must slay Paris before the tomb.

The death of this stranger is the last force furthering the sad end of the lovers. Even when Juliet now in a fortunate moment awakes, her path and Romeo's is so overflowed with blood, that any good fortune, or even life, has become improbable to them.

The task undertaken here has been only to point out in a few chief particulars the contrast between inner dramatic unification and epic narration. The piece contains still an abundance of other motives; and even the minute details are so dovetailed and riveted as to evince the dramatist's special purpose.

The internal unity of a dramatic action is not secured merely by making a succession of events appear as the deeds and sufferings of the same hero. No great fundamental law of dramatic creation is more frequently violated, even by great poets, than this one; and this disregard has always interfered with the effects of even the power of genius. The Athenian stage suffered on this account; and Aristotle attempted to meet the evil, when in his firm way he said: "The action is the first and most important thing, the characters only second;" and, "The action is not given unity by being made to concern only one person." Especially, we later ones, who are most frequently attracted by the charm of historical material, have urgent reason to cling to the law, that union about a person alone does not suffice to gather and bind the events into unity.

It still frequently happens that a poet undertakes to present the life of an heroic prince, as he is at variance with his vassals, as he wages war with his neighbors and the church, and is again reconciled to them, and as he finally perishes in one of these conflicts; the poet distributes the principal moving forces of the historical life among the five acts and three hours of the acting play, makes in speech and response an exposition of political interests and party standpoints, interweaves well or ill a love episode, and thinks to have changed the historical picture into a poetic one. He is positively a weak-hearted destroyer of history, and no priest of his proud goddess. What he has produced is not history, and not drama. He has, sure enough, yielded to some of the demands of his art; he has omitted weighty events which did not suit his purpose; he has fashioned the character of his hero simply and according to rule, has not been sparing in additions, small and great, has here and there substituted for the complicated connections of historical events, invented ones. Through all this, however, he has attained a general effect which is at best a weak reflection of the sublime effect that the life of the hero would have produced, if well presented by the historian; and his error has been in putting the historic idea in the place of the dramatic idea.

Even the poet who thinks more worthily of his art, is in danger, when busied with historical matter, of seeking a false unity. The historical writer has taught him that the shifting events of historic life are accounted for by the peculiarities of characters, which assume results, which conjure up a fatality. The effect which the intimate connections of an historic life produce, is powerful, and excites wonder. Determined by such a force of the real, the poet seeks to comprehend the inner connections of events in the characteristic elements of the hero's life. The character of the hero is to him the last motive in laying the foundation for the various vicissitudes of an active existence. A German prince, for example, powerful and high spirited, is forced by sheer violence into conflicts and submission; in heart-rending humiliation and deepest abasement, he finds again his better self, and subdues his soaring pride; such a character may possess all the qualities of a dramatic hero,—what is universally comprehensible and significant gushes forth powerfully from the casual in his earthly life; and his lot in life shows a relation between guilt and punishment, which takes hold of men's minds; he appears as the artificer of his own happiness or misery; the germ and essence of his life may be very like a poetic idea. But just before such a similarity, let the poet pause in distrust. He has to ask himself whether through his art he can infuse anything more powerful or effective than the story itself offers; or, indeed, whether he is at all in a position to enlarge through his art any part of the effects which, perceiving in advance, he admires in the historical material. Of course he may intensify the character of his hero. What was working in the soul of Henry IV. as he journeyed toward Canossa and stood in his penitential garment by the castle wall, is the secret of the poet; the historian knows very little to tell about it. To such impelling forces of a real life, the poet has an inalienable right. But the disposition and transformations of the historical hero do not fashion themselves completely in short periods of personal isolation; and what the poet was lured by was exactly an heroic nature whose original texture showed itself in various occurrences. Now these occurrences which the historian reports, are very numerous. The poet is obliged to limit himself to a very few. He is obliged to remodel these few in order to give them the significance which in reality the course of the whole had. He will see with astonishment how difficult this is, and how by this means his hero becomes smaller and weaker, and that his historic idea is completed with so little. But, even in the representation of these selected events, the poet is poorer than the historian. Every one of his impelling forces must have an introduction that will account for it; he must introduce to the spectator his Hannos, his Ottos, his Rudolphs and Henrys; he must to a certain extent make their affairs attractive; two or three times in the piece he will create excitement, then allay it; the persons will throng and conceal each other on the narrow stage; the rising interest of hearers will every now and then relapse. He will make the astonishing discovery that the hearer's suspense is usually not produced by the characters, however interesting these may be, but only through the progress of the action; and he will at best attain only one or the other greatly elaborated scene with pure dramatic life, which stands alone in a desert of sketchy, brief suggestions of mutilated history, and cramped invention.

Engaged in such labor upon the abundant beautiful material offered in history, the poet has probably often abandoned the material without seeing its beauty. To idealize an entire political human life is a prodigious undertaking. Cyclic dramas, trilogies, tetralogies, may in most cases scarcely suffice for this. A single historic movement may give the dramatist superabundant material. For, as faith begins when knowledge ends, so poetry begins when history leaves off. What history is able to declare can be to the poet only the frame within which he paints his most brilliant colors, the most secret revelations of human nature; how shall space and inward freedom remain to him for this, when he must toil and moil to present a succession of historical events? Schiller has made use, in his two greatest historical pieces, of the historical catastrophe only, the last scenes of a real historical life; and for so small an historic segment he has required in *Wallenstein* three dramas. Let this example be taken to heart. It is true *Götz von Berlichingen* will always be considered a very commendable poem, because the chivalric anecdotes which are excellently presented with short, sharp strokes, hold the reader spellbound ; but upon the stage the piece is not an effective drama ; and the same is true of *Egmont*, although its feeble action, and the lack of characterization of its hero, is to a certain extent compensated for in the greater elaboration of its vigorous female characters.

Concerning the artless treatment of historical material through the epic traditions of our old stage, Shakespeare, above all others, has given hints to the Germans. His historic plays, taken from English history, the structure of which, except *Richard III.* we should not imitate, had a far different justification. At that time there was no writing of history, as we understand the term ; and as the poet made use of material from historic resources for his artistic figures, he wrought from an abundance, and opened up the immediate past to his nation, in a multitude of masterly character sketches. But he, himself, achieved for the stage of his time the wonderful advance to a complete action ; and we owe to him, after he began to make use of the material in Italian novels, our comprehension of how irreplaceable the noble effects are which are produced by a unified and well-ordered action. His Roman plays, if one makes allowance for a few of the practices of his stage, and the third act of *Antony and Cleopatra*, are models of an established construction. We do not do well to imitate what he has overcome.

Without doubt, the influence of the characters on

the texture of the action, is greater in the modern drama than on the stage of the ancients. As the first impulse toward creation comes to the Germanic mind frequently through the characteristic features of an historic hero ; as the delineation of the characters and their representation by actors have received a finer finish than was possible in the Greek masque tragedy, so will the character of the hero exert greater influence on the structure of the action, but only that we may thereby account for the inner, consistent, unified action through the characteristic peculiarities of the hero. Such an establishing of motive was not unknown to the Greeks. Already in one of the older plays of Æschylus, *The Suppliants*, the vacillating character of the King of Argos is made so prominent that one distinctly recognizes how, in the missing piece which followed, the poet had laid the motive in this for the surrender of the Danaids, who were begging protection. Sophocles is specially skilful in introducing as controlling motive some marked trait of his characters, for example, Antigone, Ajax, Odysseus. Indeed, Euripides is even more like the Germans than Sophocles in this, that he delights in making more prominent the peculiarities of his characters. In general, however, the epic trend of the fable was much stronger than with us ; as a rule the persons were fashioned according to the demands of a well known and already prepared network of events, as in the case of Agamemnon, Clytemnestra, Orestes. This was an advantage to the Greeks, but to us it seems a restraint. With us the poet not seldom finds himself in the position, that his hero is seeking an action which shall be a luminous center, throwing light on everything that approaches it. We will be able to explain, from his nature, what is more profound and hidden. But however rigidly we construct the action according to his needs, it must always be composed of individual parts which belong to the same event, and this must extend from the beginning to the end of the piece. Among the Greeks, Sophocles is our master in the management of this dramatic unity, Euripides unconscionably against it. How, in his serious plays, Shakespeare disclosed this law to himself, and gradually to us, in the face of the sixteenth century stage, has already been mentioned. Among the Germans, Lessing preserves the unity with great care ; Goethe, in the short action of *Clavigo*, and in the later plays in which he had thought of the stage—*Tasso* and *Iphigenia*. Schiller has observed the law faithfully in *Love and Intrigue*. Is it an accident that in his last plays, in *Tell*, and in *Demetrius*, so far as this play may be judged from notices of it, he has neglected the law? Whenever he approached the bounds of license, it occurred through his delight in episodes and in double heroes, as in *Don Carlos*, *Mary Stuart*, and *Wallenstein*.

Of kinds of material, those taken from epic legends make it not difficult to preserve the unity of action ; but their action does not easily permit dramatic elaboration of characters. Material from novels preserves well the unity of action, but the characters, on account of the entangled action, are easily thrown about with too little freedom of movement, or they are restrained in their movement through the portrayal of situations. Historical material offers the greatest and most beautiful opportunities; but it is very difficult to combine it into a good action.

The poet's interest in the characters of his counter-players easily mounts so high that to them is accorded a rich, detailed portrayal, a sympathetic exposition of their striving and their fighting moods, and a peculiar destiny. Thereby arises a double action for the drama; or the action of the piece may be of such a nature as to require for its illumination and completion a subordinate action, which through the exposition of concurrent or opposing relations brings into greater prominence the chief persons, with what they do and what they suffer.

Various defects — especially one-sidedness — in material, may make such a completion desirable. One play is not to run through the whole wide range of affecting and thrilling moods; it is not to play from its sober ground color, through all the possible color-tones; but a variation in mood and modest contrasts in color are as necessary to the drama as it is that in a painting in which there are many figures, the swing of the lesser lines should be in contrast with the greater lines and groups, and that in contrast with the ground color, use should be made of dependent, supplementary colors. A specially somber material renders necessary the introduction of bright accessory figures. To contrast with the defiant characters of Iphigenia and Creon, the milder counterparts, Ismene and Hæmon, were invented; through the introduction of Tecmessa, the despair of Ajax receives an affecting tone, the magic charm of which we still feel to-day. The gloomy, pathetic Othello requires opposed to him some one in whom the unrestrained freedom of humor is apparent. The somber figure of Wallenstein and his companions in intrigue imperatively demands that the brilliant Max be joined with them.

If, for this reason, the Greeks classed their plays into those with single action, and those with double action, the modern drama has much less avoided the extension of counter-play into an accessory action. The interweaving of this with the main action has occurred sometimes at the expense of the combined effect. The Germans, especially, who are always inclined, during their labor, to grasp the significance of the accessory persons with great ardor, must guard themselves against too wide an extension of the subordinate action. Even Shakespeare has occasionally, in this way, injured the effect of the drama, most strikingly in *Lear*, in which the whole parallel action of the house of Gloucester, but loosely connected with the main action, and treated with no particular fondness, retards the movement, and needlessly renders the whole more bitter. The poet allowed the episodes in both parts of *Henry IV.* to develop into an accessory action, the immortal humor of which outshines the serious effect of the play; and this has made these dramas favorites of the reader. Every admirer of Falstaff will grant, however, that the general effect on the stage has not the corresponding power, in spite of this charm. Let it be noticed, in passing, that in Shakespeare's comedies the double action belongs to the nature of the play; he strives to take from his clowns the episodical, while he interweaves them with the serious action. The genial humor which beams from their scenes must sometimes conceal the harder elements in the material; as when the constables must help to prevent the sad fate threatening the heroine. Among German poets, Schiller was most in danger of injury from the double action. The disproportion of the accessory action in *Don Carlos* and *Mary Stuart* rests upon this, that his ardor for the character set in contrast to the hero, becomes too great; in *Wallenstein*, the same principle has extended the piece to a trilogy.[4] In *Tell*, three actions run parallel.[5]

It is the business of the action to represent to us the inner consistency of the event, as it corresponds to the demands of the intellect and the heart. Whatever, in the crude material, does not serve this purpose, the poet is in duty bound to throw away. And it is desirable that he adhere strictly to this principle, to give only what is indispensable to unity. Yet he may not avoid a deviation from this; for there will be occasional deviations desirable which may strengthen the color of the piece, in a manner conformable to its purpose; which may intensify the meaning of the characters, and enhance the general effect by the introduction of a new color, or a contrast. These embellishing additions of the poet are called episodes. They are of various kinds. At a point where the action suffers a short pause, a characterizing moment may be enlarged into a situation; opportunity may be given a hero to exhibit some significant characteristic of his being in an attractive manner, in connection with some subordinate person; some subordinate rôle of the piece may, through ampler elaboration, be developed into an attractive figure. By a modest use, which must not take time from what is more important, these may become an embellishment to the drama. And the poet has to treat them as ornaments, and to compensate for them with serious work, if they ever retard the action. The episodes perform different duties, according to the parts of the drama in which they appear. While at the beginning they enter into the rôles of the chief persons to delineate these in their idiosyncracies, they are allowed in the last part as enlargements of those new rôles which afford lesser aids to the movement of the action; in each place, however, they must be felt to be advantageous additions.[6]

The Greeks understood this word in a somewhat broader sense. That which in the plays of Sophocles his contemporaries called episode, we no longer so name: for the ingenious art of this great master consisted, among other things, in this, that he interwove his beautifying additions very intimately with his action, for the most part to set the characters of the chief heroes in a stronger light, by means of contrast. Thus, in *Electra*, in addition to the Ismene scene, mentioned later, Chrysomethis is indispensable according to our feeling for the chief heroine, and no longer as episode, but as part of the action. Moreover, where he paints a situation more broadly, as in the beginning of *Œdipus at Colonos*, such a portrayal corresponds throughout to the customs of our stage. Shakespeare treats his episodes almost exactly in the same way. Even in those serious plays, which have a more artistic construction, there are, in almost every act, partly extended scenes, partly whole rôles of episodical elaboration; but there is so much of the beautiful worked in and with this, so much that is efficient for the combined effect, that the severest manager of our stage, who may be compelled to shorten the drama, rarely ever allows these passages to be expunged. Mercutio, with his Queen Mab, and the jests of the nurse, the interviews of Hamlet with the players and courtiers, as well as the grave-digger scene, are such examples as recur in almost all his plays. Almost superabundantly, and with apparent carelessness, the great artist adorns all parts of his piece with golden ornaments; but he who approaches to unclasp them, finds them fastened as if with steel, grown inseparably into what they adorn. Of the Germans, Lessing, with a reverential regularity joined his episodes to the carefully planned structure of his piece, according to his own method, which was transferred to his successors. His episodes are little character rôles. The painter and countess Orsina, in *Emilia Galotti* (the last, the better prototype of Lady Milford), Riccault, in *Minna von Barnhelm*, indeed, even the Dervise in *Nathan The Wise*, became models for the German episodes of the eighteenth century. Goëthe has not honored them with a place in his regular plays, *Clavigo*, *Tasso*, *Iphigenia*. In Schiller, they throng abundantly in every form, as portrayals, as detailed situations, as accessory figures in the conjoined action. Frequently, through their peculiar beauty, they are adapted to be effective adjuncts to the stilted, tedious movement, but not always; for we would gladly spare some single ones, like Parricida in *William Tell*, just because in this case the understood purpose is so striking; and The Black Knight in the *Maid of Orleans;* and not seldom the long-drawn observations and delineations in his dialogue-scenes.

IV.

PROBABILITY OF THE ACTION.

The action of the serious drama must be probable.

Poetic truth is imparted to material taken from real life, by its being raised above its casual connections and receiving a universally understood meaning and significance. In dramatic poetry, this transformation of reality with poetic truth is effected thus : the essential parts, bound together and unified by some causative connection, and all the accessory inventions, are conceived as probable and credible motives of the represented events. But more than this, poetic truth is needed in the drama. The entertained hearer surrenders himself gladly to the invention of the poet; he gladly lets the presumption of a piece please him, and is in general quite inclined to approve of the invented human relations in the world of beautiful illusion; but he is not able entirely to forget the reality; he holds close to this poetic picture, which rises full of charm before him, the picture of the real world in which he breathes. He brings with him before the stage a certain knowledge of historical relations, definite, ethical and moral demands upon human life, presages and a clear knowledge of the course of events. To a certain extent, it is impossible for him to renounce this purport of his own life; and sometimes he feels it very strongly when the poetic picture contradicts it. That ocean vessels should land on the coast of Bohemia, that Charlemagne should use cannon, appears to our spectators a serious mistake.

That the Jew, Shylock, is promised mercy if he will turn Christian, shocks the moral sense of the spectator, and he is probably not inclined to concede that a just judge has so decided. That Thoas, who in so refined and dignified a manner seeks the hand of the priestess Iphigenia, allows human sacrifices in his kingdom, appears as an internal contradiction between the noble personality of the characters and the presuppositions of the piece; and however shrewdly the poet conceals this irrational element, it yet may be injurious to the effect of the play. That Œdipus rules many years without troubling himself about the death of Laius, appears to the Athenians, even at the first presentation of the play, as a doubtful supposition.

Now it is well known that this picture of the real, which the spectator holds up against the single drama, does not remain the same in every century, but is changed by each advance of human culture. The interpretation of past times, moral and social demands, the social relations, are nothing firmly established; but every spectator is a child of his time; for each the comprehension of what is commonly acceptable, is limited through his personality and the culture of his age.

And it is further clear that this picture of real life shades off differently in the mind of each person, and that the poet, however fully and richly he has taken into his own life the culture of his race, still is confronted with conceptions of reality in a thousand different tones. He has, indeed, the great calling to be, in his time, the apostle of the highest and most liberal culture, and without posturing as a teacher, to draw his hearers upward toward himself. But to the dramatic poet there are for this reason private bounds staked out. He must not exceed these bounds. He must not, in many cases, leave vacant any of the space which they enclose. Where they arise invisible, they may be divined in each single case only through delicate sensibility and trustworthy feeling.

The effects of dramatic art are, so to speak, sociable. As the dramatic work of art, in a combination of several arts, is represented through the general activity of numerous adjuncts, so is the audience of the poet a body composed of many changing individuals and yet, as a whole, a unit, which like every human congregation, mightily influences the individuals who compose it; a certain agreement in feeling and contemplation develops, elevates one, depresses another, and to a great extent equalizes mood and judgment through a common opinion. This community of feeling in the audience expresses itself continually by its reception of the dramatic effects; it may increase their power prodigiously, it may weaken them in an equal degree. Scarcely will a single hearer escape the influence which an unsympathetic house or an enthusiastic audience exercises on him. Indeed, everyone has felt how different the impression is which the same piece makes, equally well presented on different stages before a differently constituted audience. The poet, while composing, is invariably directed, perhaps without knowing it, by his conception of the intelligence, taste, and intellectual requirements of his audience. He knows that he must not attribute too much to it, nor dare he offer it too little. He must, moreover, so arrange his action that it shall not bring into collision with its presuppositions a good average of his hearers, who bring these from actual life before the stage; that is, he must make the connection of events and the motives and outlines of his heroes probable. If he succeeds in this respect with the groundwork of his piece, the action and the outlines of his characters, as for the rest, he may trust to his hearers the most refined culture and the keenest understanding which his performance contains.

This consideration must guide the poet most when he is tempted to put forward what is strange or marvellous. To make charming what is strange, is, indeed, possible. The dramatic art specially has rich means of making it understood, and of laying stress upon what is intelligible to us; but for this there is needed a special expenditure of force and time; and frequently the question is justified, whether the effect aimed at warrants the expenditure of time and compensates for the limitation of the essentials occasioned. Especially the newer poets, with no definitely marked out field of material, in the midst of a period of culture to which the ready reception of extraneous pictures is peculiar, can easily be enticed to gather material from the culture-relations, the civilization of a dark age, of remote peoples. Perhaps just what is marvellous in such material has appeared peculiarly valuable for sharply delineating individual portraiture. Already a minute observation of early times in Germany, or of the old world, offers numerous peculiarities, circumstances unknown to the life of later times, in which a striking and significant meaning is manifested of highest import to the historian of culture. These can be used by the poet, however, only in exceptional cases, with most skilful treatment, and as accessories which deepen a color. For not out of the peculiarities of human life, but out of its immortal import, out of what is common to us and to the old times, blossom his successes. Still more he will avoid presenting such strange peoples as stand entirely outside the great forward movements of civilization. That which is unusual in their manners and customs, their costumes, or even the color of their skins, is distracting and excites attendant images which are unfavorable to serious art effects. In a crude way, the ideal world of poetry is joined in the hearer's mind with a picturing of real circumstances, which can claim an interest only because they are real. But even the inner life of such foreigners is unsuitable for dramatic expression; for, without exception, the capability is in reality wanting in them of presenting in any fulness the inner mental processes which our art finds necessary. And the transferring of such a degree of culture into their souls, rightly arouses in the hearer a feeling of impropriety. Anyone who would lay the scene of his action among the ancient Egyptians or the present-day fellahs, among the Japanese or even Hindoos, would perhaps awaken an ethnographic interest by the strange character of his people; but this interest of curiosity in the unusual would not increase for the hearer before the stage the real interest in what may be the poetical meaning, but would thwart it and prejudice it. It is no accident that only such peoples are a fitting basis for the drama as have advanced so far in the development of their intellectual life that they themselves could produce a popular drama—Greeks, Romans, cultured peoples of modern times; after these, a people nearly like them, whose nationality has grown up with ours, or with the ancient culture, like the Hebrews—scarcely yet the Turks.

How far the marvellous may be deemed worthy of the drama, cannot be doubtful even to us Germans, upon whose stage the most spirited and most amiable of all devils has received citizenship. Dramatic poetry is poorer and richer than her sisters, lyric and epic, in this respect, that she can represent only men, and, if one looks more closely, only cultivated men, these, however, fully and profoundly as no other art can. She must arrange historical relations by inventing for them an inner consistency which is thoroughly comprehensible to human understanding. How shall she embody the supernatural?

But granted that she undertakes this, she can do it only in so far as the superhuman, already poetically prepared through the imagination of the people, and provided with a personality corresponding to the human, is personifiable through sharply stamped features even to details. Thus given form, the Greek gods lived in the Greek world among their people; thus hover among us still, fashioned with affection, images of many of the holy ones of Christian legend, almost numberless shadowy forms, from the household faith of German primitive times. Not a few of the images of fancy have, through poetry, legend, painting, and the spirit of our people, which, credulous or incredulous, is still busied with them, received so rich an amplification, that they surround the creating artist during his labor like old, trusted friends. The Virgin Mary, St. Peter at the gate of heaven, many saints, archangels, and angels, and not last the considerable swarm of devils, live among our people, credulously associated with women in white, the wild huntsman, elves, giants and dwarfs. But, however alluringly the colors gleam which they wear in their twilight, before the sharp illumination of the tragic stage, they vanish into unsubstantial shadows. For it is true they have received through the people a share in human feeling, and in the conditions of human life. But this participation is only of the epic kind; they are not fashioned for dramatic mental processes. In some of the most beautiful legends, the Germans make the little spirits complain that they cannot be happy; that is that they have no human soul. The same difference, which already in the middle ages the people felt, keeps them in a different way from the modern stage—inward struggles are wanting in them, freedom fails to test and to choose, they stand outside of morals, law, right; neither a complete lack of changeableness, nor perfected purity, nor complete wickedness are presentable, because they exclude all inward agitation. Even the Greeks felt this. When the gods should rather be represented on the stage than speak a command *ex machina*, they must either become entirely men, with all the pain and rage, like Prometheus, or they must sink beneath the nobility of human nature, without the poets being able to hinder, down to blank generalizations of love and hate, like Athene, in the prologue of *Ajax*.

While gods and spirits have a bad standing in the serious drama, they have far better success in the comedy. And the now worn-out magic tricks give only a very pale representation of what our spirit world could be to a poet, in whimsical and humorous representation. If the Germans shall ever be ripe for political comedy, then will they learn to use the wealth, the inexhaustible treasure of motives and resistance which can be mined from this world of phantasy, for droll freaks, political satire, and humorous portraiture.

For what has been said, *Faust* is the best proof; and in this play, the rôle of Mephistopheles. Here the genius of the greatest of German poets has created a stage problem which has become the favorite task of our character players. Each of them seeks in his own manner to solve, with credit to himself, the riddle which can not be solved; the one brings out the mask of the old wood-cut devil, another, the cavalier youth Voland; at best, the player will succeed with the business who contents himself prudently and with spirit to render intelligible the fine rhetoric of the dialogue, and exhibits in the comic scenes a suitable bearing and good humor. The poet has indeed made it exceedingly difficult for the player, of whom, during the composition of the piece, he did not think at all; for the rôle changes into all colors, from the true-hearted speech of Hans Sachs, to the subtle discussion of a Spinozist, from the grotesque to the terrifying. And if one examines more closely how the representation of this piece still becomes possible on the stage, the ultimate reason is the entrance of a comic element. Mephistopheles appears in some serious situations, but is a comic figure treated in a grand style; and so far as he produces an effect on the stage, he does it in this direction.

By this is not meant that the mysterious, that which has no foundation in human reason, should be entirely banished from the province of the drama. Dreams, portents, prophesyings, ghost-seers, the intrusion of the spirit world upon human life, everything for which there may be supposed to be a certain susceptibility in the soul of the hearer, the poet may employ as a matter of course for the occasional strengthening of his effects. It is understood in this that he must appreciate rightly the susceptibility of his contemporaries; we are no longer much inclined to care for this, and only very sparing use of side effects is now accorded to the poet. Shakespeare was allowed to use this kind of minor accessories with greater liberty; for in the sentiments of even his educated contemporaries, the popular tradition was very vivid, and the connection with the world of spirits was universally conceived far differently. The soul-processes of a man struggling under a heavy burden, were, not only among the people but with the more pretentious, very differently thought of. In the case of intense fear, qualm of conscience, remorse, the power of imagination conjured up before the sufferer the image of the frightful, still as something external; the murderer saw the murdered rise before him as a ghost; clutching into the air, he felt the weapon with which he committed the crime; he heard the voice of the dead ringing in his ear. Shakespeare and his hearers conceived, therefore, Macbeth's dagger even on the stage, and the ghosts of Banquo, Cæsar, the elder Hamlct, and the victims of Richard III., far differently from ourselves. To them this was not yet a bold, customary symbolizing of the inward struggles of their heroes, an accidental, shrewd invention of the poet, who supported his effects by this ghostly trumpery; but it was to them the necessary method, customary in their land, in which themselves experienced, dread, horror, struggles of soul. Dread was not artistically excited by recollection of nursery tales; the stage presented only what had been frightful in their own lives, or what could be. For while young Protestantism had laid the severest struggles in men's consciences, and while the thoughts and the most passionate moods of the excited soul had been already more carefully and critically observed by individuals, the mode of thinking natural to the middle ages, had not, for that reason, quite disappeared. Therefore Shakespeare could make use of this kind of effects, and expect more from them than we can.

But he furnishes at the same time the best example of how these ghost-like apparitions may be rendered artistically worthy of the drama. Whoever must present heroes of past centuries according to the view of life of their time, will not entirely conceal men's lack of freedom from and dependence on legendary figures; but he will use them as Shakespeare used his witches in the first act of *Macbeth*, as arabesques which mirror the color and mood of the time, and which only give occasion for forcing from the inner man of the hero what has grown up in his own soul, with the liberty necessary for a dramatic figure.

It is to be observed that in the work of the modern poet, such accessories of the action serve especially to give color and mood. They belong also to the first half of the play. But even when they are interwoven with the effects of the later parts, their appearance must be arranged for in the first part, by a coloring in harmony with them; and besides this, the way must be paved for them otherwise, with great care. Thus the appearance of The Black Knight in the *Maid of Orleans* is a disturbing element, because his ghostly form comes to view with no preparation of the audience, and is thoroughly unsuitable to the brilliant, thoughtful language of Schiller, to the tone and color of the piece. The time and the action would, in themselves, have very well allowed such an apparition; and it appeared to the poet a counterpart to the Blessed Virgin who bears banner and sword in the play.

But Schiller did not bring the Blessed Virgin herself upon the stage; he only had her reported in his magnificent fashion. Had the prologue presented the decisive interview between the shepherdess and the Mother of God in such language and with such naïve address as the material from the middle ages would suggest, then there would have been a better preparation for the later appearance of the evil spirit. In costume and speech, the rôle is not advantageously equipped. Schiller was an admirable master in the disposition of the most varied historical coloring; but the glimmer of the legendary was not to the taste of one who always painted in full colors, and if a playful simile is allowed, used most fondly, gleaming golden yellow, and dark sky blue. On the other hand, Goethe, the unrestrained master of lyric moods, has made an admirable use of the spirit-world to give color to *Faust*, but not at all with a view to its presentation on the stage.

V.

IMPORTANCE AND MAGNITUDE OF THE ACTION.

The action of the serious drama must possess importance and magnitude.

The struggles of individual men must affect their inmost life; the object of the struggle must, according to universal apprehension, be a noble one, the treatment dignified. The characters must correspond to such a meaning of the action, in order that the play may produce a noble effect. If the action is constructed in conformity with the stated law, and the characters are inadequate to the demands thus created, or if the characters evince strong passion and extreme agitation, while these elements are wanting to the action, the incongruity is painfully apparent to the spectator. Euripides' *Iphigenia in Aulis* contains what affords to the stage the most frightful struggles of the human soul; but the characters, at least with the exception of Clytemnestra, are poorly invented, disfigured either through unnecessary meanness of sentiment, or through lack of force, or through sudden, unwarranted change of feeling; thus Agamemnon, Menelaus, Achilles, Iphigenia. Again, in Shakespeare's *Timon of Athens*, the character of the hero, from the moment when he is aroused to activity, has an ever-increasing energy and power, to which a gloomy grandeur is not at all lacking, but idea and action stand in incongruity with it. That a warm-hearted, trusting spendthrift should, after the loss of external possessions, become a misanthrope through the ingratitude and meanness of his former friends, presupposes the weakness of his own character and the pitiableness of his surroundings; and this instability, lamentableness of all the relations represented, restrains the sympathy of the hearer in spite of great poetic skill.

But even the environment, the sphere of life of the hero, influences the dignity and magnitude of the action. We demand rightly that the hero whose fate is to hold us spellbound, shall possess a character whose force and worth shall exceed the measure of the average man. This force of his being, however, does not lie wholly in the energy of his will and the violence of his passion, but as well in his possessing a rich share of the culture, manners, and spiritual capacity of his time. He must be represented as superior in the important relations of his surroundings; and his surroundings must be so created as easily to awaken in the hearer a keen interest. It is, therefore, no accident that when an action is laid in past time, it always seeks the realm in which what is greatest and most important is contained, the greatest affairs of a people, the life of its leaders and rulers, those heights of humanity that have developed not only a mighty spiritual significance, but also a significant power of will. Scarce any but the deeds and destinies of such commanding figures have been handed down to us from the former times.

With material from later times, the relations, of course, are changed. No longer are the most powerful passions and the sublimest soul-struggles to be recognized at courts and among political rulers alone, nor even generally. There remains, however, to these figures for the drama a pre-eminence which may be, for their life and that of their contemporaries, a positive disadvantage. They are now less exposed to the compulsion which middle-class society exercises on the private citizen. They are not, to the same degree as the private citizen, subjected to civil law, and they know it. In domestic and foreign conflicts, their own self has not greater right but greater might. So they appear exposed to freer, more powerful temptation, and capable of greater self-direction. It must be added that the relations in which they live, and the directions in which they exert influence, offer the greatest wealth of colors and the most varied multiplicity of figures. Finally the counterplay against their characters and against their purposes is most effective; and the sphere of the interests for which they should live, embraces the most important affairs of the human race.

The life of the private citizen has also been for centuries freeing itself from the external restraint of restricting traditions, has been gaining nobility and spiritual freedom, and become full of contradictions and conflicts. In any realm of reality, where worldly aims and movements resulting from the civilization of the times have penetrated, a tragic hero may be generated and developed in its atmosphere. It depends only on whether a struggle is possible for him, which, according to the general opinion of the audience, has a great purpose, and whether the opposition to this develops a corresponding activity worthy of consideration. Since, however, the importance and greatness of the conflict can be made impressive only by endowing the hero with the capability of expressing his inmost thought and feeling in a magnificent manner, with a certain luxuriance of language; and since these demands increase among such men as belong to the life of modern times,— to the hero of the modern stage a suitable measure of the culture of the time is indispensable. For only in this way does he receive freedom of thought and will. Therefore, such classes of society as remain until our own time under the sway of epic relations, whose life is specially directed by the customs of their circle; such classes as still languish under the pressure of circumstances which the spectator observes and decides to be unjust; finally, such classes as are not specially qualified to transpose, in a creative manner, their thoughts and emotions into discourse,—such are not available for heroes of the drama, however powerfully passion works in their natures, however their feeling, in single hours, breaks out with spontaneous, native force.

From what has been said, it follows that tragedy must forego grounding its movement on motives which the judgment of the spectator will condemn as lamentable, common, or unintelligible. Even such motives may force a man into violent conflicts with his environment; but the dramatic art, considered in general, may be in a position to turn such antagonisms to account. He who from a desire for gain, robs, steals, murders, counterfeits; who from cowardice, acts dishonorably; who through stupidity, short-sightedness, frivolity, and thoughtlessness, becomes smaller and weaker than his relations demand,— he is not at all suitable for hero of a serious play.

If a poet would completely degrade his art, and turn to account in the action of a play full of contention and evil tendency, the social perversion of real life, the despotism of the rich, the torments of the oppressed, the condition of the poor who receive from society only suffering,—by such work he would probably excite the sympathy of the audience to a high degree; but at the end of the play this sympathy would sink into a painful discord. The delineating of the mental processes of a common criminal belongs to halls where trial by jury is held; efforts for the improvement of the poor and oppressed classes should be an important part of our labor in real life; the muse of art is no sister of mercy.

VI.

MOVEMENT AND RISE OF THE ACTION.

The dramatic action must represent all that is important to the understanding of the play, in the strong excitement of the characters, and in a continuously progressive increase of effects.

The action must, first of all, be capable of the strongest dramatic excitement; and this must be universally intelligible. There are great and important fields of human activity, which do not make the growth of a captivating emotion, a passionate desire, or a mighty volition easy; and again, there are violent struggles which force to the outside men's mental processes, while the subject of the struggle is little adapted to the stage, though importance and greatness are not lacking to it. For example, a politic prince, who negotiates with the powerful ones of his land, who wages war and concludes peace with his neighbors, will perhaps do all this without once exhibiting the least excited passion; and if this does come to light as secret desire or resentment toward others, it will be noticeable only by careful observation, and in little ripples. But even when it is allowed to represent his whole being in dramatic suspense, the subject of his volition, a political success or a victory, is capable of being shown only very imperfectly and fragmentarily in its stage setting. And the scenes in which this round of worldly purposes is specially active, state trials, addresses, battles, are for technical reasons not the part most conveniently put on the stage. From this point of view, warning must be given against putting scenes from political history on the boards. Of course the difficulties which this field of the greatest human activity offers, are not unsurmountable; but it requires not only maturity of genius but very peculiar and intimate knowledge of the stage to overcome them. But the poet will never degrade his action by reducing it to an imperfect and insufficient exposition of such political deeds and aims; he will need to make use of a single action, or a small number of actions, as a background, before which he presents — and in this he is infinitely superior to the historian — a most minute revelation of human nature, in a few personages, and in their most intimate emotional relations with each other. If he fails to do this, he will in so far falsify history without creating poetry.

An entirely unfavorable field for dramatic material is the inward struggles which the inventor, the artist, the thinker has to suffer with himself and with his time. Even if he is a reformer by nature, who knows how to impress the stamp of his own spirit on thousands of others; indeed, if his own material misfortunes may lay claim to unusual sympathy, the dramatist will not willingly conclude to bring him forward as the hero of the action. If the mental efforts, the mode of thought of such a hero, are not sufficiently known to the living audience, then the poet will have first to show his warrant for such a character by artful discourse, by a fulness of oral explanation, and by a representation of spiritual import. This may be quite as difficult as it is undramatic. If the poet presupposes in his auditors a living interest in such personages, acquaintance with the incidents of their lives, and makes use of this interest in order to avail himself of an occurrence in the life of such a hero, he falls into another danger. On the stage the good which is known beforehand of a man, and the good that is reported of him, have no value at all, as opposed to what the hero himself does on the stage. Indeed, the great expectations which the hearer brings with him in this case, may be prejudicial to the unbiased reception of the action. And if the poet succeeds, as is probable in the case of popular heroes, in promoting the scenic effects through the already awakened ardor of the audience for the hero, he must credit his success to the interest which the audience brings with it, not to the interest which the drama itself has merited. If the poet is conscientious, he will adopt only those moments from the life of the artist, poet, thinker, in which he shows himself active and suffering quite as significantly toward others as he was in his studio. It is clear that this will be the case only by accident; it is quite as clear that in such a case it will be only an accident, if the hero bears a celebrated name. Therefore, the making use of anecdotes from the life of such great men, the meaning of which does not show itself in the action but in the non-representable activity of their laboratory, is intrinsically right undramatic. The greatness in them is non-representable; and what is represented borrows the greatness of the hero from a moment of his life lying outside the piece. The personality of Shakespeare, Goethe, Schiller, is in this respect worse on the stage than in a novel or romance, and all the worse the more intimately their lives are known.

Of course, opinions as to what may be represented on the stage, and what is effective, are not the same in all ages. National custom as well as the arrangement of the theatre direct the poet. We have no longer the susceptibility of the Greeks to epic narratives which are brought upon the scene by a messenger; we have greater pleasure in what can be acted, and risk upon our stage the imitation of actions which would have appeared entirely impossible on the Athenian stage, in spite of its machines, its devices for flying and its perspective painting,—popular tumults, collision of armies, and the like. And as a rule the later poet will be inclined to do too much rather than too little in this direction.

It may happen to him rather than to the Greek, therefore, that through full elaboration of the action, the inner perturbation of the chief figures may be disproportionately restricted, and that an important transition, a portentous series of moods, remains unexpressed. A well known example of such a defect is in *Prince of Homburg*, the very piece in which the poet has superbly achieved one of the most difficult scenic tasks, the disposition of an army for battle and the battle itself. The prince has taken his imprisonment light-heartedly; when his friend, Hohenzollern, brings him the news that his death-warrant is awaiting the signature, his mood naturally becomes serious, and he determines to entreat the intercession of the electoral princess. And in the next scene, the young hero throws himself powerless, and without self-control, at the feet of his protectress, because, as he relates, he has seen on his way to her, men digging his grave by torchlight; he begs for his life, though he may be shamefully degraded. This sudden plunge to a cowardly fear of death, does painful violence to the character of a general. It is certainly not untrue in itself, even if we unwillingly tolerate lack of self-control in a general under such circumstances. And the drama demanded the severest humiliation of the hero; just this lack of courage is the turning point of the piece; in his confusion he must plunge down to this, in order to redeem himself worthily in the second part of the action. It was therefore a chief task to present the abasement of a youthful heroic nature even to the fear of death, and indeed, in such a manner that the sympathy of the hearer should not be dissipated through contempt. That could happen only by an accurate exhibition of the inner perturbations, even to the bursting forth of the death anguish, which terminated in the prostration at the princess's feet—a difficult task for even powerful poetic genius, but one which must be performed. And here a rule may be mentioned, which has force for the poet as well as for the actor: it is preposterous to hasten over parts of the action which for any reason are necessary to the play, but have not the merit of pleasing motives; on the contrary, upon such passages, the highest technical art must be expended, in order to give poetic beauty to what is in itself unsuitable. Before just this kind of tasks, the artist must achieve the proud feeling that for him there are no unconquerable difficulties.

Another case in which the forcing forward of the chief effect has been neglected, is the third act of *Antony and Cleopatra.* A defect in Shakespeare does not, indeed, originate in want of insight, nor in haste. The striking thing is that the piece lacks climax. Antony has withdrawn from Cleopatra, has been reconciled with Octavianus, and has re-established his authority. But the spectator has long had a presentiment that he will return to Cleopatra. The inner necessity of this relapse is amply motived from the first act. Notwithstanding this, one demands rightly to see this momentous relapse, with its violent passions and mental disturbances; it is the point on which all that has gone before is suspended, and which must account for all that follows, the degradation of Antony, even to his cowardly flight, and his death. And yet, it is presented in only brief sections; the culmination of the action is divided up into little scenes, and the joining of these into one well-executed scene was the more desirable, because the important occurrence in the last half of the play, that flight of Antony from the naval battle, cannot be represented on the stage, but can be made intelligible only through the short account of the subordinate commander and the thrilling struggle of the broken-down hero which follows.'

But the poet has not the task, let it be understood, of representing through what is done on the stage every individual impulse which is necessary to the inner connection of the action as actually occurring. Such a representation of accessories would rather conceal the essentials than make them impressive, by taking time from the more important; it would also divide up the action into too many parts and thereby injure the effects. Upon our stage, also, many heroic accounts of events are necessary in vivid representation. Since they always produce resting places in the action, however excitedly the declaimer may speak, the law applies to them, that they must come in as relief from a strongly worked-up suspense. The spectator must be previously aroused by the excited emotion of the persons concerned. The length of the narration is to be carefully calculated; a line too much, the least unnecessary elaboration, may cause weariness. If the narrative contains individual parts of some extent, it must be divided and interspersed with short speeches of other characters, which indicate the narrator's mood; and the parts must be carefully arranged in the order of climax, both as to meaning and style. A celebrated example of excellent arrangement is the Swedish captain's story in *Wallenstein.* An elaborate narrative must not occur when the action is moving forward with energy and rapidity.

One variety of messenger scene is the portrayal of an occurrence thought of as behind the scenes, when the persons on the stage are represented as observers; also the presentation of an occurrence from the impressions which it has made on the characters. This kind of recital allows more easily of dramatic excitement; it may be almost a mere, quiet narrative; it may possibly occasion or increase passionate excitement on the stage.

The grounds upon which the poet has something happening behind the scenes, are of various kinds. First of all, occasion is given by unavoidable incidents which, because of their nature, cannot be represented on the stage at all, or only through elaborate machinery — a conflagration, a naval battle, a popular tumult, battles of cavalry and chariot-eers — everything in which the mighty forces of nature or great multitudes of men are active in widespread commotion. The effect of such reflected impressions may be greatly enhanced by little scenic indications: calls from without, signals, lurid lights, thunder and lightning, the roar of cannon, and similar devices which excite the fancy, and the appropriateness of which is easily recognized by the hearer. These indications and shrewd hints of something in the distance, will be most successful when they are used to show the doings of men; not so favorable are the representation of the unusual operations of nature, descriptions of landscape, all spectacles to which the spectator is not accustomed to give himself over before the stage. In such a case the designed effect may entirely fail, because the audience is accustomed to strive against attempts to produce strange illusions.

This representation of mirrored impressions, the laying a part of the action behind the scene, has peculiar significance for the drama in moments when what is frightful, terrifying, or horrible is to be exhibited. If it is desired by the present-day poet that he should follow the example of the Greeks, and discreetly lay the decisive moment of a hideous deed as much as possible behind the scenes, and bring it to light only through the impressions which it makes on the minds of those concerned, then an objection must be made against this restriction in favor of the newer art; for an imposing deed is sometimes of the greatest effect on our stage, and is indispensable to the action. First, if the dramatically presentable individual parts of the deed give significance to what follows; next, if we recognize in such a deed the sudden culmination of an inner process just perfected; third, if only through the contemplation of the action itself the spectators may be convinced how the affair really happened, —nowhere need we fear the effects on the stage, of death, murder, violent collision of figures, though in themselves not the highest effects of the drama. While the Greek stage was developed out of a lyric representation of passionate emotions, the German has arisen from the epic delineation of events. Both have preserved some traditions of their oldest conditions; the Greek remained just as inclined to keep in the background the moment of the deed, as the Germans rejoiced to picture fighting and rapine.

But if the Greeks avoided violent physical efforts, blows, attacks, wrestlings, overthrows, perhaps not the foresight of the poet, but the need of the actors was the ultimate reason. The Greek theatre costume was very inconvenient for violent movements of the body; the falling of a dying person in the cothurnus must be gradual and very carefully managed if it would not be ridiculous. And the mask took away any possibility of representing the expression of the countenance, indispensable in the moments of highest suspense. Æschylus appears to have undertaken something also in this direction; and the shrewd Sophocles went just as far as he dared. He ventured to have even Antigone dragged by an armed force from the grove of Colonos, but he did not venture, in *Electra*, to have Ægisthos killed on the stage; Orestes and Pylades must pursue him with drawn swords behind the scenes. Perhaps Sophocles perceived, as well as we, that in such a place this was a disadvantage, a restriction which was laid upon him by the leather and padding of his actors, and, too, by the religious horror which the Greeks felt for the moment of death. Then this is one of the places in the drama where the spectator must *see* that the action completes itself. Even if pursued by two men, Ægisthos could either have defended himself against them or have escaped them.

Through the greater ease and energy of our imitation, we are freed from such considerations; and in our pieces, numerous effects, great and small, rest on the supreme moment of action. The scene in which Coriolanus embraces Aufidius before the household altar of the Volscians, receives its full significance only through the battle scene in the first act, in which the embittered antagonists are seen to punish each other. The contest is necessary between Prince Henry and Percy. And again in *Love and Intrigue*, how indispensable, according to the premises, is the death of the two lovers on the stage. In *Romeo and Juliet*, how indispensable the death of Tybalt, of Paris, and of the loving pair, before the eyes of the spectators. Could we believe it, were Emilia Galotti stabbed by her father behind the scenes? And would it be possible to dispense with the great scene in which Cæsar was murdered?

On the other hand, again, there is an entire series of great effects, when the deed itself does not busy the eye, but is so concealed that the attending circumstances stimulate the imagination, and cause the terrible to be felt through those impressions which fall into the soul of the hero. Wherever there is room to make impressive the moments preparatory to a deed; wherever the deed does not enter into the sudden excitement of the hero; finally, wherever it is more useful to excite horror, and hold in suspense, than sorrowfully to relax excited suspense,—the poet will do well to have the deed itself performed behind the scenes. We are indebted to such a concealment for many of the most powerful effects which have been produced at all. When in the *Agamemnon* of Æschylus, the captive Cassandra announces the individual circumstances of the murder which occurs in the house; when Electra, as the death shrieks of Clytemnestra press upon the stage, cries to her brother behind the scene, "Strike once more!"—the fearful power of these effects has never been surpassed. Not less magnificent is the murdering of King Duncan in *Macbeth*—the delineating of the murderer's frame of mind before and after the deed.

For the German stage, the suspense, the undefined horror, the unearthly, the exciting, produced by skilful treatment, through this concealing of momentous deeds, are especially to be esteemed in the part of the action tending toward climax. In the more rapid course and the more violent excitement of the second part, they will not be so easily made use of. At the last exit of the hero, they can be used only in cases where the moment of death itself is not capable of presentation on the stage,— execution on the scaffold, military execution, and where the impossibility of any other solution is a matter of course, on account of the undoubtedly greater strength of the death-dealing antagonist. An interesting example of this is the last act of *Wallenstein*. The gloomy figure of Buttler, the soliciting of the murderers, the drawing together of the net about the unsuspecting one,—all this is impressed upon the soul of the spectator, in a long and powerfully exciting climax; after such a preparation, the accomplishment of the murder itself would not add intensity; one sees the murderer press into the sleeping room; the creaking of the last door, the clanking of arms, the succeeding sudden silence, hold the imagination in the same unearthly suspense which colors the whole act; and the slow awakening of the fancy, the anxious expectation, and the last concealment of the deed itself, are exceedingly well adapted to what is visionary and mysterious in the inspired hero, as Schiller has conceived him.

The poet has not only to exhibit, but as well to keep silence. First of all, there are certain illogical ingredients of the material, which the greatest art is not able always to manage,—this will be further treated in the discussion of dramatic material.

Then there is the repulsive, the disgusting, the hideous, all that shocks dramatic taste, which depends on the crudeness of otherwise serviceable material; what, in this respect may be repugnant to art, the artist must himself feel; it cannot be taught him.

But further, the poet must continually heighten his effects from the beginning to the end of his play. The listener is not the same in every part of the performance. At the beginning of the piece, he acquiesces with readiness, as a rule, in what is offered, and with slight demands; and as soon as the poet has shown his power by some respectable effect, and has shown his manly judgment, through his language, and a firm kind of characterization, the hearer is inclined to yield himself confidently to the poet's leading. This frame of mind lasts till toward the climax of the piece. But in the further course, the listener becomes more exacting; his capability for receiving what is new becomes less; the effects enjoyed have been exciting more powerfully, have in many respects afforded satisfaction; with increasing suspense, comes impatience; with the greater number of impressions received, weariness comes more easily. With all this in view, the poet must carefully arrange every part of his action. Indeed, so far as the import of the play is concerned, he need not, with a skilful arrangement of tolerable material, be anxious about the listener's increasing interest. But he must see to it, that the performance becomes gradually greater and more impressive. During the first acts, in general, a light and brief treatment may be made possible; and here sometimes the heavy exaction is laid on the poet, perhaps even to moderate a great effect; but the last acts from the climax on, require the summoning of all his resources. It is not a matter of indifference, where a scene is placed, whether a messenger recites his narrative in the first or in the fourth act, whether an effect closes the second or the fourth act. It was wise foresight that made the conspiracy scene in *Julius Cæsar* so brief, in order not to prejudice the climax of the piece, and the great tent scene.

Another means of heightening effects lies in the multiplicity of moods that may be aroused, and of characters which may bear forward the action. Every piece, as has been said, has a ground mood, which may be compared to a musical chord or a color. From this controlling color, there is necessary a wealth of shadings, as well as of contrasts. In many cases the poet does not find it essential to make this necessity apparent by cool investigation; for it is an unwritten law of all artistic creation, that anything discovered suggests its opposite,—the chief character, his counterpart, one scene effect, that which contrasts with it. Among the Germans, particularly, there is need that they fondly and carefully infuse into everything which they create, a certain totality of their feeling. Yet, during the work, the critical examination of the figures, which by natural necessity have challenged one another, will supply many important gaps. For in our plays, rich in figures, it is easily possible, by means of a subordinate figure, to give a coloring which materially aids the whole. Even Sophocles is to be admired for the certainty and delicacy with which, in every tragedy, he counterbalances the one-sidedness of some of his characters, by means of the suggested opposites. In Euripides, again, this feeling for harmony is very weak. All great poets of the Germanic race, from Shakespeare to Schiller, considered all together, create, in this direction, with admirable firmness; and in their works we seldom find a character which is not demanded by a counterpart, but is introduced through cool deliberation, like Parricida in *William Tell.* It is a peculiarity of Kleist that his supplementary characters come to him indistinctly; here and there arbitrariness or license violates, in the ground lines of his figures.

From this internal throng of scenic contrasts in the action, there has originated what, to the Germans, is the favorite scene of tragedy — the luminous and fervid part which, as a rule, embraces the touching moments, in contrast with the thrilling moments of the chief action. These scenic contrasts, however, are produced not only through a variation of meaning, but also through a change of amplified and concise scenes, of scenes of two, and of many persons. Among the Greeks, scenes moved in a much narrower circle, both as to matter and form. The variation is made in this way: the scenes have a peculiar, regular, recurring construction, each according to its contents; dialogues and messenger scenes are interrupted by pathos scenes; for each of these kinds there arose, in essentials, an established form.

Not only sharp contrast, but the repetition of the same scenic motive, may produce a heightened effect, as well through parallelism as through fine contrarieties in things otherwise similar. In this case, the poet must give diligent care, that he lay peculiar charm in the returning motive, and that before the recurrence, he arouse suspense and enjoyment in the motive. And in this he will not be allowed to neglect the law, that on the stage, in the last part of the action, even very fine work will not easily suffice to produce heightened effects by means already used, provided the same receive a broader elaboration. There is special danger if the performer wants the peculiar art of setting in strong contrast the repeated motive, and one that has preceded it. Shakespeare is fond of repeating a motive to heighten effects. A good example is the heavy sleepiness of Lucius in *Julius Cæsar*, which in the oath scene shows the contrast in the temper of the master and the servant, and in the tent scene is repeated almost word for word. The second sounding of the chord has to introduce the ghost here, and its soft minor tone reminds the hearer very pleasingly of that unfortunate night and Brutus's guilt. Similarly, in *Romeo and Juliet*, the repetition of the deed with fatal result, works as well through consonance as through contrasted treatment. Further, in *Othello*, the splendid recurring variations of the same theme in the little scenes between Iago and Roderigo. But success with these effects is not always accorded to even great poets. The repetition of the weird-sister motive, in the second half of *Macbeth*, is no strengthening of the effect. The ghostly resists, indeed, a more ample elaboration in the second place. A very remarkable example of such a repetition is the repeated wooing of Richard III., the scene at the bier, and the interview with Elizabeth Rivers.[8] That the repetition stands here as a significant characterizing of Richard, and that a strong effect is intended, is perfectly clear from the great art and full amplification of both scenes. The second scene, also, is treated with greater fondness ; the poet has made use of a technique, new to to him, but very fine ; he has treated it according to antique models, giving to speech and response the same number of lines. And our criticism is accustomed to account for a special beauty of the great drama from this scene. It is certainly a disadvantage on the stage. The monstrous action presses already toward the end, with a power which takes from the spectator the capability of enjoying the extended and artistic battle of words in this interview. A similar disadvantage for our spectators, is the thrice-repeated casket scene in the *Merchant of Venice*. The dramatic movement of the first two scenes is inconsiderable, and the elegance in the speeches of those choosing has not sufficient charm. Shakespeare might gladly allow himself such rhetorical niceties, because his more constant audience found peculiar pleasure in polite, cultured discourse.

VII.

WHAT IS TRAGIC?

It is well known how busily the German poets since Lessing's time, have been occupied in exploring that mysterious property of the drama which is called the tragic. It should be the quality which the poet's moral theory of life deposits in the piece; and the poet should be, through moral influences, a fashioner of his time. The tragic should be an ethical force with which the poet has to fill his action and his characters; and in this case, there have been only diverse opinions as to the essential nature of dramatic ethical force. The expressions, tragic guilt, inner purification, poetic justice, have become convenient watchwords of criticism, conveying, however, a different meaning to different persons. But in this all agree, that the tragic effect of the drama depends on the manner in which the poet conducts his characters through the action, portions their fate to them, and guides and terminates the struggle of their one-sided desire against opposing forces.

Since the poet with freedom joins the parts of his action so as to produce unity, and since he produces this unity by setting together the individual elements of the represented events in rational, internal consistency, it is, of course, clear that the poet's representations of human freedom and dependence, his comprehension of the general consistency of all things, his view of Providence and destiny, must be expressed in a poetic invention, which derives from the inner nature of some important personage sustaining great relations, his deeds and his sorrows. It is further plain that it devolves on the poet to conduct this struggle to such a close as shall not shock the humanity and the reason of the hearer, but shall satisfy it; and that for the good effect of his drama, it is not at all a matter of indifference whether in deducing guilt from the soul of the hero, and in deriving retribution from the compelling force of the action, he shows himself a man of good judgment and just feeling. But it is quite evident that the feeling and judgment of poets have been quite unlike in different centuries, and in individual poets, cannot be graduated in the same manner. Manifestly he who has developed in his own life a high degree of culture, a comprehensive knowledge of men, and a manly character, will, according to the view of his contemporaries, best direct the destiny of his hero; for what shines forth from the drama is only the reflection of the poet's own conception of the great world-relations. It cannot be taught; it cannot be inserted into a single drama like a rôle or a scene.

Therefore, in answer to the question, how the poet must compose his action so that it may be tragic in this sense, the advice, meant in all seriousness, is given that he need trouble himself very little about it. He must develop in himself a capable and worthy manhood, then go with glad heart to a subject which offers strong characters in great conflict, and leave to others the high-sounding words, guilt and purification, refining and elevating. Unsettled must is sometimes put into bottles worthy of the purest wine. What is, in truth, dramatic will have an earnest tragic effect in a strongly moving action if it was a *man* who wrote it; if not, then assuredly not.

The poet's own character determines the highest effects in an elevated drama more than in any other species of art. But the error of former art theories has been that they have sought to explain from the morale or ethics of the drama the combined effect in which sonorousness of words, gesture, costume, and not much else, are concerned.

The word, tragic, is used by the poet in two different meanings; it denotes, first, the peculiar general effect which a successful drama of elevated character produces upon the soul of the spectator; and, second, a definite kind of dramatic causes and effects which in certain parts of the drama are either useful or indispensable. The first is the physiological signification of the expression; the second, a technical denotation.

To the Greeks, a certain peculiarity in the aggregate effect of the drama was well known. Aristotle has sharply observed the special influence of the dramatic effects on the life of the spectators, and has understood them to be a characteristic property of the drama; so that he has included them in his celebrated definition of tragedy. This explanation, "Tragedy is artistic remodeling of a worthy, undivided, complete event, which has magnitude," and so forth, closes with the words, "and effects through pity and fear the purification of such passions." In another place, he explains in detail (Rhetoric, II. 8) what pity is, and how it may be awakened. Awakening pity is to him exhibiting the whole realm of human sorrows, circumstances, and actions, the observation of which produces what we call emotion and strong agitation. The word purification (*katharsis*), however, which as an expression of the old healing art, denoted the removal of diseased matter, and, as an expression of divine worship, denoted the purging of man by atonement from what polluted, is evidently an art term adopted by him for the proper effect of tragedy on the hearer. These peculiar effects which the critical observer perceived upon his contemporaries, are not entirely the same which the representation of a great dramatic masterpiece produces upon our audience, but they are closely related; and it is worth while to notice the difference.

Any one who has ever observed the influence of a tragedy upon himself, must have noticed with astonishment how the emotion and perturbation caused by the excitement of the characters, joined with the mighty suspense which the continuity of the action produces, take hold upon his nerves. Far more easily than in real life the tears flow, the lips twitch; this pain, however, is at the same time accompanied with intense enjoyment, while the hearer experiences immediately after the hero, the same thoughts, sorrows, calamities, with great vividness, as if they were his own. He has in the midst of the most violent excitement, the consciousness of unrestricted liberty, which at the same time raises him far above the incidents through which his capacity to receive impressions seems to be levied upon. After the fall of the curtain, in spite of the intense strain which he has been under for hours, he will be aware of a rebound of vital force; his eye brightens, his step is elastic, every movement firm and free. The dread and commotion are followed by a feeling of security; in his mental processes of the next hour, there is a greater elevation; in his collocation of words, emphatic force; the aggregate production, now his own, has raised him to a high pitch. The radiance of broader views and more powerful feeling which has come into his soul, lies like a transfiguration upon his being. This remarkable affection of body and soul, this elevation above the moods of the day, this feeling of unrestrained comfort after great agitation, is exactly what, in the modern drama, corresponds to Aristotle's "purification." There is no doubt that such a consequence of scenic exhibitions among the finely cultured Greeks, after a ten hours' suspense, through the most powerful effects, came out all the more heightened and more striking.

The elevating influence of the beautiful, upon the soul, is no entirely unusual art; but the peculiar effect which is produced by a union of pain, horror, and pleasure, with a great, sustained effort of the fancy and the judgment, and through the perfect satisfying of our demands for a rational consistency in all things,—this is the prerogative of the art of dramatic poetry alone. The penetrating force of this dramatic effect is, with the majority of people, greater than the force of effects produced by any other form of art. Only music is able to make its influence more powerfully felt upon the nerves ; but the thrill which the musical tone evokes, falls rather within the sphere of immediate emotions, which are not transfigured into thought ; they are more rapturous, less inspired.

Naturally the effects of the drama are no longer the same with us as they were in Aristotle's time. He, himself, makes that clear to us. He who knew so well that the action is the chief thing in the drama, and that Euripides composed his actions badly, yet called *him* the most tragic of the poets, that is, one who knew how to produce most powerfully the effects peculiar to a play. Upon us, however, scarcely a play of Euripides produces any general effect, however powerfully the stormy commotions of the hero's soul, in single ones of his better plays, thrill us. Whence comes this diversity of conception? Euripides was a master in representing excited passion, with too little regard for sharply defined personages and rational consistency of the action. The Greek drama arose from a union of music and lyric poetry ; from Aristotle's time forward, it preserved something of its first youth. The musical element remained, not in the choruses, but the rhythmical language of the hero easily rose to climaxes in song; and the climaxes were frequently characterized by fully elaborated pathos scenes. The aggregate effect of the old tragedy stood between that of our opera and our drama, perhaps still nearer the opera; it retained something of the powerful inflammatory influence of music.

On the other hand, there was another effect of the ancient tragedy, only imperfectly developed, which is indispensable to our tragedy. The dramatic ideas and actions of the Greeks lacked a rational conformity to the laws of nature, that is, such a connecting of events as would be perfectly accounted for by the disposition and one-sidedness of the characters. We have become free men, we recognize no fate on the stage but such as proceeds from the nature of the hero himself. The modern poet has to prepare for the hearer the proud joy, that the world into which he introduces him corresponds throughout to the ideal demands which the heart and judgment of the hearer set up in comparison with the events of reality. Human reason appears in the new drama, as agreeing with and identical with divine; it remodels all that is incomprehensible in the order of nature, according to the need of our spirit and heart. This peculiarity of the action specially strengthens for the spectator of the best modern plays, beautiful transparence and joyous elevation; it helps to make himself for hours stronger, nobler, freer. Here is the point in which the character of the modern poet, his frank manliness, exercises greater influence upon the aggregate effect than in ancient times.

The Attic poet also sought this unity of the divine and the rational; but it was very difficult for him to find it. This boldly tragical, of course, shines forth in single dramas of the ancient world. And that can be explained; for the vital laws of poetical creation control the poet long before criticism has found rules for it; and in his best hours, the poet may receive an inward freedom and expansion which raise him far above the restrictions of his time. Sophocles directed the character and fate of his heroes sometimes, almost in the Germanic fashion. In general, however, the Greeks did not free themselves from a servitude which seems to us, in the highest art effects, a serious defect. The epic source of their subjects was thoroughly unfavorable for the free direction of their heroes' destiny. An incomprehensible fate reached from without into their action; prophecies and oracular utterances influence the conclusion; accidental misfortunes strike the heroes; misdeeds of parents control the destiny of later generations; personifications of deity enter the action as friends and as enemies; between what excites their rage and the punishments which they decree, there is, according to human judgment, no consistency, much less a rational relation. The partiality and arbitrariness with which they rule, is frightful and terrifying; and when they occasionally grant a mild reconciliation, they remain like something foreign, not belonging here. In contrast to such cold excess of power, meek-spirited modesty of man is the highest wisdom. Whoever means to stand firmly by himself in his own might, falls first before a mysterious power which annihilates the guilty as well as the innocent. With this conception, which in its ultimate foundation was gloomy, sad, devouring, there remained to the Greek poet only the means of putting even into the characters of his fettered heroes, something that to a certain degree would account for the horrors which they must endure. The great art of Sophocles is shown, among other things, in the way he gives coloring to his personages. But this wise disposition of characters does not always extend far enough to establish the course of their destiny; it remains not seldom an inadequate motive. The greatness which the ancients produced, lay first of all in the force of passions, then in the fierceness of the struggles through which their heroes were overthrown, finally in the intensity, unfeelingness, and inexorableness, with which they made their characters do and suffer.

The Greeks felt very well that it was not advisable to dismiss the spectator immediately after such effects of the efforts of the beautiful art. They therefore closed the exhibition of the day with a parody, in which they treated the serious heroes of the tragedy with insolent jest, and whimsically imitated their struggles. The burlesque was the external means of affording the recreation which lies for us in the tragedy itself.

From these considerations, the last sentence of Aristotle's definition, not indeed without limitation, avails for our drama. For him as well as for us, the chief effect of the drama is the disburdening of the hearer from the sad and confining moods of the day, which come to us through wretchedness and whatever causes apprehension in the world. But when in another place, he knows how to account for this, on the ground that man needs to see himself touched and shaken, and that the powerful pacifying and satisfying of this desire gives him inward freedom, this explanation is, indeed, not unintelligible to us; but it accepts as the ultimate inner reason for this need pathological circumstances, where we recognize a joyous emotional activity of the hearer.

The ultimate ground of every great effect of the drama lies not in the necessity of the spectator passively to receive impressions, but in his never-ceasing and irresistible desire to create and to fashion. The dramatist compels the listener to repeat his creations. The whole world of characters, of sorrow, and of destiny, the hearer must make alive in himself. While he is receiving with a high degree of suspense, he is in most powerful, most rapid creative activity. An ardor and beatifying cheerfulness like that which the poet himself has felt, fills the hearer who repeats the poet's efforts; therefore the pain with the feeling of pleasure; therefore the exaltation which outlasts the conclusion of the piece. And this stimulation of the creative imagination is, in the new drama, penetrated with still a milder light; for closely connected with it, is an exalting sense of eternal reason in the severest fates and sorrows of man. The spectator feels and recognizes that the divinity which guides his life, even where it shatters the individual human being, acts in a benevolent fellowship with the human race; and he feels himself creatively exalted, as united with and in accord with the great world-guiding power.

So the aggregate effect of the drama, the tragic, is with us related to that of the Greek, but still no longer the same. The Greeks listened in the green youth of the human race, for the tones of the proscenium, filled with the sacred ecstacy of Dionysus; the German looks into the world of illusion, not less affected, but as a lord of the earth. The human race has since then passed through a long history; we have all been educated through historical science.

But more than the general effect of the drama is denoted by the word tragic. The poet of the present time, and sometimes also the public, use the word in a narrower sense. We understand by it, also, a peculiar kind of dramatic effects.

When at a certain point in the action, there enters suddenly, unexpectedly, in contrast with what has preceded, something sad, sombre, frightful, that we yet immediately feel has developed from the original course of events, and is perfectly intelligible from the presuppositions of the play, this new element is a tragic force or motive. This tragic force must possess the three following qualities: (1) it must be important and of serious consequence to the hero; (2) it must occur unexpectedly; (3) it must, to the mind of the spectator, stand in a visible chain of accessory representations, in rational connection with the earlier parts of the action. When the conspirators have killed Cæsar and, as they think, have bound Antony to themselves, Antony, by his speech stirs up against the murderers themselves the same Romans for whose freedom Brutus had committed the murder. When Romeo has married Juliet, he is placed under the necessity of killing her cousin, Tybalt, in the duel, and is banished. When Mary Stuart has approached Elizabeth so near that a reconciliation of the two queens is possible, a quarrel flames up between them, which becomes fatal to Mary. Here the speech of Antony, the death of Tybalt, the quarrel of the queens, are tragic forces; their effect rests upon this, that the spectator comprehends the ominous occurrences as surprising, and yet inseparably connected with what has preceded. The hearer keenly feels the speech of Antony to be a result of the wrong which the conspirators have done Cæsar; through the relation of Antony to Cæsar, and his behavior in the previous dialogue scene with the conspirators, the speech is conceived as the necessary consequence of the sparing of Antony, and the senseless and over-hasty confidence which the murderers place in him. That Romeo must kill Tybalt, will be immediately understood as an unavoidable consequence of the mortal family quarrel and the duel with Mercutio; the quarrel of the two queens, the hearer at once understands to be the natural consequence of their pride, hatred, and former jealousy.

In the same technical signification, the word tragic is also sometimes used for events in real life. The fact, for example, that Luther, that mighty champion of the freedom of conscience, became in the last half of his life an intolerant oppressor of conscience, contains, thus stated, nothing tragic. Overweening desire for rule may have developed in Luther; he may have become senile. But from the moment when it becomes clear to us, through a succession of accessory ideas, that this same intolerance was the necessary consequence of that very honest, disinterested struggle for truth, which accomplished the Reformation; that this same pious fidelity with which Luther upheld his conception of the Bible against the Roman Church, brought him to defend this conception against an adverse decision; that he would not despair when in his position outside of the church, but remained there, holding obstinately to the letter of his writings; from the moment, also, when we conceive of the inner connection of his intolerance with all that is good and great in his nature,—this darkening of his later life produces the effect of the tragic. Just so with Cromwell. That the Protector ruled as a tyrant, produces, in itself, nothing tragic. But that he must do it against his will, because the partisan relations through which he had arisen, and his participation in the execution of the king, had stirred the hearts of the conservative against him; that the great hero from the pressure which his earlier life had laid upon him, could not wrest himself free from his office,—this makes the shadow which fell upon his life through his unlawful reign, tragic for us. That Conradin, child of the Hohenstaufens, gathered a horde, and was slain in Italy by his adversary,—this is not in itself dramatic, and in no sense of the word tragic. A weak youth, with slender support,—it was in order that he should succumb. But when it is impressed upon our souls, that the youth only followed the old line of march of his ancestors toward Italy, and that in this line of march, almost all the great princes of his house had fallen, and that this march of an imperial race was not accidental, but rested on ancient, historical union of Germany with Italy,—then the death of Conradin appears to us specially tragic, not for himself, but as the final extinction of the greatest race of rulers of that time.

With peculiar emphasis, it must again be asserted that the tragic force must be understood in its rational causative connection with the fundamental conditions of the action. For our drama, such events as enter without being understood, incidents the relation of which with the action is mysteriously concealed, influences the significance of which rests on superstitious notions, motives which are taken from dream-life, prophesyings, presentiments, have merely a secondary importance. If a family picture which falls from its nail, shall portentously indicate death and destruction; if a dagger which was used in a crime, appears burdened with a mysterious, evil-bringing curse, till it brings death to the murderer,—these kinds of attempts which ground the tragic effect upon an inner connection which is incomprehensible to us, or appears unreasonable, are for the free race of the present day, either weak or quite intolerable. What appears to us as an accident, even an overwhelming one, is not appropriate for great effects on the stage. It is now several centuries since the adoption of such motives and many others, has been tried in Germany.

The Greeks, it may be remarked incidentally, were somewhat less fastidious in the use of these irrational forces for tragic effect. They could be contented if the inner connection of a suddenly entering tragic force, with what had preceded, were felt in an ominous shudder. When Aristotle cites as an effective example in this direction, that a statue erected to a man, in falling down, kills him who was guilty of the man's death, we should feel in every-day life such an accident is significant. But in art, we should not deem it worthy of success. Sophocles understands how, with such forces, to make conspicuous a natural and intelligible connection between cause and effect so far as his fables allow anything of the sort. For example, the manner in which he explains, with realistic detail, the poisonous effect of the shirt of Nessos, which Deianeira sends to Hercules, is remarkable.

The tragic force, or incident, in the drama is one of many effects. It may enter only once, as usually happens; it may be used several times in the same piece. *Romeo and Juliet* has three such forces: the death of Tybalt after the marriage; the betrothal of Juliet and Paris after the marriage night; the death of Paris before the final catastrophe. The position which this force takes in the piece, is not always the same; one point, however, is specially adapted for it, so that the cases in which it demands another place, can be considered as exceptions; and it is relevant in connection with the foregoing to speak of this here, though the parts of the drama will be discussed in the following chapter.

The point forward from which the deed of the hero reacts upon himself, is one of the most important in the play. This beginning of the reaction, sometimes united in one scene with the climax, has been noted ever since there has been a dramatic art. The embarrassment of the hero and the momentous position into which he has placed himself, must be impressively represented; at the same time, it is the business of this force to produce new suspense for the second part of the piece, and so much the more as the apparent success of the hero has so far been more brilliant, and the more magnificently the scene of the climax has presented his success. Whatever enters into the play now must have all the qualities which have been previously explained — it must present sharp contrasts, it must not be accidental, it must be pregnant with consequences. Therefore it must have importance and a certain magnitude. This scene of the tragic force either immediately follows the scene of the climax, like the despair of Juliet after Romeo's departure; or is joined by a connecting scene, like the speech of Antony after Cæsar's murder; or it is coupled with the climax scene into scenic unity, as in *Mary Stuart*; or it is entirely separated from it by the close of an act, as in *Love and Intrigue*, where Louise's writing the letter indicates the climax, and Ferdinand's conviction of the infidelity of his beloved forms the tragic force. Such scenes almost always stand in the third act of our plays, sometimes less effective in the beginning of the fourth. They are not, of course, absolutely necessary to the tragedy; it is quite possible to bring along the increasing reaction by several strokes in gradual reinforcement. This will most frequently be the case where the catastrophe is effected by the mental processes of the hero, as in *Othello*.

It is worth while for us in modern times to recognize how important this entrance of the tragic force into the action appeared to the Greeks. It was under another name exactly the same effect; and it was made still more significantly prominent by the Attic critic than is necessary for us. Even to their tragedies, this force was not indispensable, but it passed for one of the most beautiful and most effective inventions. Indeed, they classed this effect according to its producing a turn in the action itself or in the position of the chief characters relative to one another; and they had for each of these cases special names, apparently expressions of the old poetic laboratory, which an accident has preserved for us in Aristotle's *Poetics.*[9]

Revolution (*Peripeteia*), is the name given by the Greeks to that tragic force which by the sudden intrusion of an event, unforeseen and overwhelming but already grounded in the plan of the action, impels the volition of the hero, and with it the action itself in a direction entirely different from that of the beginning. Examples of such revolution scenes are the change in the prospects of Neoptolemus in *Philoctetes*, the announcement of the messenger and the shepherd to Jocasta and the king in *King Œdipus*, the account of Hyllos to Deianeira, concerning the effect of the shirt of Nessos, in *The Trachinian Women.* Through this force specially there was produced a powerful movement in the second part of the play; and the Athenians distinguished carefully between plays with revolution and those without. Those with revolution prevailed in general, being considered the better. This force of the ancient action is distinguished from the corresponding newer only in this, that it does not necessarily indicate a turning toward the disastrous, because the tragedy of the ancients did not always have a sad ending, but sometimes the sudden reversion to the better. The scenes claimed scarcely less significance, in which the position of the persons concerned in the action was changed with relation to each other, by the unexpected revival of an old and important relation between them. These scenes of the *anagnorisis*, recognition scenes, it was especially, in which the agreeable relations of the heroes became apparent in magnificent achievement. And since the Greek stage did not know our love scenes, they occupied a similar position, though good-will did not always appear in them, and sometimes even hatred flamed up. The subjects of the Greeks offered ample opportunity for such scenes. The heroes of Greek story are, almost without exception, a wandering race. Expedition and return, the finding of friends and enemies unexpectedly, are among the most common features of these legends. Almost every collection of stories contains children who did not know their parents, husbands and wives, who after long separation came together again under peculiar circumstances, host and guest, who prudently sought to conceal their names and purposes. There was, therefore, in much of their material, scenes of meetings, finding the lost, reminiscences of significant past events, some of decisive importance. Not only the recognizing of former acquaintances but the recognition of a region, of an affair having many relations, could become a motive for a strong movement. Such scenes afforded the old-time poet welcome opportunity for the representation of contrasts in perception and for favorite pathetic performances in which the excited feeling flowed forth in great waves. The woman who will kill an enemy, and just before or just after the deed recognizes him as her own son; the son who in his mortal enemy finds again his own mother, like Ion; the priestess who is about to offer up a stranger, and in him recognizes her brother, like Iphigenia; the sister who mourns her dead brother, and in the bringer of the burial urn receives back again the living; and Odysseus's nurse who, in a beggar, finds out the home-returning master by a scar on his foot,—these are some of the numerous examples. Frequently such recognition scenes became motives for a revolution, as in the case already mentioned of the account of the messenger and the shepherd to the royal pair of Thebes. One may read in Aristotle how important the circumstances were to the Greeks through which the recognition was brought about; by the great philosopher, they were carefully considered and prized according to their intrinsic worth. And it is a source of satisfaction to observe that even to the Greek, no accidental external characteristic passed for a motive suitable to art, but only the internal relations of those recognizing each other, which voluntarily and characteristically for both, manifested themselves in the dialogue. Just a glimpse assures us how refined and fully developed the dramatic criticism of the Greeks was, and how painfully conscientious they were to regard in a new drama what passed for a beautiful effect according to their theory of art.

CHAPTER II.

THE CONSTRUCTION OF THE DRAMA.

I.

PLAY AND COUNTERPLAY.

In an action, through characters, by means of words, tones, gestures, the drama presents those soul-processes which man experiences, from the flashing up of an idea, to passionate desire and to a deed, as well as those inward emotions which are excited by his own deeds and those of others.

The structure of the drama must show these two contrasted elements of the dramatic joined in a unity, efflux and influx of will-power, the accomplishment of a deed and its reaction on the soul, movement and counter-movement, strife and counter-strife, rising and sinking, binding and loosing.

In every part of the drama, both tendencies of dramatic life appear, each incessantly challenging the other to its best in play and counter-play; but in general, also, the action of the drama and the grouping of characters is, through these tendencies, in two parts. What the drama presents is always a struggle, which, with strong perturbations of soul, the hero wages against opposing forces. And as the hero must be endowed with a strong life, with a certain one-sidedness, and be in embarrassment, the opposing power must be made visible in a human representative.

It is quite indifferent in favor of which of the contending parties the greater degree of justice lies, whether a character or his adversary is better-mannered, more favored by law, embodies more of the traditions of the time, possesses more of the ethical spirit of the poet; in both groups, good and evil, power and weakness, are variously mingled. But both must be endowed with what is universally, intelligibly human. The chief hero must always stand in strong contrast with his opponents; the advantage which he wins for himself, must be the greater, so much the greater the more perfectly the final outcome of the struggle shows him to be vanquished.

These two chief parts of the drama are firmly united by a point of the action which lies directly in the middle. This middle, the climax of the play, is the most important place of the structure; the action rises to this; the action falls away from this. It is now decisive for the character of the drama which of the two refractions of the dramatic light shall have a place in the first part of the play, which shall fall in the second part as the dominating influence; whether the efflux or influx, the play or the counter-play, maintains the first part. Either is allowed; either arrangement of the structure can cite plays of the highest merit in justification of itself. And these two ways of constructing a drama have become characteristic of individual poets and of the time in which they lived.

By one dramatic arrangement, the chief person, the hero, is so introduced that his nature and his characteristics speak out unembarrassed, even to the moments when, as a consequence of external impulse or internal association of ideas, in him the beginning of a powerful feeling or volition becomes perceptible. The inner commotion, the passionate eagerness, the desire of the hero, increase; new circumstances, stimulating or restraining, intensify his embarrassment and his struggle; the chief character strides victoriously forward to an unrestrained exhibition of his life, in which the full force of his feeling and his will are concentrated in a deed by which the spiritual tension is relaxed. From this point there is a turn in the action; the hero appeared up to this point in a desire, one-sided or full of consequence, working from within outward, changing by its own force the life relations in which he came upon the stage. From the climax on, what he has done reacts upon himself and gains power over him; the external world, which he conquered in the rise of passionate conflict, now stands in the strife above him. This adverse influence becomes continually more powerful and victorious, until at last in the final catastrophe, it compels the hero to succumb to its irresistible force. The end of the piece follows this catastrophe immediately, the situation where the restoration of peace and quiet after strife becomes apparent.

With this arrangement, first the inception and progress of the action are seen, then the effects of the reaction; the character of the first part is determined by the depth of the hero's exacting claims; the second by the counter-claims which the violently disturbed surroundings put forward. This is the construction of *Antigone*, of *Ajax*, of all of Shakespeare's great tragedies except *Othello* and *King Lear*, of *The Maid of Orleans*, less surely of the double tragedy, *Wallenstein*.

The other dramatic arrangement, on the contrary, represents the hero at the beginning, in comparative quiet, among conditions of life which suggest the influence of some external forces upon his mind. These forces, adverse influences, work with increased activity so long in the hero's soul, that at the climax, they have brought him into ominous embarrassment, from which, under a stress of passion, desire, activity, he plunges downward to the catastrophe.

This construction makes use of opposing characters, in order to give motive to the strong excitement of the chief character; the relation of the chief figures to the idea of the drama is an entirely different one; they do not give direction in the ascending action, but are themselves directed. Examples of this construction are *King Œdipus, Othello, Lear, Emilia Galotti, Clavigo, Love and Intrigue.*

It might appear that this second method of dramatic construction must be the more effective. Gradually, in a specially careful performance, one sees the conflicts through which the life of the hero is disturbed, give direction to his inward being. Just there, where the hearer demands a powerful intensifying of effects, the previously prepared domination of the chief characters enters; suspense and sympathy, which are more difficult to sustain in the last half of the play, are firmly fixed upon the chief characters; the stormy and irresistible progress downward is particularly favorable to powerful and thrilling effects. And, indeed, subjects which contain the gradual rise and growth of a portentous passion which in the end leads the hero to his destruction, are exceedingly favorable for such an action.

But this method of constructing a play is not the most correct, dramatically; and it is no accident, that the greatest dramas of such a character, at the tragic close, intermingle with the emotions and perturbations of the hearer, an irritating feeling which lessens the joy and recreation. For they do not specially show the hero as an active, aggressive nature, but as a receptive, suffering person, who is too much compelled by the counter-play, which strikes him from without. The greatest exercise of human power, that which carries with it the heart of the spectator most irresistibly, is, in all times, the bold individuality which sets its own inner self, without regard to consequences, over against the forces which surround it. The essential nature of the drama is conflict and suspense; the sooner these are evoked by means of the chief heroes themselves and given direction, the better.

It is true, the first kind of dramatic structure conceals a danger, which even by genius, is not always successfully avoided. In this, as a rule, the first part of the play, which raises the hero through regular degrees of commotion to the climax, is assured its success. But the second half, in which greater effects are demanded, depends mostly on the counter-play; and this counter-play must here be grounded in more violent movement and have comparatively greater authorization. This may distract attention rather than attract it more forcibly. It must be added, that after the climax of the action, the hero must seem weaker than the counteracting figures. Moreover, on this account, the interest in him may be lessened. Yet in spite of this difficulty, the poet need be in no doubt to which kind of arrangement to give the preference. His task will be greater in this arrangement; great art is required to make the last act strong. But talent and good fortune must overcome the difficulties. And the most beautiful garlands which dramatic art has to confer, fall upon the successful work. Of course the poet is dependent on his subject and material, which sometimes leaves no choice. Therefore, one of the first questions a poet must ask, when contemplating attractive material, is "does it come forward in the play or in the counterplay?"

It is instructive in connection with this topic, to compare the great poets. From the few plays of Sophocles which we have preserved, the majority belong to those in which the chief actor has the direction, however unfavorable the sphere of epic material was for the unrestrained self-direction of the heroes. Shakespeare, however, evinces here the highest power and art. He is the poet of characters which reach conclusions quickly. Vital force and marrow, compressed energy and the intense virility of his heroes, impel the piece in rapid movement upward, from the very opening scene.

In sharp contrast with him, stands the tendency of the great German poets of the last century. They love a broad motiving, a careful grounding of the unusual. In many of their dramas, it looks as if their heroes would wait quietly in a self-controlled mood, in uncertain circumstances, if they were only let alone; and since, to most of the heroic characters of the Germans, conscious power, firm self-confidence and quick decision are wanting, so they stand in the action, uncertain, meditating, doubting, moved rather by external relations than by claims that have no regard to consequences. It is significant of the refinement of the last century, of the culture and spiritual life of a people to whom a joyful prosperity, a public life, and a self-government, were so greatly lacking. Even Schiller, who understood so well how to excite intense passion, was fond of giving the power of direction to the counter-players in the first half, and to the chief actors only in the second half, from the climax downward. In *Love and Intrigue*, therefore, Ferdinand and Louise are pushed forward by the intriguers; and only from the scene between Ferdinand and the president, after the tragic force enters, Ferdinand assumes the direction till the end. Still worse is the relation of the hero, Don Carlos, to the action; he is kept in leading strings, not only through the ascending half, but as well through the descending half. In *Mary Stuart*, the heroine has the controlling influence over her portentous fate, up to the climax, the garden scene; so far she controls the mental attitudes of her counter-players; the propelling forces are, however, as the subject demanded, the intriguers and Elizabeth.

Much better known, yet of less importance for the construction of the drama, is the distinction of plays, which originates in the last turn in the fate of the hero, and in the meaning of the catastrophe. The new German stage distinguishes two kinds of serious plays, tragedy and spectacle play (*trauerspiel* and *schauspiel*). The rigid distinction in this sense is not old even with us; it has been current in repertoires only since Iffland's time. And, if now, occasionally, on the stage, comedy, tragedy, and spectacle play are put in opposition as three different kinds of recitative representation, the spectacle play is no third, co-ordinate kind of dramatic creation, according to its character, but a subordinate kind of serious drama. The Attic stage did not have the name, but it had the thing. Even in the time of Æschylus and Sophocles, a gloomy termination was by no means indispensable to the tragedy. Of seven of the extant tragedies of Sophocles, two, *Ajax* and *Philoctetes*, indeed also, in the eyes of the Athenians, *Œdipus at Colonos* had a mild close, which turns the fate of the hero toward the better. Even in Euripides, to whom the critics attribute a love of the sad endings, there are, out of seventeen extant plays, four, besides *Alcestis*, *Helena*, *Iphigenia in Tauris*, *Andromache*, and *Ion*, the endings of which correspond to our spectacle play; in several others, the tragic ending is accidental and without motive. And it seems, the Athenians already had the same taste which we recognize in our spectators; they saw most gladly such tragedies as in our sense of the word were spectacle plays, in which the hero was severely worried by fate, but rescued at length, safely bore off his hide and hair.

On the modern stage, it cannot be denied, the justification of the spectacle play has become more pronounced. We have a nobler and more liberal comprehension of human nature. We are able to delineate more charmingly, more effectively, and more accurately inner conflicts of conscience, opposing convictions. In a time in which men have debated the abolition of capital punishment, the dead at the end of a play may be more easily dispensed with. In real life, we trust to a strong human power that it will hold the duty of living very high, and expiate even serious crimes, not with death but by a purer life. But this changed conception of earthly existence does not bring an advantage to the drama in every respect. It is true the fatal ending is, in the case of modern subjects, less a necessity than in the dramatic treatment of epic legends, or older historical events; but not that the hero's at last remaining alive makes a piece a spectacle play, but that he proceeds from the strife as conqueror, or by an adjustment with his opponent, goes away reconciled. If he must be the victim at last, if he must be crushed, then the piece retains not only the character but the name of tragedy. *The Prince of Homburg* is a spectacle play, *Tasso* is a tragedy.

The drama of modern times has embraced in the circle of its subjects, a broad field which was unknown to the tragedy of the ancient Greeks, indeed, in the main, to Shakespeare's art: the middle-class life of the present time, the conflicts of our society. No doubt, the strifes and sufferings of modern life make a tragic treatment possible; and this has fallen too little to their lot; but what is full of incident, what is quiet, what is full of scruple, connected as a rule with this species of material, affords artistic conception full justification; and just here it brings forward such strifes as in real life we trust to have and want to have adjusted peaceably. With the broad and popular expansion which this treatment has won, it is proper to propose two things: first, that the laws for the construction of the spectacle play and the life of the characters are, in the main, the same as for the tragedy, and that it is useful for the playwright to recognize these laws as found in the drama of elevated character, where every violence done them may be dangerous to the success of the piece; and second, that the spectacle play in which a milder adjustment of conflicts is necessary in the second part, has a double reason for laying motives in the first half by means of fine characterization, for the hero's stout-hearted and vigorous desire in the second half of the play. Otherwise, it is exposed to the danger of becoming a mere situation-piece, or intrigue-play; in the first case, by sacrificing the strong movement of a unified action to the more easy depiction of circumstances and characteristic peculiarities; in the second case, by neglecting to develop the characters, on account of the rapid chess-board performance of a restless action. The first is the tendency of the Germans; the second of the Latins; both kinds of preparation of a subject are unfavorable to a dignified treatment of serious conflicts; they belong, according to their nature, to comedy, not to serious drama.

II.

FIVE PARTS AND THREE CRISES OF THE DRAMA.

Through the two halves of the action which come closely together at one point, the drama possesses — if one may symbolize its arrangement by lines — a pyramidal structure. It rises from the *introduction* with the entrance of the exciting forces to the *climax*, and falls from here to the *catastro-*

phe. Between these three parts lie (the parts of) the *rise* and the *fall*. Each of these five parts may consist of a single scene, or a succession of connected scenes, but the climax is usually composed of one chief scene.

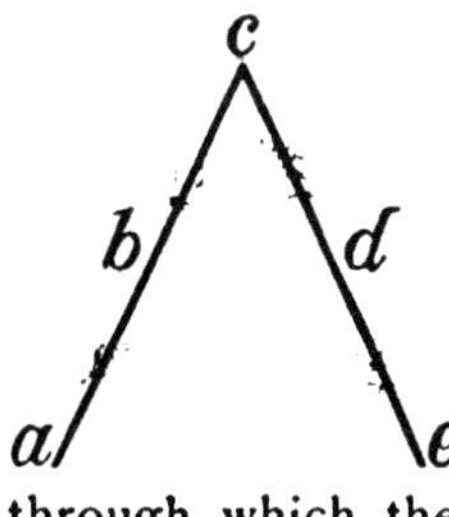

These parts of the drama, (*a*) introduction, (*b*) rise, (*c*) climax, (*d*) return or fall, (*e*) catastrophe, have each what is peculiar in purpose and in construction. Between them stand three important scenic effects, through which the parts are separated as well as bound together. Of these three dramatic moments, or crises, one, which indicates the beginning of the stirring action, stands between the introduction and the rise; the second, the beginning of the counter-action, between the climax and the return; the third, which must rise once more before the catastrophe, between the return and the catastrophe. They are called here the exciting moment or force, the tragic moment or force. and the moment or force of the last suspense. The operation of the first is necessary to every play; the second and third are good but not indispensable accessories. In the following sections, therefore, the eight component parts of the drama will be discussed in their natural order.

The Introduction.— It was the custom of the ancients to communicate in a prologue, what was presupposed for the action. The prologue of Sophocles and also of Æschylus is a thoroughly necessary and essential part of the action, having dramatic life and connection, and corresponding exactly to our opening scene; and in the old stage-management signification of the word, it comprised that part of the action which lay before the entrance song of the chorus. In Euripides, it is, by a careless return to the older custom, an epic messenger announcement, which a masked figure delivers to the audience, a figure who never once appears in the play, — like Aphrodite in *Hyppolitus* and the ghost of the slain Polydorus in *Hecuba.* In Shakespeare, the prologue is entirely severed from the action; it is only an address of the poet; it contains civility, apology, and the plea for attention. Since it is no longer necessary to plead for quiet and attention, the German stage has purposely given up the prologue, but allows it as a festive greeting which distinguishes a single representation, or as the chance caprice of a poet. In Shakespeare, as with us, the introduction has come back again into the right place; it is filled with dramatic movement, and has become an organic part of the dramatic structure. Yet, in individual cases, the newer stage has not been able to resist another temptation, to expand the introduction to a situation scene, and set it in advance as a special prelude to the drama. Well-known examples are *The Maid of Orleans* and *Kätchen of Heilbronn*, *Wallenstein's Camp*, and the most beautiful of all prologues, that to *Faust.*

That such a severing of the opening scene is

hazardous, will be readily granted. The poet who treats it as a separate piece, is compelled to give it an expansion, and divide it into members which do not correspond to their inner significance. Whatever seems separated by a strong incision, becomes subject to the laws of each great dramatic unit; it must again have an introduction, a rise, a proportionate climax, and a conclusion. But such presuppositions of a drama, the circumstances previous to the entrance of the moving force, are not favorable to a strongly membered movement; and the poet will, therefore, have to bring forward his persons in embellished and proportionately broad, elaborated situations. He will be obliged to give these situations in some fulness and abundance, because every separate structure must awaken and satisfy an independent interest; and this is possible only by using sufficient time. But two difficulties arise in this: first, that the time of the chief action, not too amply allotted on our stage without this, will be shortened; and second, that the prelude, through its broad treatment and quiet subject matter, will probably contain a color which is so different from that of the drama, that it distracts and satisfies, instead of preparing the spectator for the chief part. It is nearly always the convenience of the poet and the defective arrangement of the material, which occasion the construction of a prelude to an acting play. No material should keep further presuppositions than such as allow of reproduction in a few short touches.

Since it is the business of the introduction of the

drama to explain the place and time of the action, the nationality and life relations of the hero, it must at once briefly characterize the environment. Besides, the poet will have opportunity here, as in a short overture, to indicate the peculiar mood of the piece, as well as the time, the greater vehemence or quiet with which the action moves forward. The moderate movement, the mild light in *Tasso*, is introduced by the brilliant splendor of the princely garden, the quiet conversation of the richly attired ladies, the garlands, the adornment of the poet painter. In *Mary Stuart*, there is the breaking open of closets, the quarrel between Paulet and Kennedy —a good picture of the situation. In *Nathan the Wise*, the excited conversation of the returning Nathan with Daja is an excellent introduction to the dignified course of the action and to the contrasts in the inwardly disturbed characters. In *Piccolomini*, there are the greetings of the generals and Questenberg, an especially beautiful introduction to the gradually rising movement. But the greatest master of fine beginnings is Shakespeare. In *Romeo and Juliet*, day, an open street, brawls and the clatter of the swords of the hostile parties; in *Hamlet*, night, the startling call of the watch, the mounting of the guard, the appearance of the ghost, restless, gloomy, desperate excitement; in *Macbeth*, storm, thunder, the unearthly witches and dreary heath; and again in *Richard III.*, no striking surroundings, a single man upon the stage, the old despotic evil genius, who controls the entire dramatic life of the piece, himself speaking the prologue. So in each of his artistic dramas.

It may be asserted that, as a rule, it is expedient soon after the opening scene, to strike the first chords firmly and with as much emphasis as the character of the piece will allow. Of course, *Clavigo* is not opened with the rattle of the drum, nor *William Tell* with the quarrelling of children in the quiet life of the household; a brief excited movement, adapted to the piece, conducts without violence to the more quiet exposition. Occasionally this first exciting strain in Shakespeare, to whom his stage allowed greater liberty, is separated from the succeeding exposition by a scenic passage. Thus in *Hamlet*, a court scene follows it; in *Macbeth*, the entrance of Duncan and the news of the battle. So in *Julius Cæsar*, where the conference and strife between the tribunes and the plebeians form the first strong stroke, to which the exposition, the conversation of Cassius and Brutus, and the holiday procession of Cæsar, is closely joined. Also in *Mary Stuart*, after the quarrel with Paulet, comes the exposition, the scene between Mary and Kennedy. So in *William Tell*, after the charming, only too melodramatic opening situation, comes the conversation of the country people.

Now certainly this note, sounded at the beginning, is not necessarily a loud unison of the voices of different persons; brief but deep emotions in the chief characters may very well indicate the first ripple of the short waves which has to precede the storms of the drama. So in *Emilia Galotti*, the exposition of the restless agitation of the prince at the work-table goes through the greater beating of waves in the conversation with Conti even into the scene with Marinelli, which contains the exciting force, the news of the impending marriage of Emilia. Similarly but less conveniently in *Clavigo*, it goes from the conversation at Clavigo's desk, through Mary's dwelling, to the beginning of the action itself,—the visit of Beaumarchais to Clavigo. Indeed, the action may arise so gradually that the quiet preserved from the beginning forms an effective background, as in Goethe's *Iphigenia*.

If Shakespeare and the Germans of the earlier times,—*Sara Sampson*, *Clavigo*—have not avoided the changing of scenes in the introduction, their example is not to be imitated on our stage. The exposition should be kept free from anything distracting; its task, to prepare for the action, it best accomplishes if it so proceeds that the first short introductory chord is followed by a well-executed scene which by a quick transition is connected with the following scene containing the exciting force. *Julius Cæsar*, *Mary Stuart*, *Wallenstein*, are excellent examples in this direction.

The difficulty of giving also to the representative of the counter-play a place in the introduction, is not insurmountable. In the arrangement of scenes, at least, the poet must feel the full mastery of his material; and it is generally an embarrassment of his power of imagination when this seems impossible to him. However, should the fitting of the counter-party into the exposition be impracticable, there is always still time enough to bring them forward in the first scenes of the involution.

Without forcing all possible cases into the same uniform mould, therefore, the poet may hold firmly to this: the construction of a regular introduction is as follows: a clearly defining keynote, a finished scene, a short transition into the first moment of the excited action.

The Exciting Force.—The beginning of the excited action (complication) occurs at a point where, in the soul of the hero, there arises a feeling or volition which becomes the occasion of what follows; or where the counter-play resolves to use its lever to set the hero in motion. Manifestly, this impelling force will come forward more significantly in those plays in which the chief actor governs the first half by his force of will; but in any arrangement, it remains an important motive force for the action. In *Julius Cæsar*, this impelling force is the thought of killing Cæsar, which, by the conversation with Cassius, gradually becomes fixed in the soul of Brutus. In *Othello*, it comes into play after the stormy night-scene of the exposition, by means of the second conference between Iago and Roderigo, with the agreëment to separate the Moor and Desdemona. In *Richard III.*, on the contrary, it rises in the very beginning of the piece along with the exposition, and as a matured plan in the soul of the hero. In both cases, its position helps to fix the character of the piece; in *Othello*, where the counter-play leads at the conclusion of a long introduction; in *Richard III.*, where the villain alone rules in the first scene. In *Romeo and Juliet*, this occasioning motive comes to the soul of the hero in the interview with Benvolio, as the determination to be present at the masked ball; and immediately before this scene, there runs as parallel scene, the conversation between Paris and Capulet, which determines the fate of Juliet; both scenic moments, in such significant juxtaposition, form together the impelling force of this drama, which has two heroes, the two lovers. In *Emilia Galotti*, it sinks into the soul of the prince, as he receives the announcement of the impending marriage of the heroine; in *Clavigo*, it is the arrival of Beaumarchais at his sister's; in *Mary Stuart*, it is the confession which Mortimer makes to the queen.

Scarcely will any one cherish the opinion that *Faust* might have become better as a regular acting drama; but it is quite instructive to conceive from this greatest poem of the Germans, how the laws of creation, even with the freest exercise of invention, demanded obedience to dramatic form. This poem, too, has its exciting force, the entrance of Mephistopheles into Faust's room. What precedes is exposition; the dramatically animated action includes the relations of Faust and Gretchen; it has its rising, and its falling half; from the appearance of Mephistopheles, it ascends to the climax, to the scene which refers to the surrender of Gretchen to Faust; from there it descends to the catastrophe.

The unusual form of the structure lies, aside from the later episodes, only in this, that the scenes of the introduction, and of the exciting force, occupy half of the play, and that the climax is not brought out with sufficient strength. As for the rest, the piece, the scenes of which glitter like a string of pearls, has a little complete, well-ordered action, of a simple and even regular character. It is necessary only to think of the meeting with Gretchen as at the end of the first act.

Shakespeare treats the inception of the animated movement with special care. If the exciting force is ever too small and weak for him, as in *Romeo and Juliet*, he understands how to strengthen it. Therefore, Romeo, after his conclusion to intrude upon the Capulets, must pronounce his gloomy forebodings before the house. In three pieces, Shakespeare has yielded to his inclination to repeat a motive, each time with increased effect. As in the scene in *Othello*, "Put money in thy purse," is a variation of the introductory note, so are the weird sisters, who excite the bloody thought in Macbeth, so is the ghost which announces the murder to Hamlet. What at the beginning of the piece indicated tone and color, becomes the inciting force for the soul of the hero.

From the examples cited, it is evident that this force of the action treads the stage under very diverse forms. It may fill a complete scene; it may be comprised in a few words. It must not always press from without into the soul of the hero or his adversary; it may be, also, a thought, a wish, a resolution, which by a succession of representations may be allured from the soul of the hero himself. But it always forms the transition from the introduction to the ascending action, either entering suddenly, like Mortimer's declaration in *Mary Stuart*, and the rescue of Baumgarten in *William Tell*, or gradually developing through the speeches and mental processes of the characters, like Brutus's resolve to do the murder, where in no place in the dialogue the fearful words are pronounced, but the significance of the scene is emphasized by the suspicion which Cæsar, entering meantime, expresses.

Yet it is for the worker to notice, that this force seldom admits of great elaboration. Its place is at the beginning of the piece, where powerful pressure upon the hearer is neither necessary nor advisable. It has the character of a motive which gives direction and preparation, and does not offer a single resting-place. It must not be insignificant; but it must not be so strong that, according to the feeling of the audience, it takes too much from what follows, or that the suspense which it causes, may modify, or perhaps determine, the fate of the hero. Hamlet's suspicion can not be raised to unconditional certainty by the revelation of the ghost, or the course of the piece must be entirely different. The resolution of Cassius and Brutus must not come out in distinct words, in order that Brutus's following consideration of the matter, and the administration of the oath, may seem a progress.

The poet will, probably, sometimes have to moderate the importance attached to this force, which has made it too conspicuous. But he must always bring it into operation as soon as possible; for only from its introduction forward does earnest dramatic work begin.

A convenient arrangement for our stage is to give the exciting force in a temperate scene after the introduction, and closely join to this the first following rising movement, in greater elaboration. *Mary Stuart*, for example, is of this regular structure.

The Rising Movement.—The action has been started; the chief persons have shown what they are; the interest has been awakened. Mood, passion, involution have received an impulse in a given direction. In the modern drama of three hours, they are no insignificant parts, which belong to this ascent. Its arrangement has comparatively little significance. The following are the general rules:

If it has not been possible to accord a place in what has gone before, to the most important persons in the counter-play, or to the chief groups, a place must be made for them now, and opportunity must be given for an activity full of meaning. Such persons, too, as are of importance in the last half, must eagerly desire now to make themselves known to the audience. Whether the ascent is made by one or several stages to the climax, depends on material and treatment. In any case, a resting place in the action, and even in the structure of a scene, is to be so expressed that the dramatic moments, acts, scenes, which belong to the same division of the action, are joined together so as to produce a unified chief scene, subordinate scene, connecting scene. In *Julius Cæsar*, for instance, the ascent, from the moment of excitation to the climax, consists of only one stage, the conspiracy. This makes, with the preparatory scene, and the scene of the contrast belonging to it, an attractive scene-group very beautifully constructed, even according to the demands of our stage; and with this group, those scenes are closely joined which are grouped about the murder-scene, the climax of the play. On the other hand, the rising movement in *Romeo and Juliet*, runs through four stages to the climax. The structure of this ascending group is as follows. First stage: masked ball; three parts, two preparatory scenes (Juliet with her mother, and nurse) (Romeo and his companions); and one chief scene (the ball itself, consisting of one suggestion—conversation of the servants—and four forces—Capulet stirring up matters; Tybalt's rage and setting things to rights; conversation of the lovers; Juliet and the nurse as conclusion). Second stage: The garden scene; short preparatory scene (Benvolio and Mercutio seeking Romeo) and the great chief scene (the lovers determining upon marriage). Third stage: The marriage; four parts; first scene, Laurence and Romeo; second scene, Romeo and companions, and nurse as messenger; third scene, Juliet, and nurse as messenger; fourth scene, Laurence and the lovers, and the marriage. Fourth stage: Tybalt's death; fighting scene.

Then follows the group of scenes forming the climax, beginning with Juliet's words, "Gallop apace you fiery footed steeds," and extending to Romeo's farewell, "It were a grief, so brief to part with thee; farewell." In the four stages of the rise, one must notice the different structure of individual scenes. In the masked ball, little scenes are connected in quick succession to the close; the garden scene is the elaborate great scene of the lovers; in beautiful contrast with this, in the marriage scene-group, the accomplice, Laurence, and the nurse are kept in the foreground, the lovers are concealed. Tybalt's death is the strong break which separates the aggregate rise from the climax; the scenes of this part have a loftier swing, a more passionate movement. The arrangement of the piece is very careful; the progress of both heroes and their motives are specially laid for each in every two adjoining scenes with parallel course.

This same kind of rise, slower, with less frequently changing scenes, is common with the Germans. In *Love and Intrigue*, for example, the exciting force of the play is the announcement of Wurm to his father that Ferdinand loves the daughter of the musician. From here the piece rises in counterplay through four stages. First stage: (the father demands the marriage with Milford) in two scenes; preparatory scene (he has the betrothal announced through Kalb); chief scene (he compels the son to visit Milford). Second stage: (Ferdinand and Milford) two preparatory scenes; great chief scene (the lady insists on marrying him). Third stage: Two preparatory scenes; great chief scene (the president will put Louise under arrest, Ferdinand resists). Fourth stage: Two scenes (plan of the president with the letter, and the plot of the villains). The climax follows this: Chief scene, the composition of the letter. This piece also has the peculiarity of having two heroes—the two lovers.

The import of the play is, it must be owned, painful; but the construction is, with some awkwardness in the order of scenes, still, on the whole, regular, and worthy of special consideration, because it is produced far more through the correct feeling of the young poet, than through a sure technique.

As to the scenes of this rising movement, it may be said, they have to produce a progressive intensity of interest; they must, therefore, not only evince progress in their import, but they must show an enlargement in form and treatment, and, indeed, with variation and shading in execution; if several steps are necessary, the next to the last, or the last, must preserve the character of a chief scene.

The Climax.—The climax of the drama is the place in the piece where the results of the rising movement come out strong and decisively; it is almost always the crowning point of a great, amplified scene, enclosed by the smaller connecting scenes of the rising, and of the falling action. The poet needs to use all the splendor of poetry, all the dramatic skill of his art, in order to make vividly conspicuous this middle point of his artistic creation. It has the highest significance only in those pieces in which the hero, through his own mental processes, impels the ascending action; in those dramas which rise by means of the counter-play, it does not indicate an important place, where this play has attained the mastery of the chief hero, and misleads him in the direction of the fall. Splendid examples are to be found in almost every one of Shakespeare's plays and in the plays of the Germans. The hovel scene in *King Lear*, with the play of the three deranged persons, and the judgment scene with the stool, is perhaps one of the most effective that was ever put on the stage; and the rising action in *Lear*, up to the scene of this irrepressible madness, is of terrible magnificence. The scene is also remarkable because the great poet has here used humor to intensify the horrible effect, and because this is one of the very rare places, where the audience, in spite of the awful commotion, perceives with a certain surprise that Shakespeare uses artifices to bring out the effect. Edgar is no fortunate addition to the scene. In another way, the banquet scene in *Macbeth* is instructive. In this tragedy, a previous scene, the night of the murder, had been so powerfully worked out, and so richly endowed with the highest dramatic poetry, that there might easily be despair as to the possibility of any further rise in the action. And yet it is effected;

the murderer's struggle with the ghost, and the fearful struggles with his conscience, in the restless scene to which the social festivity and royal splendor give the most effective contrasts, are pictured with a truth, and in a wild kind of poetic frenzy, which make the hearer's heart throb and shudder. In *Othello*, on the other hand, the climax lies in the great scene in which Iago arouses Othello's jealousy. It is slowly prepared, and is the beginning of the convulsing soul-conflict in which the hero perishes. In *Clavigo*, the reconciliation of Clavigo with Marie, and in *Emilia Galotti*, the prostration of Emilia, form the climax, concealed in both cases by the predominating counter-play. Again, in Schiller, it is powerfully developed in all plays.

This outburst of deed from the soul of the hero, or the influx of portentous impressions into the soul; the first great result of a sublime struggle, or the beginning of a mortal inward conflict,—must appear inseparably connected with what goes before as well as with what follows; it will be brought into relief through broad treatment or strong effect; but it will, as a rule, be represented in its development from the rising movement and its effect on the environment; therefore, the climax naturally forms the middle point of a group of forces, which, darting in either direction, course upward and downward.

In the case where the climax is connected with the downward movement by a tragic force, the structure of the drama presents something peculiar, through the juxtaposition of two important passages which stand in sharp contrast with each other. This tragic force must first .receive attention. This beginning of the downward movement is best connected with the climax, and separated from the following forces of the counter-play to which it belongs by a division—our close of an act; and this is best brought about not immediately after the beginning of the tragic force, but by a gradual modulation of its sharp note. It is a matter of indifference whether this connection of the two great contrasted scenes is effected by uniting them into one scene, or by means of a connecting scene. A splendid example of the former is in *Coriolanus*.

In this piece, the action rises from the exciting force (the news that war with the Volscians is inevitable) through the first ascent (fight between Coriolanus and Aufidius) to the climax, the nomination of Coriolanus as consul. The tragic force, the banishment, begins here; what seems about to become the highest elevation of the hero, becomes by his untamable pride just the opposite; he is overthrown. This overthrow does not occur suddenly; it is seen to perfect itself gradually on the stage—as Shakespeare loves to have it—and what is overwhelming in the result is first perceived at the close of the scene. The two points, bound together here by the rapid action, form together a powerful group of scenes of violent commotion, the whole of far-reaching and splendid effect. But, also, after the close of this double scene, the action is not at once cut into; for there is immediately joined to this, as contrast, the beautiful, dignified pathos scene of the farewell, which forms a transition to what follows; and yet after the hero has departed, this helps to exhibit the moods of those remaining behind, as a trembling echo of the fierce excitement, before the point of repose is reached.

The climax and the tragic force are still more closely united in *Mary Stuart*. Here, also, the beginning of the climax is sharply denoted by the monologue and the elevated lyric mood of Mary, after the style of an ancient pathos scene; and this mood scene is bound by a little connecting song to the great dialogue scene between Mary and Elizabeth; but the dramatic climax reaches even into this great scene, and in this lies the transition to the ominous strife, which again in its development is set forth in minute detail.

Somewhat more sharply are the climax and tragic force in *Julius Cæsar* separated from each other by a complete connecting scene. The group of murder scenes is followed by the elaborate scene of the conspirators' conversation with Antony—this interpolated passage of beautiful workmanship—and after this the oration scenes of Brutus and Antony; and after this follow little transitions to the parts of the return.

This close connection of the two important parts gives to the drama with tragic force a magnitude and expanse of the middle part, which—if the playful comparison of the lines may be carried out,

—changes the pyramidal form into one with a double apex.

The most difficult part of the drama is the sequence of scenes in the downward movement, or, as it may well be called, the return; specially in powerful plays in which the heroes are the directing force, do these dangers enter most. Up to the climax, the interest has been firmly fixed in the direction in which the chief characters are moving. After the deed is consummated, a pause ensues. Suspense must now be excited in what is new. For this, new forces, perhaps new rôles, must be introduced, in which the hearer is to acquire interest. On account of this, there is already danger in distraction and in the breaking up of scenic effects. And yet, it must be added, the hostility of the counter-party toward the hero cannot always be easily concentrated in one person nor in one situation; sometimes it is necessary to show how frequently, now and again, it beats upon the soul of the hero; and in this way, in contrast with the unity and firm advance of the first half of the play, the second may be ruptured, in many parts, restless; this is particularly the case with historical subjects, where it is most difficult to compose the counter-party of a few characters only.

And yet the return demands a strong bringing out and intensifying of the scenic effects, on account of the satisfaction already accorded the hearer, and on account of the greater significance of the struggle. Therefore, the first law for the construction of this part is that the number of persons be limited as much as possible, and that the effects be comprised in great scenes. All the art of technique, all the power of invention, are necessary to insure here an advance in interest.

One thing more. This part of the drama specially lays claims upon the character of the poet. Fate wins control over the hero; his battles move toward a momentous close, which affects his whole life. There is no longer time to secure effects by means of little artifices, careful elaboration, beautiful details, neat motives. The essence of the whole, idea and conduct of the action, comes forward powerfully; the audience understands the connection of events, sees the ultimate purpose of the poet; he must now exert himself for the highest effects; he begins, testing every step in the midst of his interest, to contribute to this work from the mass of his knowledge, of his spiritual affinities, and of what meets the wants of his own nature. Every error in construction, every lack in characterization, will now be keenly felt. Therefore the second rule is valuable for this part; only great strokes, great effects. Even the episodes which are now ventured, must have a certain significance, a certain energy. How numerous the stages must be through which the hero's fall passes, cannot be fixed by rule, farther than that the return makes a a less number desirable than, in general, the rising movement allows. For the gradual increase of these effects, it will be useful to insert, just before the catastrophe, a finished scene which either shows the contending forces in the strife with the hero, in the most violent activity, or affords a clear insight into the life of the hero. The great scene, Coriolanus and his mother, is an example of the one case; the monologue of Juliet, before taking the sleep potion, and the sleep-walking scene of Lady Macbeth, of the other case.

The Force of the Final Suspense.—It is well understood that the catastrophe must not come entirely as a surprise to the audience. The more powerful the climax, the more violent the downfall of the hero, so much the more vividly must the end be felt in advance; the less the dramatic power of the poet in the middle of the piece, the more pains will he take toward the end, and the more will he seek to make use of striking effects. Shakespeare never does this, in his regularly constructed pieces. Easily, quickly, almost carelessly, he projects the catastrophe, without surprising, with new effects; it is for him such a necessary consequence of the whole previous portion of the piece, and the master is so certain to bear forward the audience with him, that he almost hastens over the necessities of the close. This talented man very correctly perceived, that it is necessary, in good time to prepare the mind of the audience for the catastrophe; for this reason, Cæsar's ghost appears to Brutus; for this reason, Edmund tells the soldier he must in certain circumstances slay Lear and Cordelia; for this reason, Romeo must, still before Juliet's tomb, slay

Paris, in order that the audience, which at this moment, no longer thinks of Tybalt's death, may not, after all, cherish the hope that the piece will close happily; for this reason, must the mortal envy of Aufidius toward Coriolanus be repeatedly expressed before the great scene of the return of the action; and Coriolanus must utter these great words, "Thou hast lost thy son;" for this reason the king must previously discuss with Laertes the murdering of Hamlet by means of a poisoned rapier. Notwithstanding all this, it is sometimes hazardous to hasten to the end without interruption. Just at the time when the weight of an evil destiny has already long burdened the hero, for whom the active sympathy of the audience is hoping relief, although rational consideration makes the inherent necessity of his destruction very evident,—in such a case, it is an old, unpretentious poetic device, to give the audience for a few moments a prospect of relief. This is done by means of a new, slight suspense; a slight hindrance, a distant possibility of a happy release, is thrown in the way of the already indicated direction of the end. Brutus must explain that he considers it cowardly to kill one's self; the dying Edmund must revoke the command to kill Lear; Friar Laurence may still enter before the moment when Romeo kills himself; Coriolanus may yet be acquitted by the judges; Macbeth is still invulnerable from any man born of woman, even when Burnam Wood is approaching his castle; even Richard III. receives the news that Richmond's fleet is shattered and dispersed by the storm. The use of this artifice is old; Sophocles used it to good purpose in *Antigone;* Creon is softened, and revokes the death sentence of Antigone; if it has gone so far with her as he commanded, yet she may be saved. It is worthy of note that the Greeks looked upon this fine stroke far differently from the way we regard it.

Yet it requires a fine sensibility to make good use of this force. It must not be insignificant or it will not have the desired effect; it must be made to grow out of the action and out of the character of the persons; it must not come out so prominent that it essentially changes the relative position of the parties. Above the rising possibility, the spectator must always perceive the downward compelling force of what has preceded.

The Catastrophe.—The catastrophe of the drama is the closing action; it is what the ancient stage called the *exodus.* In it the embarrassment of the chief characters is relieved through a great deed. The more profound the strife which has gone forward in the hero's soul, the more noble its purpose has been, so much more logical will the destruction of the succumbing hero be.

And the warning must be given here, that the poet should not allow himself to be misled by modern tender-heartedness, to spare the life of his hero on the stage. The drama must present an action, including within itself all its parts, excluding all else, perfectly complete; if the struggle of a hero has in fact, taken hold of his entire life, it is not old tradition, but inherent necessity, that the poet shall make the complete ruin of that life impressive. That to the modern mind, a life not weak, may, under certain circumstances, survive mortal conflicts, does not change anything for the drama, in this matter. As for the power and vitality of an existence which lies subsequent to the action of the piece, the innumerable reconciling and reviving circumstances which may consecrate a new life, these, the drama shall not and can not represent; and a reference to them will never afford to the audience the satisfaction of a definite conclusion.

Concerning the end of the heroes, however, it must be said, the perception of the reasonableness and necessity of such a destruction, while reconciling and elevating, must be vivid. This is possible only when, by the doom of the heroes, a real adjustment of conflicting forces is produced. It is necessary, in the closing words of the drama, to recall that nothing accidental, nothing happening but a single time, has been presented, but a poetic creation, which has a universally intelligible meaning.

To the more recent poets, the catastrophe is accustomed to present difficulties. This is not a good sign. It requires unembarrassed judgment to discover the reconciliation which is not opposed to the feeling of the audience, and yet embraces collectively the necessary results of the piece. Crudeness and a weak sensibility offend most where the entire work of the stage should find its justification and confirmation. But the catastrophe contains only the necessary consequences of the action and the characters; whoever has borne both firmly in his soul, can have little doubt about the conclusion of his play. Indeed, since the whole construction points toward the end, a powerful genius may rather be exposed to the opposite danger of working out the end too soon, and bearing it about with him finished; then the ending may come into contradiction with the fine gradations which the previous parts have received during the elaboration. Something of this kind is noticeable in *The Prince of Homburg*, where the somnambulism at the close, corresponding to the beginning, and manifestly having a firm place in the soul of the poet, is not at all in accord with the clear tone and free treatment of the fourth and fifth acts. Similarly in *Egmont*, the conclusion, Clara, as freed Holland in transfiguration, can be conceived as written sooner than the last scene of Clara herself in the piece, with which this conclusion is not consistent.

For the construction of the catastrophe, the following rules are of value: First, avoid every unnecessary word, and leave no word unspoken whereby the idea of the piece can, without effort, be made clear from the nature of the characters. Further, the poet must deny himself broad elaboration of scenes; must keep what he presents dramatically, brief, simple, free from ornament; must give in diction and action, the best and most impressive; must confine the scenes with their indispensable connections within a small body, with quick, pulsating life; must avoid, so long as the action is in progress, new or difficult stage-effects, especially the effects of masses.

There are many different qualities of a poetic nature, which are called into operation in these eight parts of the drama on which its artistic structure rests. To find a good introduction and a stimulating force which arouses the hero's soul and keeps it in suspense, is the task of shrewdness and experience; to bring out a strong climax is specially the business of poetic power; to make the closing catastrophe effective requires a manly heart and an exalted power of deliberation; to make the return effective is the most difficult. Here neither experience nor poetic resource, nor yet a wise, clear vision of the poetic spirit, can guarantee success; it requires a union of all these properties. In addition, it requires a good subject and some good ideas, that is, good luck. Of the component parts discussed, all of them, or such as are necessary, every artistic drama of ancient or modern times is composed.

III.

SOPHOCLES' CONSTRUCTION OF THE DRAMA.

The tragedy of the Athenians still exercises its power over the creative poet of the present; not only the imperishable beauty of its contents, but its poetic form influences our poetic work; the tragedy of antiquity has essentially contributed to separate our drama from the stage productions of the middle ages, and give it a more artistic structure and more profound meaning. Therefore, before an account is given of the technical arrangement in the tragedies of Sophocles, it will be necessary to recall those peculiarities of the ancient stage, which, so far as we can judge, with their demands and limitations, controlled the Athenian poet. What is easily found elsewhere will be but briefly mentioned here.

The tragedy of the old world grew out of the dithyrambic solo songs with choruses, which were used in the Dionysian spring-time festivals; gradually the speeches of individuals were introduced between the dithyrambs and choruses, and were enlarged to an action. The tragedy retained from these beginnings, the chorus, the song of single leading rôles in the moments of highest excitement, the alternating songs of the actors and of the chorus. It was a natural consequence that the part of the tragedy won the mastery, and the chorus receded. In the oldest plays of Æschylus, *The Persians* and *The Suppliants*, the choral songs are by far the larger part. They have a beauty, a magnitude, and so powerful a dramatic movement that neither in our oratorios nor in our operas is there much that can be compared with them. The short incidental sentences interpolated, spoken by individual characters, and not lyric-musical, serve almost entirely as motives to produce new moods in the solo singer and the chorus. But already in the time of

Euripides, the chorus had stepped into the background, its connection with the developed action was loose, it sank from its position of guide and confidant of the chief characters to a quite unessential part of the drama, choral songs of one drama were used for another; and at last they represented nothing but the song which completed the interval between acts. But the lyric element remained fixed in the action itself. Well-planned, broadly elaborated sentimental scenes of the performers, sung and spoken, remained in important places of the action an indispensable component part of the tragedy. These pathos-scenes, the renown of the first actor, the centre of brilliance for ancient acting, contain the elements of the lyric situation in a completeness which we can no longer imitate. In them are comprised the touching effects of the tragedy. These long-winded gushings of inner feeling had so great a charm for the audience that to such scenes unity and verisimilitude of action were sacrificed by the weaker poets. But however beautiful and full the feeling sounds in them, the dramatic movement is not great. There are poetic observations upon one's own condition, supplications to the gods, feeling portrayal of peculiar relations. The first of these may perhaps be compared with the monologues of modern times, although in them the chorus sometimes represents the sympathising hearer, sometimes the hearer who responds.

That extension of the old dithyrambic songs, first tô oratorios, the solo-singers in which appeared in festal costume with simple pantomime, then to dramas with a well-developed art of representation, was effected by means of an action which was taken almost exclusively from the realm of Hellenic heroic legend and the epic. Isolated attempts of poets to extend this realm remained, on the whole, without success. Even before Æschylus, a composer of oratorios had once attempted to make use of historical material; the oldest drama of Æschylus which has been preserved for us, made use of historical material of the immediate past; but the Greeks had, at that time, no historical writings at all, in our sense of the word. A successful attempt to put on the stage material freely invented, had in the flourishing time of the Greek tragedy little imitation.

Such a restriction to a well-defined field of material was a blessing as well as a doom to the Attic stage. It confined the dramatic situations and the dramatic effects to a rather narrow circle, in which the older poets with fresh power attained the highest success, but which soon gave occasion to the later poets to seek new effects along side-lines; and this made the decay of the drama unavoidable. Indeed, there was between the world from which the material was taken and the essential conditions of the drama, an inherent opposition which the highest skill did not suffice to conquer, and at which the talents of Euripides grew powerless.

The species of poetry which before the development of the drama had made legendary subjects dear to the people, maintained a place in certain scenes of the play. It was a popular pleasure among the Greeks to listen to public speeches, and later, to have epic poems read to them. This custom gave to the tragedy longer accounts of occurrences which were essential to the action, and these occupied more space than would be accorded to them in the later drama. For the stage, the narrative was imbued with dramatic vividness. Heralds, messengers, soothsayers, are standing rôles for such recitals; and the scenes in which they appear have, as a rule, the same disposition. After a short introduction, the informants give their narration; then follow a few longer or shorter verses of like measure, quickly exchanged question and answer; at last the result of the announcement is compassed in brief words. The narrative comes in where it is most striking, in the catastrophe. The last exit of the hero is sometimes only announced.

In another way, the conduct of the scenes was influenced through the great opportunity of the Attic market, the judicial proceedings. It was a passion of the people to listen to the speeches of the accuser and of the defender. The highest artistic development of Greek judicial oratory, but also the artificial manner in which it was sought to produce effects, fine sophistical rhetoric, intruded upon the Attic stage, and determined the character of the speaking scenes. These scenes, also, considered as a whole, are fashioned according to established rules. The first actor delivers a little speech; the second answers in a speech of similar, sometimes exactly equal length; then follows a sort of rotation verses, each four answered by another four, three by three, two by two, one by one; then both actors resume their position and condense what they have to say, in second speeches; then follows the rattle of rotation verses, till he who is to be victor, once more briefly explains his point of view. The last word, a slight preponderance in verses, turns the scale. This structure, sometimes interrupted and divided by interpolated speeches of the chorus, has not the highest dramatic movement, despite the interchange of finished oratory, and in spite of the externally strong and progressive animation; it is an oratorical exposition of a point of view; it is a contest with subtle arguments, too oratorical for our feeling, too calculated, too artificial. One party is seldom convinced by the other. Indeed this had still another ground; for it is not easily allowed to an Attic hero to change his opinion on account of the orations of some one else. When there was a third rôle on the stage, the colloquy preserved the character of a dialogue; sudden and repeated interlocking of the characters was infrequent, and only momentary; if the third rôle entered into the colloquy, the second retreated; the change was usually made conspicuous by the insertion of a choral line. Mass-scenes, as we understand the word, were not known on the ancient stage.

The action ran through these pathos-scenes, messenger-scenes, colloquy-scenes, orations, and announcements of official persons to the chorus. If one adds to these the revolution-scenes, and the recognition-scenes, the aggregate contents of the piece will be found arranged according to the forms prescribed by the craft. The endowment of the poets is preserved for us in the way they knew how to give animation to these forms. Sophocles is greatest; and for this reason, what is constant in his works is most varied and, as it were, concealed.

In another way, the construction of the drama was modified through the peculiar circumstances under which its production took place. The Attic tragedies were presented in the flourishing time of Athens, on the days of the Dionysian festivals. At these festivals the poet contested with his rivals, not as author of the dramas; but when he did not also appear himself as actor, he appeared as manager or director. As such, he was united with his actors and the leader of the chorus in a partnership. To each poet, a day was allotted. On this day he must produce four plays, the last being, as a rule, a burlesque-play. It may be wondered which was the most astonishing, the creative power of the poet, or the endurance of the audience. If we conceive of a burlesque-play added to the trilogy of Æschylus, and estimate the time required for the performance according to the experience of our stage, and take into account the slowness with which it must be delivered, because of the peculiar acoustics of the great hall, and the necessity of a sharp, well-marked declamation, this representation on the stage must have required, with its brief interruptions at the end of pieces, at least nine hours. Three tragedies of Sophocles, together with the burlesque, must have claimed at least ten hours.[10]

The three serious plays were, in the earlier times, bound into one consistent action, which was taken from the same legendary source. So long as this old trilogy-form lasted, they had the nature of colossal acts, each of which brought a part of the action to a close. When Sophocles had disregarded this custom, and as contestant for the prize, put on the stage three independent, complete plays, one after another, the pieces stood worthy of confidence for their inner relations. How far a heightening of aggregate effect was secured by significant combination of ideas and action, by parallelism and contrast of situations, we can no longer ignore; but it follows from the nature of all dramatic representation, that the poet must have aspired to a progressive rise, a certain aggregation of the effects then possible.[11]

And as the spectators sat before the stage in the exalted mood of the holy spring-festival, so the chief actors were clothed in a festal costume. The costume of the individual rôles was usually prescribed strictly according to the custom of the festival; the actors wore masks with an aperture for the mouth, the high cothurnus on their feet, the body padded, and decked with long garments. Both sides of the stage, and the three doors in the background, through which the actors entered and made their exits, were arranged appropriately for their use in the piece.

But the poet contested on his theatre day, through

four plays, with the same players, who were called prize-contestants. The older Attic oratorios had only one actor, who entered in different rôles in a different costume; Æschylus added a second, Sophocles added a third. The Attic theatre never, in its most palmy days, exceeded three solo actors. This restriction of the number of players determined the technique of the Greek tragedy, more than any other circumstance. It was, however, no restriction which any resolute will could have dispensed with. Not external reasons alone hindered an advance; old tradition, the interest which the state took in the representations, and perhaps not less the circumstance, that the immense open auditorium on the Acropolis, which seated 30,000 persons, demanded a metallic quality of voice, a discipline of utterance possessed certainly by very few. To this must be added, that at least two of the actors, the first and the second, must be ready singers, before an exacting audience with a delicate ear for music. Sophocles' first actor must, during an effort of ten hours, pronounce about 1,600 lines, and sing at least six greater or less song pieces.[12]

This task would be great, but not inconceivable to us. One of the most exacting of our rôles is Richard III. This includes in the printed text, 1128 lines, of which more than 200 are usually omitted. Our lines are shorter, there is no song, the costume is much more convenient, the voice is of a different kind, comparatively less wearying; the effort for gesture, on the other hand, is incomparably greater;

on the whole, the creative work for the moment, much more significant; there is a very different expenditure of nervous energy. For our actors to compass the task of the ancients, would present no unconquerable difficulties, but just that which presents itself to the inexperienced as an alleviation, the prolonging the work through ten hours. And if they set up in opposition to the actor's art of the ancients, with some show of justice, that their present task is a greater and higher one, it is performed not with voice alone, but with facial expression and gesture freely invented, yet they must not forget that the scantiness of Greek pantomime, which remained restricted through masks and conventional movements and attitudes, found a supplement again in a remarkably fine culture in dramatic enunciation. Old witnesses teach us that a single false tone, a single incorrect accent, a single hiatus in a line, could arouse the universal ill-will of the audience against the player, and rob him of his victory; that the great actor was passionately admired, and that the Athenians, on account of the actor's art, would neglect politics and the prosecution of war. One must certainly not put a low value on the independent, creative work of the Hellenic actor; for we do not at all know how creatively his soul worked in the usual inflections of dramatic delivery.

Among these three actors, all the rôles of the three tragedies and the burlesque were divided. In each play, the actor had, in addition to his chief rôle — in which, according to custom, he wore the festal costume — subordinate parts corresponding to his character, or for which he could be spared. But even in this matter the poet was not allowed full liberty.

The personality of the actor on the stage was not so completely forgotten in his rôle, by his audience, as is the case with us. He remained in the consciousness of the Athenian, in spite of his various masks and changes of costume, always more the genial *person* performing, than the player who sought to hide himself entirely in the character of his rôle. And so in this respect, even at the time of Sophocles, the representation on the stage was more like an oratorio or the reading aloud of a piece, with parts assigned, than like our production on the stage. This is an important circumstance. The effects of the tragedy were not, for this reason, injured, but somewhat differently colored.

The first player was, therefore, made somewhat significantly conspicuous on the stage. To him belongs the middle door of the background — "the royal" — for his entrances and exits; he played the most distinguished persons, and the strongest characters. It would have been against his professional dignity to represent on the stage, anyone who allowed himself to be influenced or led by any other character in the piece — the gods excepted. He specially was the player of pathetic parts, the singer and hero, of course for both masculine and feminine rôles; his rôle alone gave the piece its name, in case he was the controlling spirit, in the action; otherwise the name of the piece was taken from the costume and character of the chorus. Next him stood the second contestant, as his attendant and associate; over against him stood the third, a less esteemed actor, as character player, intriguer, representative of the counter-play.

This appointment was strictly adhered to by Sophocles, in the preparation and distribution of parts. There were in his plays, the chief hero, his attendant, and his adversary. But the subordinate parts, also, which each of them must undertake, and which corresponded to each of the chief rôles, were, so far as was at all possible, distributed according to their relations to the chief rôles. The chief actor, himself, took the part of his representative and companion in sentiment; the parts of friends and retainers, so far as possible, the second player took; the third, or adversary, took the parts of strangers, enemies, opposing parties; and in addition to these, sometimes with the second, he assumed further accessory rôles.

From all this there originated a peculiar kind of stage effects, which we might call inartistic, but which had for the Attic poet, and the Attic stage, not a little significance. The next duty of the actor was specially to indicate every one of the rôles he assumed in a piece, by a different mask, a different tone of voice, a different carriage, and different gestures. And we recognize that here, too, there was much that had conformed to custom, and become established; for example, in the make-up and delivery of a messenger, in the step, bearing, gesture of young women, and of old women. But a second peculiarity of this established distribution of parts was that what was constant in the actor, became apparent in his individual parts, and was felt by the audience as something proper to himself, and effective. The actor on the Attic stage became an ideal unity which held its rôles together. Above the illusion that different persons were speaking, the feeling remained to the hearer, that they were one and the same; and this circumstance the poet used for peculiar dramatic effects. When Antigone was led away to death, the whole excited soul of Tiresias rang behind the tone of voice in which his threat was made to Creon; the same tone, the same spiritual nature in all the words of the messenger who announced the sad end of Antigone and of Hæmon, again touched the spirit of the audience. Antigone, after she had gone away to death, came continually back to the stage. By this means there arose, sometimes during the performance, a climax of tragic effects, where we, in reading, notice a bathos. When in *Electra*, the same actor presents Orestes and Clytemnestra, son and mother, murderer and victim, the same quality of voice suggests the blood relation to the audience, the same cold determination and cutting sharpness of tone—it was the rôle of the third actor—suggests the inner kinship of the two natures; but this sameness moderated, perhaps, the horror which the fearful action of the play produced.

When, in *Ajax*, the hero of the piece kills himself at the climax, this must have been, in the eyes of the Greeks, a danger to the effect of the play, not because this circumstance in this case affected the unity of the action, but probably put too much of the weight toward the beginning. But when, immediately afterwards, from the mask of Teucros, the same honest, true-hearted nature still rang in the voice, only more youthful, fresher, unbroken, the Athenian not only felt with satisfaction the blood relation, but the soul of Ajax took a lively part in the struggle continued about his grave. Particularly attractive is the way Sophocles makes use of this means—of course, not he alone,—to present effectively, in the catastrophe, the ruin of a chief character, which can only be announced. In each of the four pieces, which contain the very conspicuous rôle of a messenger in the catastrophe (in the *Trachinian Women* it is the nurse) the actor who has played the part of the hero whose death is announced, became himself the messenger, who related the affecting circumstances of the death, sometimes in a wonderfully animated speech; to the Athenians, in such a case, the voice of the departed came back from Hades, and pierced their souls—the voice of Œdipus at Colonos, of Jocasta, of Antigone, of Deianeira. In *Philoctetes*, the return of the same actor in various rôles is most peculiarly prized for dramatic effects,—of this there will be a discussion later on.[18]

Such a heightening of the effect through a lessening of the scenic illusion, is foreign to our stage, but not unheard of. A similar effect depends on the representation of women's parts by men, which Goethe saw in Rome.

This peculiarity of the Attic stage gave the poet some liberties in the structure of the action, which we no longer allow. The first hero could be spared from his chief rôle during longer parts of the play —as in *Antigone* and *Ajax*. When, in the *Trachinian Women*, the chief hero, Hercules, does not enter at all till the last scene, yet he has been effective through his representatives from the beginning forward. The maid of the prologue, who refers to the absent Hercules, Lichas, his herald, who gives accounts of him, speak with the subdued voice of the hero.

And this keeping back of the hero was frequently necessary to the poet as a prudent aid in concealing the indulgence which, before all others, the first actor must claim for himself. The almost superhuman effort of a day's acting could be endured only when the same actor did not have the longest and most exacting groups of rôles in all three tragedies. The chief rôle among the Greeks, remained that of the protagonist, who had the dignity and the pathos requiring great effort, even if to this part, perhaps, only a single scene was given. But the poet was compelled, in individual pieces of the festival occasion, to give to the second and third actors what we call the chief parts, the most comprehensive parts; for he must be considerate enough to make a somewhat even distribution of the lines of the three tragedies, among his three contestants.[14]

The plays of Sophocles which have been preserved, are distinguished more by the character of their action than by their construction, from the Germanic drama. The section of the legend, which Sophocles used for the action of his piece, had peculiar presuppositions. His plays, as a whole, represent the restoration of an already disturbed order, revenge, penance, adjustment; what is supposed to have preceded is also the direst disturbance, confusion, crime. The drama of the Germans, considered in general, had for its premises, a certain if insufficient order and rest, against which the person of the hero arose, producing disturbance, confusion, crime, until he was subdued by counteracting forces, and a new order was restored. The action of Sophocles began somewhat later than our climax. A youth had in ignorance slain his father, had married his mother; this is the premise—how this already accomplished, unholy deed, this irreparable wrong comes to light, is the play. A sister places her happiness in the hope that a young brother in a foreign land will take vengeance upon the mother for the murder of the father. How she mourns and hopes, is terrified at the false news of his death, is made happy by his arrival, and learns about the avenging deed—this is the play. Everything of misfortune, of atrocity, of the guilt, of the horrible revenge, which preceded, yes, the horrible deed itself, is represented through the reflections that fall upon the soul of a woman, the sister of the avenger, the daughter of the murderess and of the murdered man. An unfortunate prince, driven from his home, gratefully communicates to the hospitable city which receives him the secret blessing which, according to an oracle, hangs over the place of his burial. A virgin, contrary to the command of the prince, buries her brother, who lies slain on the field; she is therefore sentenced to death, and involves the son and the wife of the inexorable judge with herself in destruction. To a wandering hero, there is sent into the foreign land, by his wife who has heard of his infidelity, and wishes to regain his love, a magic garment which consumes his body; on account of her grief at this, the wife kills herself and has her body burned.[15] A hero, who through a mad delusion has slain a captured herd instead of the abhorred princes of his people, kills himself for shame; but his associates achieve for him an honorable burial. A hero, who on account of an obstinate disease of his army, is left exposed on an uninhabited island, is brought back, because an oracle, through those who hated him and banished him, has demanded his return as a means of restoring health to the army. What precedes the play is always a great part of what we must include in the action.[16]

But if from the seven plays of Sophocles which have been preserved, it is allowable to pass a guarded judgment on a hundred lost plays, this treatment of myths does not seem universal among the Greeks, but seems to distinguish Sophocles. We recognize distinctly that Æschylus in his trilogies considered longer portions of the legends — the wrong, the complication, the adjustment. Euripides sometimes exceeded the definite end piece of the legend, or with more convenience than art, announced what had preceded, in an epic prologue. In both of his best pieces, *Hyppolitus* and *Medea*, the action is built on premises, which would also have been possible in newer pieces.

This order of the action in Sophocles allowed not only the greatest excitement of passionate feeling, but also a firm connection of characters; but it excluded numerous inner changes, which are indispensable to our plays. How these monstrous premises affected the heroes, he could represent with a mastery now unattainable; but there were given most unusual circumstances, through which the heroes were influenced. The secret and ecstatic struggles of the inner man, which impel from a comparative quiet, to passion and deed, despair and the stings of conscience, and again the violent changes which are produced in the sentiment and character of the hero himself through an awful deed, the stage of Sophocles did not allow to be represented. How any one gradually learned something fearful little by little, how any one conducted himself after reaching a momentous conclusion, this invited picturing; but how he struggled with the conclusion, how the terrible calamity that pressed upon him, was prepared by his own doings,—this, it appears, was not dramatic for the stage of Sophocles. Euripides is more flexible in this, and more similar to us; but in the eyes of his contemporaries, this was no unconditional excellence. One of the most finished characters of our drama is Macbeth; yet it may be well said, to the Athenians before the stage he would have been thoroughly intolerable, weak, unheroic; what appears to us most human in him, and what we admire as the greatest art of the poet, his powerful conflict with himself over the awful deed, his despair, his remorse,— this would not have been allowed to the tragic hero of the Greeks. The Greeks were very sensitive to vacillations of the will; the greatness of their heroes consisted, before all, in firmness. The first actor would scarcely have represented a character who would allow himself in any matter of consequence, to be influenced by another character in the piece. Every mental disturbance of the leading persons, even in subordinate matters, must be carefully accounted for and excused. Œdipus hesitates about seeing his son; Theseus makes all his representations of obstinacy in vain; Antigone must first explain to the audience; to listen is not to yield.

If Philoctetes had yielded to the reasonable arguing of the second player, he would have fallen greatly in the regard of the audience; he would have been no longer the strong hero. To be sure, Neoptolemus changes his relation to Philoctetes, and the audience was extremely heated over it; that he did so, however, was only a return to his own proper character, and he was only second player. We are inclined to consider Creon in *Antigonè* as a grateful part; to the Greeks he was only a rôle of third rank; to this character, the justification of pathos was entirely wanting. Just the trait that makes him appeal to us, his being convulsed and entirely unstrung by Tiresias,—that artifice of the poet to bring a new suspense into the action—this lessened to the Greeks the interest in the character. And that the same trait in the family and in the play comes out once more, that Hæmon, too, will kill his father only after the messenger's announcement, but then kills himself—for us a very characteristic and human trait—Attic criticism seems to have established as a reproach against the poet, who brought forward such undignified instability twice in one tragedy. If ever the conversion of one character to the point of view of another is accomplished, it does not occur—except in the catastrophe of *Ajax*—during the scene in which the parties fight each other with long or short series of lines; but the change is laid behind the scenes; the convert comes entirely altered, into his new situation.

The struggle of the Greek hero was egotistic; his purpose ended with his life. The position of the Germanic hero, with reference to his destiny, is therefore, very different, because to him the purpose of his existence, the moral import, his ideal consciousness, reaches far out beyond his individual life, love, honor, patriotism. The spectators bring with them to the Germanic play, the notion that the heroes of the stage are not there entirely for their own sake, not even specially for their own sake, but that just they, with their power of free self-direction, must serve higher purposes, let the higher which stands above them be conceived as Providence, as the laws of nature, as the body politic, as the state. The annihilation of their life is not ruin, in the same sense as in the ancient tragedy. In *Œdipus at Colonos*, the greatness of the import took a strong hold upon the Athenians; they felt here forcibly the humanity of a life which, beyond mere existence, and indeed by its death, rendered a high service to the universal existence. From this, too, arises the great closing effect of *The Furies*. Here the sufferings and fate of the individual are used as blessings to the universal. That the greatest unfortunates of the legend—Œdipus and Orestes—pay so terrible a penance for their crime, appeared to the Greeks as a new and sublime dignifying of man upon the stage, not foreign to their life, but to their art. The undramatic climax of pity, produced by practical closing results, however useful to home and country, leaves us moderns unmoved. But it is always instructive to note that the two greatest dramatists of the Hellenes once raised their heroes to the same theory of life in which we are accustomed to breathe and to see the heroes of our stage.

How Sophocles fashioned his characters and his situations under such constraint is remarkable. His feeling for contrasts worked with the force of a power of nature, to which he himself could not afford resistance. Notice the malicious hardness of Athene, in *Ajax*. It is called out by contrast with the humanity of Odysseus, and shows the needed contrast in color with an unscrupulous sharpness, whereby naturally the goddess comes short of herself, because she will sagaciously illuminate with her divinity the shadowing of her nature, which is like Menelaus's. The same piece gives in every scene a good insight into the manner of his creation, which is so spontaneous, and withal so powerful in effects, so carelessly sovereign, that we easily understand how the Greeks found in it something divine. Everywhere here, one mood summons another, one character another, exact, pure, certain; each color, each melody, forces forward another corresponding to it. The climax of the piece is the frame of mind of Ajax after the awakening. How nobly and humanly the poet feels the nature of the man under the adventurous presuppositions of the piece! The warm-hearted, honest, hot-headed hero, the ennobled Berlichingen of the Greek army, had been several times churlish toward the gods; then misfortune came upon him. The convulsing despair of a magnificent nature, which is broken by disgrace and shame, the touching concealment of his determination to die, and the restrained pathos of a warrior, who by voluntary choice performs his last act,—these were the three movements in the character of the first hero which gave the poet the three great scenes, and the requirements for the entire piece. First, as contrast with the prologue, the picture of Ajax himself. Here he is still a monster, stupid as if half asleep. He is the complete opposite of the awakened Ajax, immediately the embodiment of shrewdness. The situation was as ridiculous on the stage as it was dismal; the poet guarded himself, indeed, from wishing to make anything different out of it. Both counter-players must accommodate themselves to the depressing constraint. Odysseus receives a slight tinge of this ridiculous element, and Athene receives the cold, scornful hardness. It is exactly the right color, which was needed by what was being represented, a contrast developed with unscrupulous severity, created, not by cold calculation, not through unconscious feeling, but as a great poet creates, with a certain natural necessity, yet with perfect, free consciousness.

In the same dependence upon the chief heroes, the collective rôles are fashioned, according to the conditions under which the Greek composed for each of the three actors; associate player, accessory player, counter-player. In *Ajax* for instance, there was the "other self" of Ajax, the true, dutiful brother Teucros; then, there were the second rôles, his wife, the booty of his spear, Tecmessa, loving, anxious, well knowing, however, how to oppose the hero; and there was his friendly rival, Odysseus; finally, the enemies, again three degrees of hate; the goddess, the hostile partisan, and his more prudent brother, whose hatred was under control out of regard for policy. When, in the last scene, the counter-player and the hostile friend of the hero were reconciled at the grave, from the compact which they made, the Athenian would recognize very distinctly the opposite of the opening scene, where the same voices had taken sides against the madman.

Within the individual characters of Sophocles, also, the unusual purity and power of his feeling for harmony, and the same creation in contrasts, are admirable. He perceived here surely and with no mistake, what could be effective in them, and what was not allowable. The heroes of the epic and of the legend, resist violently, being changed into dramatic characters: they brook only a certain measure of inner life and human freedom; whoever will endow them with more, from him they snatch away and tear into shreds the loose web of their myths—barbarous on the stage. The wise poet of the Greeks recognizes very well the inward hardness and untamableness of the forms which he must transform into characters. Therefore, he takes as little as possible from the legend itself into the drama. He finds, however, a very simple and comprehensible outline of its essential characteristic as his action needs it, and he always makes the best of this one peculiarity of character, with peculiar strictness and logical congruity. This determining trait is always one impelling toward a deed: pride, hate, connubial sense of duty, official zeal. And the poet conducts his characters in no way like a mild commander; he exacts from them according to their disposition, what is boldest, and most extreme; he is so insatiably hard and pitiless, that to us weaker beings, a feeling of real horror comes, on account of the fearful one-sidedness into which he has them plunge; and that even the Athenians compared such effects to the loosing of bloodhounds. The defiant sisterly love of Antigone, the mortally wounded pride of Ajax, the exasperation of the tormented Philoctetes, the hatred of Electra, are forced out in austere and progressive intensity, and placed in the deadly conflict.

But over against this groundwork of the characters, he perceives again with marvellous beauty and certainty just the corresponding gentle and friendly quality which is possible to his characters, with their peculiar harshness. Again, this contrast appears in his heroes, with the power of the required complementary color; and this second and opposite quality of his persons—almost always the gentle, cordial, touching side of their nature, love opposed to hate, fidelity to friends opposed to treachery, honest candor against sheer irascibility—is almost always adorned with the most beautiful poetry, the most delicate brilliancy of color. Ajax, who would have slain his foes in mad hatred, displays an unusual strength of family affection, true-hearted, deep, intense love toward his companions, toward the distant brother, toward the child, toward his wife; Electra, who almost lives upon her hatred of her mother, clings with the gentlest expressions of tenderness about the neck of her longed-for brother.

The tortured Philoctetes, crying out in pain and anguish, demanding the sword that he may hew asunder his own joints, looks up, helpless, grateful, and resigned, to the benevolent youth who can behold the odious suffering and give no expression to his horror. Only the chief characters exhibit this unfolding of their powerfully conceived unity, in two opposite directions; the accessory persons, as a rule show only the required supplementary colors; Creon thrice, Odysseus twice, both in each of their pieces differently shaded off, Ismene, Theseus, Orestes.

Such a uniting of two contrast colors in one chief character was possible to the Greek only because he was a great poet and student of human nature; that is, because his creative soul perceived distinctly the deepest roots of a human existence, from which these two opposite leaves of his characters grew. And this exact observation of the germ of every human life is the highest prerogative of the poet, which causes the simple bringing out of two opposite colors in character to produce the beautiful appearance of wealth, of fulness, of symmetry. It is an enchanting illusion, in which he knows how to place his hearers; it gives his pictures exactly the kind of life which has been possible in his material on the stage. With us, the characters of the great poets show much more artistic fashioning than those ancient ones, which grew up so simply, leaf opposite to leaf, from the root; Hamlet, Faust, Romeo, Wallenstein, cannot be traced back to so simple an original form. And they are, of course, the evidence of a higher degree of development of humanity. But on this account, the figures of Sophocles are not at all less admirable and enchanting. For he knows how to design them with simplicity, but with a nobility of sentiment, and fashion them in a beauty and grandeur of outline that excited astonishment even in ancient times. Nowhere are loftiness and power wanting in either chief characters or accessory characters; everywhere is seen from their bearing, the insight and unrestrained master-power of a great poet nature.

Æschylus embodied in the characters of the stage a single characteristic feature, which made their individuality intelligible; in Prometheus, Clytemnestra, Agamemnon, Sophocles intensified his great rôles, while he attributed to them two apparently contradictory qualities, which were in reality requisite and supplementary; when Euripides went further, and created pictures imitating reality, which were like living beings, the threads of the old material flew asunder, and curled up like the dyed cloth of Deianeira in the sunlight.

This same joyousness, and the sure perception of contrasts, allowed the poet, Sophocles, also to overcome the difficulty which his choice of fables prepared for him. The numerous and monstrous premises of his plot seemed peculiarly unfavorable to a powerful action proceeding from the hero himself. In the last hours of its calamity, it appears, the heroes are almost always suffering, not freely acting. But the greater the pressure the poet lays upon them from without, so much higher the power becomes with which they battle against it. Whatever already in the first ascending half of the piece, fate or a strange power works against the hero, he does not appear as receiving it, but as thrusting his whole being emphatically against it. He is, in truth, impelled; but he appears in a distinctive manner to be the impelling force; thus Œdipus, Electra, even Philoctetes, taken together, are efficient natures, which rage, impel, advance. If any one ever stood in a position of defence dangerous to a play, it was poor King Œdipus. Let it be observed how Sophocles represents him, as far as the climax, fighting in increasing excitement, against opposition; the more dismal his cause becomes to himself, so much the more violently does he beat against his environment.

These are some of the conditions under which the poet created his action. If the plays of Sophocles together with the chorus, claimed about the same time as our plays, on the average, require, yet the action is much shorter than ours. For aside from the chorus, and from the lyric and epic parts inserted, the whole design of the scenes is greater and, on the whole, broader. The action, according to our way of presenting, would scarcely occupy half an evening. The transitions from scene to scene are short, but accurately motived; entrance and exit of new rôles are explained, little connecting parts between elaborate scenes are infrequent. The number of divisions was not uniform; only in the later time of the ancient tragedy was the division into five acts established. The different parts of the action were separated by choral songs. Every one of such parts,—as a rule, corresponding to our finished scene—was distinguished from the one preceding it, by its meaning, but not so sharply as our acts. It appears, almost, that the single pieces of the day—not the parts of a piece—were separated by a curtain drawn across the stage. Indeed, the tableau in the beginning of Œdipus may be explained otherwise; but since the decoration of Sophocles already plays a part in the piece—and he was as fond of referring to this as Æschylus was to his chariot and flying machine—its fastenings must have been taken from the view of the spectator before the beginning of a new piece.

Another characteristic of Sophocles, so far as it is recognizable to us, lies in the symmetrical proportions of his piece.

The introduction and the conclusion of the old drama were set off from the rest of the structure, much more markedly than at present. The introduction was called the prologue; embraced one appearance or more of the solo-players, before the first entrance of the chorus; contained all the essentials of the exposition; and was separated by a choral song from the rising action. The conclusion, *exodus*, likewise separated from the falling action by a choral song, was composed of scene-groups, carefully worked out, and included the part of the action which we moderns call the catastrophe. In Sophocles, the prologue is, in all the plays preserved, an artfully constructed dialogue scene, with a not insignificant movement, in which two, sometimes all three, actors appear and show their relation to each other. It contains, first, the general premises of the piece, and second, what appears to be peculiar to Sophocles, a specially impressive introduction of the exciting force which shall impel the action, after the choral song.

The first choral song follows the prologue; after this comes the action with the entrance of the first excitement. From here the action rises in two or more stages to the climax. There are in Sophocles, sometimes, very fine motives, insignificant in themselves, which occasion this ascent. The summit of the action arises mightily; for bringing out this moment, the poet uses all the splendor of color, and all the sublimest poetic fervor. And when the action allows of a broad turn, the scene of this turn, revolution, or recognition, follows not suddenly and unexpectedly, but with fine transition, and always in artistic finish. From here, the action plunges swiftly to the end, only occasionally, before the *exodus*, a slight pause, or level, is arranged. The catastrophe itself is composed like a peculiar action; it consists not of a single scene, but of a group of scenes,—the brilliant messenger part, the dramatic action, and sometimes lyric pathos scenes, lie in it, connected by slight transition scenes. The catastrophe has not the same power, in all the plays, nor is it treated with effects of progressive intensity. The relation of the piece to the others of the same day may, also, have controlled the work of the conclusion.

The play of *Antigone* contains—besides prologue and catastrophe—five parts, of which the first three form the rising movement; the fourth, the climax; the fifth, the return. Each of these parts, separated from the others by a choral song, embraces a scene of two divisions. The idea of the piece is as follows: A maiden, who contrary to the command of the king, buries her brother, slain in a battle against his native city, is sentenced to death by the king. The king, on this account, loses his son and his consort, by self-inflicted death. In a dialogue scene, which affords a contrast between the heroine and her friendly helpers, the prologue explains the basis of the action, and makes an exposition of the exciting force,—the resolution of Antigone to bury her brother. The first step of the ascent is, after the introduction of Creon, the message that Polynices is secretly buried, the wrath of Creon, and his command to find the perpetrator of the deed. The second step is the introduction of Antigone, who has been seized, the expression of her resistance to Creon, and the intrusion of Ismene, who declares that she is an accomplice of Antigone and will die with her. The third step is the entreaty of Hæmon, and when Creon remains inexorable, the despair of the lover. The messenger scene has been followed so far by dialogue scenes, continually increasing in excitement. The pathos scene of Antigone, song and recitation, forms the climax. This is followed by Creon's command to lead her away to death. From this point the action falls rapidly. The prophet, Tiresias, announces calamity awaiting Creon, and punishes his obstinacy. Creon is softened, and gives orders that Antigone be released from the burial vault where she is imprisoned. And now begins the catastrophe, in a great scene-group; announcement by messenger of Antigone's death, and Hæmon's, the despairing departure of Eurydice, the lament of Creon, another message, announcing the death of Eurydice, and the concluding lament of Creon. The continuance of Antigone herself is the seer, Tiresias, and the messenger of the catastrophe; the friendly accessory players are Ismene and Hæmon; the counter-player, with less power and with no pathos, is Creon. Eurydice is only an assisting rôle.

The most artistic play of Sophocles is *King Œdipus*. It possesses all the fine inventions of the Attic drama, besides variations in songs and chorus, revolution scene, recognition scene, pathos scene, finished announcement of the messenger at the close. The action is governed by the counter-play, has a short ascent, comparatively weak climax, and a long descent. The prologue brings out all three actors, and announces, besides the presupposed conditions, Thebes under Œdipus during a plague, the exciting force, an oracular utterance,—that Laius's murder shall be avenged, and with this the city shall be delivered from the pestilence. From here the action rises by two steps. First, Tiresias, called by Œdipus, hesitates to interpret the oracle; rendered suspicious by the violent Œdipus, he hints in ambiguous, enigmatical terms, at the mysterious murderer, and departs in wrath. Second step, strife of Œdipus with Creon, separated by Jocasta. After this, climax; interview of Œdipus and Jocasta. Jocasta's account of the death of Laius, and Œdipus's words, "O woman, how, at your words, a sudden terror seizes me!" are the highest point of the action. Up to this passage, Œdipus has summoned up a violent resistance to the crowding conjectures; although he has been gradually growing anxious, now the feeling of an infinite danger falls upon his soul. His rôle is the conflict between defiant self-consciousness and unfathomable self-contempt; in this place the first ends, the second begins. From here the action goes again in two steps downward, with magnificent execution; the suspense is increased by the counterplay of Jocasta; for what gives her the fearful certainty once more deceives Œdipus; the effects of the recognitions are here masterfully treated. The catastrophe has three divisions, messenger scene, pathos scene, closing with a soft and reconciling note.

On the other hand, *Electra* has a very simple construction. It consists—besides prologue and catastrophe—of two stages of the ascent and two of the fall; of these, the two standing nearest the climax are united with this into a great scene-group, which makes specially conspicuous the middle point of the play. The play contains not only the strongest dramatic effect which we have received from Sophocles, but it is also, for other reasons, very instructive, because in comparing it with the *Libation Pourers* of Æschylus and the *Electra* of Euripides, which treat the same material, we recognize distinctly how the poets prepared for themselves, one after another, the celebrated legend. In Sophocles, Orestes, the central point of two pieces in Æschylus's trilogy, is treated entirely as an accessory figure; he performs the monstrous deed of vengeance by command of and as the tool of Apollo, deliberate, composed, with no trace of doubt or vacillation, like a warrior who has set out upon a dangerous undertaking; and only the catastrophe represents this chief part of the old subject dramatically. What the piece presents is the mental perturbations of an extremely energetic and magnificent female character, but shaped for the requirements of the stage in a most striking manner, by changes in feeling, through will and deed. In the prologue, Orestes and his warden give the introduction and the exposition of the exciting force (arrival of the avengers), which works at first in the action as a dream and presentiment of Clytemnestra. The first stage of the rising action follows this: Electra receives from Chrysothemis the news that she, the ever-complaining one, will be put into prison; she persuades Chrysothemis not to pour upon the grave of the murdered father the expiating libation which the mother has sent. Second stage: Conflict of Electra and Clytemnestra, then climax; the warden brings the false report of the death of Orestes; different effect of this news on the two women; pathos scene of Electra added to this, the first step of the return. Chrysothemis returns joyfully from her father's grave, announces that she found a strange lock of hair, as a pious benediction there; a friend must be near. Electra no longer believes the good news, challenges the sister to unite with herself and kill Ægisthos, rages against the resisting Chrysothemis, and resolves to perform the deed alone. Second stage: Orestes as a stranger, with the urn containing Orestes's ashes; mourning of Electra, and recognition scene of enrapturing beauty. The *exodus* contains the representation of the avenging deed, first in the fearful mental convulsions of Electra, then the entrance of Ægisthos and his death.

What is contained in *Œdipus at Colonos* appears, if one considers the idea of the piece, extremely unfavorable for dramatic treatment. That an old man, wandering about the country, should bestow the blessing which, according to an oracle, was to hang over his grave, not upon his ungrateful native city, but upon hospitable strangers—such a subject seems to the casual patriotic feeling of an audience, rather offensive. And yet Sophocles has understood how to charge even this with suspense, progressive elevation, passionate strife between hatred and love. But the piece has a peculiarity of construction. The prologue is expanded into a greater whole, which in its extreme compass corresponds to the catastrophe; it consists of two parts, each composed of three little scenes, connected by a pathetic moment of alternating song between the solo players and the chorus, which enters at this unusually early point. The first part of the prologue contains the exposition, the second scene the exciting force—the news which Ismene brings the venerable Œdipus, that he is pursued by those of his native city, Thebes. From here the action rises through a single stage—Theseus, lord of the land, appears, offers his protection—to the climax, a great conflict scene with powerful movement. Creon enters, drags away the daughters by force, threatening Œdipus himself with violence, in order that he shall return home; but Theseus maintains his protecting power and sends Creon away. Hereupon follows the return action, in two stages: The daughters, rescued by Theseus, are brought back to the old man; Polynices, for his own selfish ends, entreats reconciliation with his father, and his father's return. Œdipus dismisses him unreconciled; Antigone expresses in touching words the fidelity of a sister. Then follows the catastrophe; the mysterious snatching away of Œdipus, a short oration scene and chorus, then grand messenger scene and concluding song. By the expansion of the prologue and the catastrophe, this piece becomes about three hundred lines longer than the other plays of this writer. The freer treatment of the permanent scene-forms, like the contents of the play, lets us perceive what we also know from old accounts, that this tragedy was one of the last works of the venerable poet.

Perhaps the earliest of the plays of Sophocles which have come down to us is *The Trachinian Women*. Here, too, is something striking in construction. The prologue contains only the introduction, anxiety of the wife, Deianeira, for Hercules remaining far away from home, and the sending of the son, Hyllos, to seek the father. The exciting force lies in the piece itself, and forms the first half of the rising action, of two parts: first, arrival of Hercules; second, Deianeira's discovery that the female captive slave whom her husband had sent in advance, was his mistress. Climax: In her honest heart, Deianeira resolves to send to the beloved man a love-charm which a foe whom he had slain had left her. She delivers the magic garment to the care of a herald. The falling action, in a single stage, announces her anxiety and regret at sending the garment; she has learned by an experiment that there is something unearthly in the magic. The returning son tells her in heartless words, that the present has brought upon the husband a fatal illness. Here follows the catastrophe, also in two parts; first, a messenger scene which announces the death of Deianeira; then Hercules himself, the chief hero of the piece, is brought forward, suffering mortal pain, as after a great pathos scene, he demands of his son the burning of his body on Mount Œta.

The tragedy, *Ajax*, contains after the prologue in three parts, a rising movement in three stages; first, the lament and family affection of Ajax,—and his determination to die; then the veiling of his plan, out of regard for the sadness which it would cause his friends; finally, without our perceiving a change of scene, an announcement by messenger, that to-day Ajax will not come out of his tent, and the departure of his wife and the chorus to seek the absent hero. Hereupon follows the climax—the pathos scene of Ajax and his suicide, especially distinguished by this, that the chorus has previously left the orchestra, so that the scene presents the character of a monologue. Now comes the return action in three parts; first, the discovery of the dead man, lament of Tecmessa and of Teucros, who now enters; then the conflict between Teucros and Menelaus, who will forbid the burial. The catastrophe at last, an intensifying of this strife in a dialogue scene between Teucros and Agamemnon, the mediation of Odysseus, and the reconciliation.

Philoctetes is noticeable for its particularly regular form; the action rises and falls in beautiful proportion. After a dialogue scene between Odysseus and Neoptolemus in the prologue has made clear the premises and the exciting force, the first part follows, the ascent, in a group of three connected scenes; after this come the climax and the tragic force in two scenes, of which the first is a two-part pathos scene splendidly finished; then the third, the return action, corresponding exactly to the first, again in a group of three connected scenes. Just as perfectly, the choruses correspond to each other. The first song is an alternating song between the second actor and the chorus; the third, just such an alternating song between the first actor and the chorus. Only in the middle stands a full choral song. The resolution of the chorus into a dramatically excited play in concert—not only in *Philoctetes* but in *Œdipus*—is not an accident. It may be concluded from the firm command of form, and the masterly conduct of the scenes, that this drama belongs to the later time of Sophocles.[17]

Here, also, the first actor, Philoctetes, has the pathetic rôle. His violent agitation, represented with marvellous beauty and in rich detail, goes through a wide circle of moods, and arises in the climax, the great pathos scene of the play, with soul-convulsing power. The circumstance of horrible physical suffering, so important to the drama, and immediately following, soul-devouring mental anguish, have never been delineated so boldly and so magnificently. But the honest, embittered, obstinate man affords no opportunity to the action itself for dramatic movement. This, therefore, is placed in the soul of the second actor, and Neoptolemus is leader of the action. After he has, in the prologue, not without reluctance, acceded to the wily counsels of Odysseus, he attempts in the first part of the action to lead Philoctetes forward by deception. Philoctetes confidently leans for support upon him as the helper who promises to bring him into his own land; and he delivers to this helper the sacred bow. But the sight of the sick man's severe sufferings, the touching gratitude of

Philoctetes for the humanity which is shown him, arouse the nobler feelings of the son of Achilles; and with an inward struggle, he confesses to the sick man his purpose of taking him with his bow to the Greek army. The reproaches of the disappointed Philoctetes increase the other's remorse, and his excitement is still further augmented when Odysseus, hastening by, has Philoctetes seized by violence. At the beginning of the catastrophe, the honesty of Neoptolemus is in strife against Odysseus himself; he gives back to Philoctetes the deadly bow, summons him once more to follow to the army; and, as Philoctetes refuses, promises him once more what he falsely promised at the beginning of the play; now his achievement must be to defy the hatred of the whole Greek army, and lead the suffering man and his ship home. Thus, through the transformations in the character of the hero who directs the action, this is concluded dramatically, but in direct opposition to the popular tradition; and in order to bring the unchanging material of the piece into harmony with the dramatic life of the play, Sophocles has seized upon a device which is nowhere else found in his plays; he has the image of Hercules appear in the closing scene and unsettle the resolution of Philoctetes. This conclusion, according to our sense of fitness, an excrescence, is still instructive in two directions: it shows how even Sophocles was restricted by the epic rigor of a traditional myth, and how his high talent struggled against dangers upon which, shortly after his time, the old tragedy was to be wrecked. Further, he gives us instruction concerning the means by which a wise poet might overcome the disadvantage of an apparition out of keeping, not with our feeling, but with the sensibility of his spectators. He pacified his artistic conscience first of all by previously concluding the inner dramatic movement entirely. So far as the piece plays between Neoptolemus and Philoctetes, it is at an end. After a violent conflict, the two heroes have nobly come to a mutual agreement. But they have arrived at a point against which both the oracle and the advantage of the Grecian army offer objections. The third actor, the wily, unscrupulous statesman, Odysseus, now represents the highest interest. With the fondness which Sophocles also elsewhere shows for even his third man, he has here specially dignified that personage. After the counter-player has in the prologue agreeably expressed the well-known character of Odysseus, the latter appears immediately in a disguise in which the spectator not only knows in advance that the strange figure is a shrewd invention of Odysseus, but also recognizes the voice of Odysseus and his sly behavior. Three times more he appears as Odysseus in the action, in order to point to the necessity of the seizure as an advantage of the whole; his opposition becomes continually bolder and more emphatic. At last, in the catastrophe, shortly before the divine hero becomes visible on high, the warning voice of Odysseus rings out; his form, apparently protected by the rock, appears in order once more to express opposition; and this time his threatening cry is sharp and conscious of victory. When, only a short time afterwards, perhaps above the same spot where Odysseus's figure was seen for a moment, the transfigured form of Hercules is visible, and again with the voice of the third actor, makes the same demand in a mild and reconciling tone, Hercules himself appears to the spectator as an intensifying of Odysseus; and in this last repetition of the same command, the spectator perceived nothing new entering from without; but rather he perceived more vividly the irresistible power of the keen human intelligence which had struggled through the entire play against the impassioned confusion of the other actor. The prudence and calculation of this intensification, the spiritual unity of the three rôles of the third actor, were confidently believed by the audience to be a beauty of the piece.

IV.

THE GERMANIC DRAMA.

That enjoyment of exhibitions, the representation of unusual occurrences by acting on the stage, governed the beginnings of the Germanic drama, is still recognized by the works of higher art as well as by the inclination of the public, and most of all by the first attempts of our dramatic poets.

Shakespeare filled with dramatic life the old customs of a play-loving people; from a loosely woven narrative, he created an artistic drama. But even up to his time and that of his romantic contemporaries, there shot across nearly two thousand years some brilliant rays from the splendid time of the Attic theater.

To him also, the arrangement of a piece depended on the construction of his stage. This had, even in his later time, scarcely side curtains and a simple scaffolding in the rear, which formed a smaller raised stage, with pillars at the sides, and a balcony above, from which steps led to the front stage below. The chief stage had no drop curtain; the divisions of the piece could be separated only by pauses; there were, therefore, fewer divisions than with us now. It was not possible, as it is on our stage, to begin in the midst of a situation, nor to leave it incomplete. In Shakespeare's plays, all the players must enter before they could address the audience, and they must all make their exit before the eyes of the audience; even the dead must thus be borne off in an appropriate manner. Only the inner stage was concealed behind curtains, which could be drawn apart and drawn together without trouble, and denote a convenient change of scene. First, the front space was the street,—on which, for instance, Romeo and his companions entered in masks; when they had departed, the curtains were drawn apart, and there was the guest-room of the Capulets, as indicated by the servants in attendance. Capulet came forward from the middle of the background and greeted his friends; his company poured in upon the stage, and spread about the foreground. When the guests had departed, the middle curtain was drawn behind Juliet and the nurse, and the stage became a street again, from which Romeo slipped behind the curtain to be out of sight of his boisterous friends who were calling him. When these were gone, Juliet appeared on the balcony, the stage became a garden, Romeo appeared,[18] and so on. Everything must be more in motion, lighter, quicker changing of scene-groups, a more rapid coming and going, a more nimble play, a closer concentration of the aggregate impression. Attention is called to this oft discussed arrangement of the stage, because this dispensing with changes of scenes, this former accustoming of the spectator to make every transition of place and time with his own active fancy, exerted a decided influence on Shakespeare's manner of dividing his plays. The number of the smaller divisions could be greater than with us, because they disturbed the whole less; sometimes little scenes were inserted with no trouble at all. What seems to us a breaking up of the action, was less perceptible on account of the technical arrangement.

Moreover, Shakespeare's audience, accustomed to the spectacular from former times, had a preference for such plays as presented great numbers of men in violent commotion. Processions, battles, scenes full of figures, were preferably seen and belonged, notwithstanding the scanty equipment which on the whole the spectacular drama of the time possessed, to the cherished additions of a play. Like the Englishmen of that time, Shakespeare's heroes are fond of company. They like to appear with a train of attendants, and talk confidentially in unrestrained conversation about the important relations of their lives, on the market place and on the street.

In Shakespeare's time, still, the actor must assume several rôles ; but his task now was to conceal his own distinctive personality entirely, and clothe beautiful truth with the appearance of reality. Only the parts of women, which were still played by men, preserved something of the ancient character of stage play, which made the spectator a confidant in the illusion which was to be produced.

Upon such a stage appeared Germanic dramatic art in its first and most beautiful bloom. Shakespeare's technique is the same, in essential respects, that we still strive to attain. And he has, on the whole, established the form and construction of our pieces. In the following pages the discussion must recur to him continually ; therefore, in this place, only a few of the characteristics of his time and of his manner, which we can no longer imitate, will be mentioned.

In the first place, the change of his scenes is too frequent for our stage ; above all, the little side scenes are disturbing. Where he binds together a number of scenes, we must form the corresponding part of the action into a single scene. When, for example, in Coriolanus, the dark figure of Aufidius or of another Volscian appears from the first act forward in short scenes, in order to indicate the counter-play, up to the second half of the piece where this presses powerfully to the front, we are entirely at a loss, on our stage, to make these fleeting forces effective, with the exception of the battle scene in the beginning of the rising action. But we are obliged to compose the scenes more strictly for the chief heroes and represent their emotions and movements in a smaller number of situations, and therefore with fuller elaboration.

In Shakespeare we admire the mighty power with which, after a brief introduction, he throws excitement in the way of his heroes and impels them swiftly in rapid upward stages to a momentous height. His method of leading the action and the characters beyond the climax, in the first half of the play, may also serve as a model to us. And in the second half, the catastrophe itself is planned with the sureness and scope of genius, with no attempt at overwhelming effect, without apparent effort, with concise execution, a consequence of the play, following as a matter of course. But the great poet does not always have success with the forces of the falling action, between climax and catastrophe, the part which fills about the fourth act of our plays. In this important place, he seems too much restrained by the customs of his stage. In many of the greatest dramas of his artistic time, the action is divided up, in this part, into several little scenes, which have an episodical character and are inserted only to make the connection clear. The inner conditions of the hero are concealed, the heightening of effects and the concentration so necessary here fails. It is so in *Hamlet*, in *King Lear*, in *Macbeth*, somewhat so in *Antony and Cleopatra*. Even in *Julius Cæsar*, the return action contains, indeed, that splendid quarrel scene and the reconciliation between Brutus and Cassius, and the appearance of the ghost ; but what follows is again much divided, fragmentary. In *Richard III.*, the falling action is indeed drawn together into several great impulses ; but yet these do not in a sufficient degree correspond in stage effect to the immense power of the first part.

We explain this characteristic of Shakespeare from a relic of the old custom of telling the story on the stage by means of speech and responsive speech. As the dark suspicion against the king works upon Hamlet ; as Macbeth struggles with the idea of murder ; as Lear is continually plunged deeper into misery ; as Richard strides from one crime to another,—this must be represented in the first half of the drama. The *ego*, the *self* of the hero, which strives to achieve its design, here concentrates almost the entire interest in itself. But from this point on, where the will has become deed, or where the impassioned embarrassment of the hero has reached the highest degree, where the consequences of what has happened are at work and the victory of the counter-play begins, the significance of the opponent becomes, of course, greater. As soon as Macbeth has murdered the king and Banquo, the poet must turn the efforts of the murderous despot toward other men and events ; other opponents must bring the conflict with him to an end. When Coriolanus is banished from Rome, he must be brought forward in new relations and with new purposes. When Lear flies about as a deranged beggar, the piece must either close, a thing which is not possible without something further, or the remaining persons must make apparent new uses of his terrible fate.

It is also natural that from the climax downward, a greater number of new motives, perhaps, too, of new persons, may be introduced into the piece ; it is further natural that this play of the opposing party must set forth the influences which are exerted upon the hero from without, and therefore makes necessary more external action and a broader elaboration of the engrossing moment. And it is also not at all surprising that Shakespeare right here yielded more to curiosity and to the very convenient scene-connection of his time than is allowable on our stage.

But it is not this alone. Sometimes one can not repel the feeling that the poet's ardor for his heroes is lessened in the second part. It is certainly not so in *Romeo and Juliet.* In the return action, Romeo, indeed, is concealed ; but the poet's darling, Juliet, is so much the more powerfully delineated. It is not so in *Coriolanus*, where the two most beautiful scenes of the play, that in the house of Aufidius, and the grand scene with the hero's mother, lie in the return action. But it is strikingly so in *King Lear*. What follows the hovel scene is only an episode or a divided narrative in dialogue, with insufficient effect; the second mad scene of Lear is also no intensifying of the first. Similarly in Macbeth, after the frightful banquet scene, the poet is through with the inner life of his hero. The finished witch scene, the prophesying, the dreary episode in Macduff's house,— few attractive figures of the counter-play fill this part, in an arrangement of scenes which we may not imitate; and only occasionally the great power of the poet blazes up, as in the catastrophe of Lady Macbeth.

Manifestly, it is his greatest joy, to fashion from the most secret depths of human nature, a will and a deed. In this he is inexhaustibly rich, profound, and powerful. No other poet equals him. If he has once rendered his hero this service, if he has represented the spiritual processes culminating in a portentous deed, then the counter-influence of the world, the later destiny of the hero, does not fill him with the same interest.

Even in *Hamlet*, there is a noticeable weakness in the return action. The tragedy was probably worked over several times by the poet; it was apparently a favorite subject; he has mysteriously infused into it the most thoughtful and penetrating poetry. But these workings-over at long intervals have taken from the play the beautiful proportion, which is only possible in a simultaneous moulding of all parts. *Hamlet* is, of course, no precipitate of poetic moods from half a human life, like *Faust;* but breaks, gaps, little contradictions in tone and speech, between characters and action, remained ineffaceable to the poet. That Shakespeare worked out the character of Hamlet so fondly, and intensified it till beyond the climax, makes the contrast in the second half only so much the greater; indeed, the character itself receives something iridescent and ambiguous, from the fact that deeper and more spirited motives were introduced into the texture of the rising action. Something of the old manner of bringing narrative upon the stage clung also to the poet's last revision; some places in Ophelia's exit and the graveyard scene appear to be new-cut diamonds, which the poet has set in while working over the earlier connection.

Nevertheless it is instructive to set forth distinctly in a scheme, the artistic combination of the drama from the constituent parts already discussed. What is according to plan, what is designed for a certain purpose, has not been found by the poet entirely through the same consideration which is necessary to the reader when instituting his review. Much is evidently without careful weighing; it has come into being as if by natural necessity, through creative power; in other places, the poet is thoughtful, considerate, has doubted, then decided. But the laws of his creation, whether they directed his invention secretly and unconsciously to himself; or whether, as rules known to him, they stimulated the creative power for certain effects, they are for us readers of his completed works, everywhere, distinctly recognizable. This self-developing organization of the drama, according to a law, will here be briefly analyzed, without regard to the customary division into acts.

Introduction. 1. The key-note; the ghost appears on the platform; the guards and Horatio. 2. The exposition itself; Hamlet in a room of state, before the beginning of the exciting force. 3. Connecting scene with what follows; Horatio and the guards inform Hamlet of the appearance of the ghost. Interpolated exposition scene of the accessory action. The family of Polonius, at the departure of Laertes.

The Exciting Force. 1. Introductory key-note; expectation of the ghost. 2. The ghost appears to Hamlet. 3. Chief part, it reveals the murder to him. 4. Transition to what follows. Hamlet and his confidants.

Through the two ghost scenes, between which the introduction of the chief persons occurs, the scenes of the introduction and of the first excitement are enclosed in a group, the climax of which lies near the end.

Ascending action in four stages. First stage: the counter-players. Polonius propounds that Hamlet has become deranged through love for Ophelia. Two little scenes: Polonius in his house, and before the king; transition to what follows. Second stage: Hamlet determines to put the king to a test by means of a play. A great scene with episodical performances, Hamlet against Polonius, the courtiers, the actors. Hamlet's soliloquy forms the transition. Third stage: Hamlet's examination by the counter-players. 1. The king and the intriguers. 2. Hamlet's celebrated monologue. 3. Hamlet warns Ophelia. 4. The king becomes suspicious. These three stages of the rising action are worked out with reference to the effect of the two others; the first becomes an introduction, the broad and agreeable elaboration of the second forms the chief part of the ascent; the third, through the continuation of the monologue, beautifully connected with the second, forms the climax of the group, with sudden descent. Fourth stage, which leads up to the climax: the play, confirmation of Hamlet's suspicion. 1. Introduction. Hamlet, the players and courtiers. 2. The rendering of the play, the king. 3. Transition, Hamlet, Horatio, and the courtiers.

Climax. A scene with a prelude, the king praying. Hamlet hesitating. Closely joined to this, the

Tragic Force or Incident. Hamlet, during an interview with his mother, stabs Polonius. Two little scenes, as transition to what follows; the king determines to send Hamlet away. These three scene-groups are also bound into a whole, in the midst of which the climax stands. At either side in splendid working-out, are the last stage of the rising action and the tragic force.

The Return. Introductory side-scene. Fortinbras and Hamlet on the way. First stage: Ophelia's madness, and Laertes demanding revenge. Side scene: Hamlet's letter to Horatio. Second stage: A scene; Laertes and the king discuss Hamlet's death. The announcement of the queen that Ophelia is dead, forms the conclusion, and the transition to what follows. Third stage: Burial of Ophelia. Introduction scene, with great episodical elaboration. Hamlet and the grave-diggers. The short, restrained chief scene; the apparent reconciliation of Hamlet and Laertes.

Catastrophe. Introductory scene: Hamlet and Horatio, hatred of the king. As transition, the announcement of Osric; the chief scene, the killing. Arrival of Fortinbras.

The three stages of the falling action are constructed less regularly than those of the first half. The little side scenes without action, through which Hamlet's journey and return are announced, as well as the episode with the grave-diggers, interrupt the connection of scenes. The work of the dramatic close is of ancient brevity and vigor.

V.

THE FIVE ACTS.

The drama of the Hellenes was built up in a regular system of parts, so that between a completed introduction and the catastrophe, the climax came out powerfully, bound by means of a few scenes of the rising and of the falling action with the beginning and the end; within these limits was an action filled with violent passion, and elaborately finished. The drama of Shakespeare led an extensive action in a varied series of dramatic forces, in frequent change of finished scenes and accessory scenes, by steep ascent, up to a lofty height; and from this summit again downward, by stages. The whole passed before the spectator tumultuously, in violent commotion, rich in figures and sublime effects prominently brought forward. The German stage, on which since Lessing our art has blossomed, collected the scenic effects into larger groups, which were separated from each other by more marked boundaries. The effects are carefully prepared, the ascent is slow, the altitude which is attained is less lofty and of longer continuance; and gradually, as it arose, the action sinks to the close.

The curtain of our stage has had a material influence on the structure of our plays. The parts of the drama, which have been presented already, must now be disposed in five separate divisions; they possessed greater independence, because they were drawn farther apart from each other. The transition from the old way of dividing the action to our five acts, was, of course, long ago prepared. The meritorious method of binding together different moods, which the ancient chorus between the single parts of the action represented, failed already in Shakespeare; but the open stage, and the pauses, certainly shorter, made, as we frequently recognize in his dramas, breaks in the connection, not always so deep as does in our time, the close by means of the curtain, and the interval with music, or without it. With the curtain, however, there came also the attempt not only to indicate the environment of the person who entered, but to carry on the performance with more pretentious elaboration by means of painting and properties. By this means, the effects of the play were essentially colored, and only occasionally supported. Moreover, by this means, the different parts of the action were more distinctly separated than they were yet in Shakespeare's time. For by means of change of decorations often brilliant, not only the acts, but the smaller parts of the action, became peculiar pictures which form a contrast in color and tone. Every such change distracts; each makes a new tension, a new intensifying, necessary.

Therefore little but important alterations were produced in the structure of the pieces. Each act received the character of a completed action. For each, a striking of chords to give the keynote, a short introduction, a climax in strong relief, an effective close, were desirable. The rich equipment for scenic surroundings compelled a restriction of the frequent change of place, which in Shakespeare's time had become too easy, a leaving out of illustrative side scenes, and the laying of longer parts of the action in the same room, and in divisions of time following immediately upon one another. Thus the number of scenes became less, the dramatic flow of the whole more quiet, the joining of greater and lesser forces more artistic. One great advantage, however, was offered by closing up the stage. It would now be possible to begin in the midst of a situation, and end in the midst of a situation. The spectator could be more rapidly initiated into the action, and more quickly dismissed, without taking in the bargain the preparation and the solution of what had held him spell-bound; and that was no small gain which was possible five times in a piece, for the beginning and the end of the effects. But this advantage offered also a danger. The depiction of situations, the presentation of circumstances with less dramatic movement, became easier now; this painting especially favored, for the quiet Germans, the longer retention of the characters in the same enclosed room. On such a changed stage, the German poets of the last century produced their acts, till the time of Schiller, planning with foresight,—introducing with care,—all with a sustained movement of scenes and effects which corresponded to the measured and formal sociability of the time.

In the modern drama, in general, each act includes one of the five parts of the older drama; the first contains the introduction; the second, the rising action; the third, the climax; the fourth, the return; the fifth, the catastrophe. But the necessity of constructing the great parts of the piece in the same fashion as to external contour, renders it impossible that the single acts should correspond entirely to the five great divisions of the action. Of the rising action, the first stage was usually in the first act, the last sometimes in the third; of the falling action, the beginning and end were sometimes taken in the third and fifth acts, and combined with the other component parts of these acts into a whole. Naturally Shakespeare had already, as a rule, made his divisions in this manner.

This number of acts is no accident. The Roman stage long ago adhered to it. But only since the development of the modern stage among the French and Germans, has the present construction of the play been established in these countries.

In passing, it may be remarked that the five parts of the action will bear contracting into a smaller number of acts, with lesser subjects of less importance and briefer treatment. The three points, the beginning of the struggle, the climax, and the catastrophe, must always be in strong contrast; the action allows then of division into three acts. Even in the briefest action, which may have its course in one act, there are five or three parts always recognizable.

But as every act has its significance for the drama, so it has also its peculiarities in construction. A great number of variations is possible here. Every material, every poetic personality demands its own right. Still, from a majority of works of art at hand, some frequently recurring laws may be recognized.

The act of the introduction contains still, as a rule, the beginning of the rising movement, and in general, the following moments or forces: the introductory or key note, the scene of the exposition, the exciting fòrce, the first scene of the rising action. It will therefore be in two parts, as a general thing, and concentrate its effects about two lesser climaxes, of which the last may be the most prominent. Thus in *Emilia Galotti*, the prince at his work-table is the key-note; the interview of the prince with the painter is the exposition; in the scene with Marinelli lies the exciting force, the approaching marriage of Emilia. The first ascent is in the following short scene, with the prince, in his determination to meet Emilia at the Dominicans'. In *Tasso*, the decking of the statues with garlands by the two women indicates the prevailing mood of the piece; their succeeding conversation and the talk with Alphonso is the exposition. Following this, the decking of Tasso with wreaths by the princess is the exciting force; the entrance of Antonio and his cool contempt for Tasso is the first stage of the rising action. So in *Mary Stuart*, the forcing of the cabinets, the confession to Kennedy, the entrance of Mortimer, and the great scene between Mary and the emissaries, follow after each other. In *William Tell*, where the three actions are interwoven, there stands after the situation near the beginning, which gives the key-note, and after a short introductory colloquy of country people, the first exciting force for the action of Tell,—Baumgarten's flight and rescue. Then follows as introduction to the action of the confederated Swiss, the scene before Stauffacher's house. After this, the first rising action for

Tell; the conversation before the hat on the pole. Finally, for the second action, the exciting force, in the conversation of Walter Fürst and Melchthal; the making of Melchthal's father blind; and as finale of the first ascent, the resolution of the three Swiss to delay at Rütli.

The act of the ascent has for its duty in our dramas, to lead up to the action with increased tension, in order to introduce the persons in the counter-play who have found no place in the first act. Whether this contains one or several stages of the progressing movement, the hearer has already received a number of impressions; therefore in this, the struggles must be greater, a grouping of several in an elaborate scene, and a good close to the act, will be useful. In *Emilia Galotti*, for instance, the act begins, as almost every act in Lessing does, with an introductory scene, in which the Galotti family are briefly presented, then the intriguers of Marinelli expose their plan. Then the action follows in two stages, the first of which contains the agitation of Emilia after the meeting with the prince; the second, the visit of Marinelli and his proposition to Appiani. Both great scenes are bound together by a smaller situation scene which presents Appiani and his attitude toward Emilia. The beautifully wrought scene of Marinelli follows the excited mood of the family as an excellent close. The regular construction of *Tasso* shows in two acts just two stages of the ascent: the approach of Tasso to the princess, and in sharp contrast, his strife with Antonio. The second act in *Mary Stuart*, in its introduction leads forward Elizabeth and the other counter-players; it contains the rising action, Elizabeth's approach to Mary, in three stages: first, the strife of the courtiers in favor of Mary and against her, and the effect of Mary's letter upon Elizabeth; further, the conversation of Mortimer with Leicester, introduced by the conversation of the queen with Mortimer; finally, Leicester's inducing Elizabeth to see Mary. *Tell*, finally, compasses in this act the exposition of its third action, the Attinghausen family; then, for the confederated Swiss, a climax in an elaborate scene: Rütli.

The act of the climax must strive to concentrate its forces about a middle scene, brought out in strong relief. This most important scene, however, if the tragic force comes in here, is bound with a second great scene. In this case, the climax scene moves well back toward the beginning of the third act. In *Emilia Galotti*, the entrance of Emilia is the beginning of this highest scene, after an introductory scene in which the prince explains the strained situation, and after the explanatory announcement regarding the attack. The prostration of Emilia and the declaration of the prince are the highest point in the piece. The outbursting rage of Claudia against Marinelli follows this closely, as a transition to the falling movement. In *Tasso*, the act begins with the climax, the confessions which the princess makes to Leonora of her attachment to Tasso. Following this, comes as first stage of the falling movement, the interview between Leonora and Antonio, in which the latter becomes interested in Tasso and resolves to establish the poet at court. In *Mary Stuart*, the climax and the tragic force lie in the great park scene, which is in two parts; following this and connected with it by a little side scene, is the outburst of Mortimer's passion to Mary, as beginning of the falling action; the dispersion of the conspirators forms the transition to the following act. The third act of *Tell* consists of three scenes, the first of which contains a short preparatory situation scene in Tell's house,—Tell's setting out; the second, the climax between Rudenz and Bertha; the third, the greatly elaborated climax of the Tell action,—the shooting of the apple.

The act of the return has been treated by the the great German poets, with great and peculiar carefulness since Lessing's time, and its effects are almost always regular and included in a scene of much significance. On the other hand, among us Germans, the introduction of new rôles into the fourth act is much more frequent than in Shakespeare, whose praiseworthy custom it was, previously to intertwine his counter-players in the action. If this is impracticable, still one must be on his guard not to distract attention by a situation scene, which a piece does not readily allow in this place. The newcomers of the fourth act must quickly take a vigorous hold of the action, and so by a powerful energy justify their appearance. The fourth act of

Emilia Galotti is in two parts. After the preparatory conversation between Marinelli and the prince, the new character, Orsina, enters as accomplice in the counter-play. Lessing understood very well how to overcome the disadvantage of the new rôle, by giving over to the impassioned excitement of this significant character, the direction of the following scenes to the conclusion of the act. Her great scene with Marinelli is followed by the entrance of Odoardo, as the second stage. The high tension which the action receives by this, closes the act effectively. In *Tasso*, the return has its course in just two scenes: Tasso with Leonora, and Tasso with Antonio; both are concluded by Tasso's monologues. The regular fourth act of *Mary Stuart* will be discussed later. In *William Tell*, the fourth act for Tell himself contains two stages for the falling action; his escape from the boat, and Gessler's death. Between these, stands the return action for the Attinghausen family, which is interwoven here with the action of the Swiss confederation.

The act of the catastrophe contains almost always, besides the concluding action, the last stage of the falling action. In *Emilia Galotti*, an introductory dialogue between the prince and Marinelli begins the last stage of the falling action, that great interview between the prince, Odoardo and Marinelli, hesitation to give back the daughter to her father, then the catastrophe, murder of Emilia. The same in *Tasso;* after the introductory conversation of Alphonso and Antonio, the chief scene;

Tasso's prayer that his poem be restored to him; then the catastrophe, Tasso and the princess. *Mary Stuart*,—otherwise a model structure in the individual acts—shows the result of using a material which has kept the heroine in the background since the middle of the piece, and has made the counter-player, Elizabeth, chief person. The first scene-group, Mary's exaltation and death, contains her catastrophe, and an episodical situation scene, and her confession, which seemed necessary to the poet, in order to win for her yet a slight increase of sympathy. Closely following her catastrophe, is that of Leicester, as connecting link to the great catastrophe of the piece, Elizabeth's retribution. The last act of *Tell*, in two parts, is only a situation scene, with the episode of Parricida.

Of all German dramas, the double tragedy of *Wallenstein* has the most intricate construction. In spite of its complexity, however, this is on the whole regular, and combines its action firmly with *Wallenstein's Death*, as well as with *The Piccolomini*. Had the idea of the piece been perceived by the poet as the historical subject presented it,—an ambitious general seeks to seduce the army to a revolt against its commander, but is abandoned by the majority of his officers and soldiers and slain,—then the idea would, of course, have given a regular drama for rising and falling action, a not insignificant excitement, the possibility of a faithful reconstruction of the historical hero.

But with this conception of the idea, what is

best is wanting to the action. For a deliberate treason, which was firmly in the mind of the hero from the beginning, excluded the highest dramatic task,—the working out of the conclusion from the impassioned and agitated soul of the hero. Wallenstein must be presented as he is turning traitor, gradually, through his own disposition, and the compulsion of his relations; so another conception of the idea, and an extension of the action became necessary,—a general is, through excessive power, contentions of his adversaries, and his own pride of heart, brought to a betrayal of his commanding officer; he seeks to seduce the army to revolt, but is abandoned by the majority of his officers and soldiers, and slain.

With this conception of the idea, the rising half of the action must show a progressive infatuation of the hero, to the climax,—to the determination upon treason; then comes a part,—the seduction of the army to revolt,—where the action hovers about the same height; finally in a mad plunge, failure and destruction. The conflict of the general and his army had become the second part of the play. The division of this action into the five acts would be about the following: First act, introduction, the assembling of Wallenstein's army at Pilsen. Exciting force; dispatching of the imperial ambassador, Questenberg. Second act, rising movement; Wallenstein seeks, in any case, the coöperation of the army, through the signatures of the generals; banquet scene. Third act, through evil suggestions, excited pride, desire of rule, Wallenstein is forced to treat with the Swedes. Climax: Scene with Wrangel, to which is closely joined, as the tragic force, the first victory of the adversary, Octavio; the gaining of General Buttler for the emperor. Fourth act, return action, revolt of the generals, and the majority of the army. Close of the act, a scene with cuirassiers. Fifth act, Wallenstein in Eger, and his death. In the broad and fine elaboration which Schiller did not deny himself, it was impossible for him to crowd the material so rich in figures and in forces, so full of meaning, into the frame of five acts.

Besides, the character of Max very soon became exceedingly important to him, for reasons which could not be put aside. The necessity of having a bright figure in the gloomy group created him; and the wish to make more significant the relations between Wallenstein and his opponents, enforced this necessity.

In intimate relation with Max, Friedland's daughter grew to womanhood; and these lovers, pictures characteristic of Schiller, quickly won a deep import in the soul of the creating poet, expanding far beyond the episodical. Max, placed between Wallenstein and Octavio, pictured to the eye of the poet a strong contrast to either; he entered the drama as a second first hero; the episodical love scenes, the conflicts between father and son, between the young hero and Wallenstein, expanded to a special action.

The idea of this second action was: A high-minded, unsuspecting youth, who loves his general's daughter, perceives that his father is leading a political intrigue against his general, and separates himself from him; he recognizes that his general has become a traitor, and separates himself from him, to his own destruction and that of the woman whom he loves. This action presents, in its rising movement, the embarrassment of the lovers and their passionate attachment, so far as the climax, which is introduced by Thekla's words, "Trust them not; they are traitors!" The relations of the lovers to each other, up to the climax, are made known only by the exalted frame of mind with which Max, in the first act, Thekla in the second, rise above and are in contrast with their surroundings. After the climax, follows the return, in two great stages, both of two scenes, the separation of Max from his father and the separation of Max from Wallenstein; after this the catastrophe: Thekla receives the announcement of the death of her lover, again in two scenes. With the illumination of two such dramatic ideas, the poet concluded to interlace the two actions into two dramas, which together formed a dramatic unit of ten acts and a prelude.

In *The Piccolomini*, the exciting force is a double one, the meeting of the generals with Questenberg, and the arrival of the lovers in the camp. The chief characters of the piece are Max and Thekla; the climax of the play lies in the interview of these two, through which the separation of the guileless

Max from his surroundings is introduced. The catastrophe is the complete renouncing of his father by Max. The passages which are brought into this play from the action of *Wallenstein's Death*, are the scenes with Questenberg, the interview of Wallenstein with the faithful ones, and the banquet scene; also, a great part of the first, second, and fourth acts.

In *Wallenstein's Death*, the exciting force is the rumored capture of Sesina, closely connected with the interview between Wallenstein and Wrangel; the climax is the revolt of the troops from Wallenstein,— farewell of the cuirassiers. But the catastrophe is double; news of the death of Max, together with Thekla's flight, and the murder of Wallenstein. The scenes interwoven from the action of *The Piccolomini* are the interview of Max with Wallenstein and with Octavio, Thekla over against her relatives, and the separation of Max from Wallenstein, the messenger scene of the Swedish captain, and Thekla's resolve to flee; also one scene and conclusion of the second act, the climax of the third, the conclusion of the fourth act.

Now, however, such an interweaving of two actions and two pieces with each other would be difficult to justify, if the union thus produced, the double drama, did not itself again form a dramatic unity. This is peculiarly the case; the interwoven action of the whole tragedy rises and falls with a certain majestic grandeur. Therefore, in *The Piccolomini*, the two exciting forces are closely coupled; the first belongs to the entire action, the second to *The Piccolomini.* The drama has likewise two climaxes lying in close proximity, of which, one is the catastrophe of *The Piccolomini*, the other the opening part of *Wallenstein's Death.* Again, at the close of the last drama, there are two catastrophes, one for the lovers, the other for Wallenstein and the double drama.

It is known that Schiller, during his elaboration of the play, laid the boundaries between *The Piccolomini* and *Wallenstein's Death.* The former embraced, originally, the first two acts of the latter, and the separation in spirit of Max from Wallenstein. This was, of course, an advantage for the action of Max. But with this arrangement, the scene with Wrangel, *i. e.* the portentous deed of Wallenstein, and besides this Buttler's apostacy to Octavio, *i, e.*, the first ascent of *Wallenstein's Death*, and the first return of the entire drama, fell into the first of the two pieces; and this would have been a considerable disadvantage; for then the second drama would have contained, with such an arrangement, only the last part of the return, and the catastrophe of the two heroes, Wallenstein and Max; and in spite of the magnificent execution, the tension would have been too much lacking to this second half. Schiller concluded, therefore, rightly, to make the division farther back, and to end the first play with the great conflict scene between father and son. By this division, *The Piccolomini* lost in compactness, but *Wallenstein's Death* gained in an indispensable order of construction. Let it be noticed that Schiller made this alteration at the last hour, and that he was probably governed less by his regard for the structure of the parts, than by regard for the unequal time which the two parts would take for representation according to the original division. The action did not form itself in the soul of the poet, as we, following his thought in the completed piece, might think. He perceived with the sureness of deliberation, the course and the poetic effect of the whole; the individual parts of the artistic structure took their places in the whole according to a certain natural necessity. What was conformable to laws, in the combination, he has in nowise made everywhere so distinct, through conscious deliberation, as we are obliged to do, getting our notion from the completed masterpiece. Nevertheless we have the right to point out what follows a law, even where he has not consciously cast it in a mould, reflecting upon it afterward as we do. For the entire drama, *Wallenstein*, in its division, which the poet adopted, partly as a matter of course, when he first planned it, and again for individual parts at a later date, perhaps for external reasons, is an entirely complete and regular work of art.[10]

It is much to be regretted that our theatrical arrangements render it impossible to represent the whole masterpiece at one performance; only in this way would be seen the beautiful and magnificent effects, which lie in the artistic sequence of parts. As the pieces are now given, the first is always at the disadvantage of not having a complete close; the second, of having very numerous presupposed circumstances, and of its catastrophe demanding too much space — two acts. With a continuous representation, all this would come into right relations. The splendid prologue, "The Camp," the beautiful pictures of which one only wants more powerfully condensed through an undivided action, could hardly be dispensed with as an introduction. It is conceivable that a time may come when it will be a pleasure to the German to witness his greatest drama in its entirety. It is not impracticable, however great the strain would be upon the players. For even when both pieces are given, one after the other, no rôle exacts what would overtax the powers of a strong man. The spectators of the present, also, are, in the great majority of cases, not incapable on special occasions of receiving a longer series of dramatic effects than our time allotted to a performance offers. But, indeed, such a performance would be possible, if only as an exception, at a great festival occasion, and if only in another auditorium than our theaters. For what exhausts the physical strength of both player and spectator in less than three hours is the unearthly glare of the gaslight, the excessive strain upon the eyes, which it produces, and the rapid destruction of the breathable air, in spite of all attempts at ventilation.

CHAPTER III.

STRUCTURE OF SCENES.

I.

ARRANGEMENT OF PARTS.

The acts—this short foreign word has driven the German term into the background—are divided for stage purposes into scenes. The entrance and exit of a person, servants and the like being excepted, begins and ends the scene. Such a division of the acts is necessary to the management, in order easily to supervise the efforts of each single rôle; and for the presentation on the stage, the scenes represent the little units by the combination of which the acts are formed. But the dramatic passages out of which the poet composes his action, sometimes embrace more than one entrance and exit, or are bound together in a greater number, by the continuance on the stage, of one person. This passage, this single dramatic movement, takes its form through the various stages in which the creative power of the poet works.

For, like the links of a chain, the nearly related images and ideas interlock themselves during the poet's labor, one evoking another with logical coercion. The single strokes of the action thus arrange themselves in such single parts, while the great outlines of the action the poet carries in his soul. However diverse the work of the creative power in different minds may be, these logical and poetical units are formed in every poetic work by necessity; and anyone who gives careful attention, may easily recognize them in the completed poem, and perceive in individual instances the greater or less power, fervor, poetic fulness, and firm, neat method of work.

Such a passage includes as much of a monologue, of dialogue, of the entrance and exit of persons as is needed to represent a connected series of poetic images and ideas, which somewhat sharply divides itself from what precedes and what follows. These passages are of very unequal length; they may consist of a few sentences, they may embrace several pages; they may alone form a short scene, they may, placed in juxtaposition, and provided with introductory words and a conclusion leading over to what follows, form a greater complete whole, within an act. For the poet, they are the links out of which he forges the long chain of the action; he is well aware of their intrinsic merit and characteristic quality, even when he, with powerful effort is creating and welding them, one immediately after another.

Out of the dramatic moments, the poet composes scenes. This foreign word is used by us with various meanings. It denotes to the director, first, the stage-room itself, then the part of the action which is presented without change of scenery. To the poet, however, scene means the union of several dramatic moments which forms a part of the action, carried on by the same chief person, perhaps an entire scene, from the director's point of view, at all events, a considerable piece of one. Since a change of scenery is not always necessary or desirable at the exit of a leading character, the scene of the poet and the scene of the director do not always exactly coincide.[20] An example may be allowed here. The fourth act of *Mary Stuart* is divided by the poet into twelve parts (entrances), separated by one shifting of scenery within the act into two director scenes. It consists of two little scenes and one great scene, —thus three dramatic scenes. The first scene, the intriguers of the court, is composed of two dramatic moments, (1) after a short key note, which gives the tone of the act, the despair of Aubespine, (2) the strife between Leicester and Burleigh. The second scene, Mortimer's end, connected with the preceding by Leicester's remaining on the stage, (1) Leicester's connecting monologue, (2) interview between Leicester and Mortimer, (3) Mortimer's death. The third great scene, the conflict about the death sentence, is more artistically constructed. It is a double scene, similar to the first and second, only with closer connection, and consists of ten movements, of which the first four, the quarrel of Elizabeth and Leicester, united in a group, and the last six, the signing of the death warrant, stand in contrast. The six movements of the second half of the scene, coincide with the last six entrances of the act; the last of these, Davison and Burleigh, is the close of this animated passage, and the transition to the fifth act.

It is not always easy to recognize these logical units of the creating spirit, from a completed drama; and now and then the critical judgment is in doubt. But they deserve greater attention than has so far been accorded to them.

It was said in the last section, that every act must be an organized structure, which combines its part of the action in an order, conformable to a purpose and an effect. In it, the interest of the spectator must be guided with a steady hand, and increased; it must have its climax a great, strong, elaborate scene. If it contains several such elaborate climaxes, these must be united by means of shorter scenes, like joints, in such a manner that the stronger interest will always rest on the later elaborate scene.

Like the act, every single scene, transition scene as well as finished scene, must have an order of parts, which is adapted to express its import with the highest effect. An exciting force must introduce the elaborate scene, the spiritual processes in it must be represented with profusion, in effective progression, and the results of the same be indicated by telling strokes after its catastrophe, toward which it sweeps forward, richly elaborated; the conclusion must come, brief, and rapid; for once its purpose attained, the tension slackened, then every useless word is too much. And as it is to be introduced with a certain rousing of expectation, so its close needs a slight intensifying, specially a strong expression of the important personalities, at the time they leave the stage. The so-called exits are no unwarranted desire of the player, however much they are misused by a crude effort for effect. The marked division at the end of the scene, and the necessity of transferring the suspense to what follows, rather justify them as an artifice, specially at the close of an act, but of course in moderate use.

The poet has frequent occasion, during the presentation of a piece on our stage, to rage against the long intervals which are caused by the shifting of the scenery, and sometimes by the useless changing of costumes. It must be the poet's concern, as much as possible to restrict the actor's excuse for this practice; and when a change of costume is necessary, have regard to it in the arrangement of the action of the piece. A longer interval—that should never be more than five minutes—may, according to the nature of the piece, follow the second or third act. The acts which stand together in closer relation, must not be separated by a pause; what follows a pause, must have the power to gather up forces, and excite a new suspense. Therefore, pauses between the fourth and fifth acts are most disadvantageous. These last two parts of the action should seldom be separated more markedly than would be allowable between two single scenes. The poet must guard against the production, in this part of the action, of closing effects which, on account of the shifting of scenery hard to manage, and the introduction of new crowds, occasion delay.

But even the shifting of scenery within the limits of an act, is no indifferent matter. For every change in the appearance of the stage during an act, makes a new, strong line of separation; and the distraction of the spectator is increased, since the custom has been adopted in modern times, of concealing the process of changing scenes from the spectator, by the drop curtain. For now it is impossible to tell, except by the color of the curtain, whether the break is made only for the sake of the management, or whether an act is ended. In view of this inconvenience, it must be the poet's zealous care to make any change of scenes in the act unnecessary; and it will be well if during the process of composition, he relies on his own power to achieve everything in this direction; for frequently a change of the scenery seems to his embarrassed soul quite inevitable, while in most cases, by slight alterations in the action, it might be avoided. But if the shifting of curtains is not entirely unavoidable during an act, care may yet be taken, at least not to have it occur in the acts which demand the greatest elaboration, specially the fourth, where without this the full skill of the poet is necessary in order to secure progressive power. Such a disturbing break is most easily overcome in the first half of the action. In the alternation of finished and connecting scenes, there lies a great effect. By this, every part of the whole is set in artistic contrast with its surroundings; the essentials are set in a stronger light, the inner connection of the action is more intelligible in the alternating light and shadow. The poet must, therefore, carefully watch his fervid feeling, and examine with care what dramatic forces are for the essentials of his action, what for accessories. He must restrain his inclination to depict fully certain kinds of characters or situations, in case these are not of importance to the action; if, however, he cannot resist the charm of this habit, if he must deviate from this law and accord to an unessential force broader treatment, he will do it with the understanding that by special beauty of elaboration and finish, he must atone for the defect thus caused in the structure.

The subordinate scene, however, whether it be the echo of a chief scene, or the preparation for a new scene, or an independent connecting member, will always give the poet the opportunity to show his talent for the rôles, in the use of the greatest brevity. Here is the place for terse, suggestive sketching, which can, in a few words, afford a gratifying insight into the inmost being of the figures in the background.

II.

THE SCENES AND THE NUMBER OF PERSONS.

The freedom in the construction of scenes for our stage, and the greater number of the actors, make it apparently so easy for the poet to conduct his action through a scene, that often, in the new drama, the customary result of an excessive lack of restraint is to be regretted. The scene becomes a jumble of speeches and responses, without sufficient order; while it has a wearying length and smooth flowing sentences, neither elevation nor contrasts are developed with any power. Of course, there is not a total lack of connection in the scenes in the most bewildered work of the amateur; for the forms are to such a degree the expression of the character, that dramatic perception and feeling, even though unschooled, is accustomed to hit what is the correct thing, in many essentials; but not always, and not every one. Let the poet, therefore, during his work, critically apply a few well known rules.

Since the scene is a part of the drama, set off from other parts, and is to prepare for the meaning of what follows in itself, to excite interest, to place a final result in a good light, and then to lead over to what may follow in the next scene,—minutely examined, it will be found to contain five parts, which correspond to the five divisions of the drama. In well wrought scenes, these parts are collectively effective. For it is impracticable to conduct the action in a straight line to the final result. A. feels, wills, demands something. B. meets him, thinking with him, disagreeing with him, opposing him. In every case, the projects of the one are checked by the other, and for a time at least, turned aside. In such scenes, whether they present a deed, a battle of words, an exhibition of feeling, it is desirable that the climax should not lie in a direct line which leads from the supposed conditions previous to the action, to the final results; but that it indicate the last point in a deviating direction, from which point the return action falls to the direct line again. Let it be the business of a scene to render B. harmless through A.; its proposed result, B's promise to be harmless. Beginning of the scene: A. entreats B. to be no longer a disturber of the peace; if B. is already willing to yield to this wish, a longer scene is not needed. If he accepts passively A's reasons, the scene moves forward in a direct line; but it is in great danger of becoming wearisome. But if B. puts himself on his defensive, and persists in continuing the disturbance or denies it, then the dialogue runs to a point where B. is as far as possible from the wish of A. From here, an approach of points of view begins, the reasons put forth by A. show themselves strongest, till B. yields.

But since every scene points to what follows, this pyramidal structure is frequently changed into the profile of a shore-beating wave, with long ascending line, and short falling side,—beginning, ascent, final result.

According to the number of persons they contain, scenes are determined differently, and are subject to varied arrangement. The monologue gives the hero of the modern stage opportunity, in perfect independence of an observing chorus, to reveal to the audience his most secret feeling and volition. It might be supposed that such confiding to the hearer would be very acceptable; but it is often not the case. So great is the influence of the struggle of each man, on every purpose of the drama, that every isolation of an individual must have a special justification. Only where a rich inner life has been concealed for a long time in the general play, does the auditor tolerate its private revelation. But in cases where artistic intrigue playing will make the audience a confidant, the spectator cares little for the quiet expression of an individual; he prefers to gather for himself the connection and the contrasts of characters, from a dialogue. Monologues have a likeness to the ancient pathos-scene; but with the numerous opportunities which our stage offers for characters to expose their inner lives, and with the changed purpose of dramatic effects through the actor's art, they are no necessary additions to the modern drama.

Since monologues represent a pause for rest in the course of the action, and place the speaker in a significant manner before the hearer, they need in advance of themselves an excited tension of feeling in the audience, and then a line of division either before or after them. But whether they open an act or close it, or are placed between two scenes of commotion, they must always be constructed dramatically. Something presented on one side, something on the other side; final result, and indeed, final result that wins something significant for the action itself. Let the two monologues of Hamlet in the rising action be compared. The second celebrated soliloquy "To be or not to be," is a profound revelation of Hamlet's soul, but no advance at all for the action, as it introduces no new volition of the hero; through the exposition of the inner struggle, it only explains his dilatoriness. The previous monologue, on the contrary, a masterpiece of dramatic emotion,—even this, the outburst resulting from the previous scene, has as its foundation a simple resolution; Hamlet says: (1) "The actor exhibits so great earnestness in mere play; (2) I sneak along inactive, in the midst of the greatest earnestness; (3) to the work! I will institute a play, in order to win resolution for an earnest deed." In this last sentence, the result of the entire preceding scene is at once concentrated, the effect which the interview with the players produces on the character of the hero, and on the course of the action.

Effective soliloquies have naturally become favorite passages with the public. In Schiller's and in Goethe's plays, they are presented with great fondness by the rising generation. Lessing would hardly have sought this kind of dramatic effects, even if he had written more than *Nathan The Wise* in our iambics.

Next to the monologues, stand the announcements by messenger in our drama. As the former represent the lyric element, the latter stand for the epic. They have been already discussed. Since it is their task to relieve the tension already produced that they may be well received, the effect which they produce on the counter-players of the messenger, or perhaps on himself, must be very apparent. An intense counter-play must accompany and interrupt a longer communication, without, of course, outdoing it. Schiller, who is very fond of these messenger speeches, gives copious examples which serve not only for imitation but for warning. *Wallenstein* alone contains a whole assortment of them. In the beautiful model speeches, "There is in human life," and "We stand not idly waiting for invasion," the poet has connected the highest dramatic suspense with the epic situations. Wallenstein's inspiration and prophetic power appear nowhere so powerful as in his narratives. In the announcement of the Swede, however, the dumb play of the mortally wounded Thekla is in the strongest contrast with the behavior and the message of the active stranger. Moreover, this drama has other descriptions,—for example, the Bohemian cup and the room of the astrologer,—the curtailing or removal of which would be an advantage on the stage.

The most important part of an action has its place in the dialogue scenes, specially scenes between two persons. The contents of these scenes,—something set forth, something set forth against it, perception against perception, emotion against emotion, volition against volition,—have with us, deviating from the uniform method of the ancients, found the most manifold elaboration. The purpose of every colloquy scene is to bring into prominence from the assertions and counter-assertions, a result which impels the action further. While the ancient dialogue was a strife, which usually exercised no immediate influence on the soul of the participants, the modern dialogue understands how to persuade, demonstrate, bring over to the speaker's point of view. The arguments of the hero and his adversary are not, as in the Greek tragedy, rhetorical word-contests; but they grow out of the character and spirit of the persons contending; and the hearer is carefully instructed how far they are to express real feeling and conviction, and how far they shall mislead.

The aggressor must arrange the grounds of his attack exactly according to the personal character of his antagonist, or he must draw his motives truly from the depths of his own being. But in order that what has a purpose, or what is true, may be fully conceived by the hearer, there is needed a certain trend of speech and reply on the stage, not in the regular course, conformable to custom, as among the Greeks or old Spanish, but essentially different from the way in which we undertake to convince any one in real life. To the character on the stage, time is limited; he has no arguments to bring forward in a continuously progressive order of effects; he has to explain impressively for his hearer, what is most effective for the time and situation. In reality, such a conflict of opinions may be in many parts, and may rest upon numerous grounds and opposing grounds; the victory may long hang doubtful; possibly an insignificant, subordinate reason may finally determine the outcome; but this is not, as a rule, possible on the stage, as it is not effective.

Therefore, it is the duty of the poet to gather up these contrasts in a few utterances, and to express their inner significance with continuous, progressive force. In our plays, the reasonings of one strike like waves against the soul of the other, broken at first by resistance, then rising higher, till, perhaps, at last they rise above the resistance itself. It happens according to an old law of composition, that frequently the third such wave-beat gives the decision; for if the proposition and counter-proposition have each made two excursions, by these two stages the hearer is sufficiently prepared for the decision; he has received a strong impulse, and has been rendered capable of conveniently comparing the weight of the reasons with the strength of the character on which they are to work. Such dialogue scenes have been finely elaborated with great attractiveness on our stage, since Lessing's time. They correspond much to the joy of the Germans in a rational discussion of a matter of business. Celebrated rôles of our stage are indebted for their success to them alone,—Marinelli, Carlos in *Clavigo*, Wrangel in *Wallenstein*.

Since the poet must so fashion the dialogue scene that the progress which it makes for the action becomes impressed upon the hearer, the technique of these scenes will be different according to the position in which they find the participants, and in which they leave them. The matter will be simplest when the intruder overcomes the one whom he attacks; then two or three approaches and separations occur, till the victory of one, or if the attacked person is more tractable, there is a gradual coming over. A scene of such persuasion, of simple structure, is the dialogue in the beginning of Brutus and Cassius' relations; Cassius presses, Brutus yields to his demands. The dialogue has a short introduction, three parts, and a conclusion. The middle part is of special beauty and great finish. Introduction, Cassius says, in effect, "You seem unfriendly toward me, Brutus." Brutus, "Not from coldness." The parts: 1. Cassius, "Much is hoped from you" (frequently interrupted with assurances that Brutus can trust him, and from cries without, calling attention to Cæsar). 2. "What is Cæsar more than we?" 3. "Our wills shall make us free." Conclusion, Brutus, "I will consider it."

But if the speakers separate without coming to terms, their position with reference to each other must not remain unchanged during the scene. It is intolerable to the audience to perceive such lack of progress in the action. In such a case, the trend of one or both must be broken, enough so, that in another place in the action they apparently agree, and after this point of apparent agreement again turn away from each other with energy. The inner emotions through which these changes of relation are affected, must be not only genuine but adapted to produce what follows, not mere conflicting whims arranged for the sake of a scenic effect but of no service to the action or the characters.

By unconnected talk, it is possible to bring into the field numerous reasons and counter-reasons, and to give the lines a sharper turn; but on the whole, the structure remains in form, as was indicated in the comparison with a roaring wave; a gradual movement upward to the climax, result, a short close. This is illustrated in the great quarrel scene between Egmont and Orange, indeed the best wrought part of the drama. It is composed of four parts, before which there is an introduction, and after which there is a conclusion. Introduction, Orange: "The queen regent will depart." Egmont: "She will not." First part, Orange: "And if another comes?" Egmont: "He will do as his predecessor did." Second part, Orange: "This time, he will seize our heads." Egmont: "That is impossible." Third part, Orange: "Alba is under way; let us go into our province." Egmont: "Then we are rebels." Here there is a turn; from this point, Egmont is the aggressor. Fourth part, Egmont: "You are acting irresponsibly." Orange: "Only with foresight." Orange: "I will go and deplore you as lost." The last uniting of these disputants into a harmonious spirit forms a fine contrast to Egmont's previous violence.

The scenes between two persons have received special significance in the new drama, scenes in which two persons seem decidedly to cherish one opinion, love scenes. They have not originated in the ephemeral taste, or passing tenderness of poets and spectators, but through an original mental characteristic of the Germans. Ever since the earliest times, love-making, the approach of the young hero to a young maiden, has been specially charming to German poetry. It has been the ruling poetic inclination of the people to surround the relations of lovers before marriage, with a dignity and a nobility of which the ancient world knew nothing. In no direction has the contrast of the Germans with ancient peoples shown itself more markedly; through all the art of the middle ages, even to the present, this significant feature is noticeable. Even in the serious drama, it prevails with a higher justification. This most attractive and lovely relation of all the earth, is brought into connection with the dark and awful, as complementary contrast, for the highest degree of tragic effect.

During the poet's work, indeed, these scenes are not the most convenient part of his creation; and everyone will not succeed in them. It is not a useless work to compare with each other the greatest love scenes in our possession, the three scenes with Romeo at the masked ball, the balcony scene, before and after the marriage night, and Gretchen in the garden. In the first Romeo scene, the poet has set the most difficult task for the actor's art; in it, the speech of the beginning passion is wonderfully abrupt and brief; from behind the polite play of words, which was current in

Shakespeare's time, the growing feeling appears only in lightning flashes. Indeed, the poet perceived into what difficulties a fuller speech would plunge him. The first balcony scene has always been considered a masterpiece of the poetic art; but when one analyzes the exalted beauty of its verses, one is astonished to find how eloquently, and with what unrestrained enjoyment, the spirits of the lovers are able to sport with their passionate feeling. Beautiful words, delicate comparisons, are so massed that we sometimes almost feel the art to be artful. For the third, the morning scene, the idea of the old *minnesongs*, and popular songs,—the song of the watchmen,—are made use of in a most charming manner.

Goethe, also, in his most beautiful love scene has made poetic use of popular reminiscences; he has composed the declaration of love, in his own manner, out of little lyric and epic moments, which —though not entirely favorable for a great effect, —he interrupts through the incisive contrast, Martha and Mephistopheles. This circumstance, also, reminds us that the dramatist was a great lyric poet, in that Faust retires for the most part, and the scenes are not much other than soliloquies of Gretchen. But each of the three little parts of which the picture is composed is of wonderful beauty.

To the enthusiastic Schiller, on the other hand, while he was writing iambics, success in this kind of scenes was not accorded. He succeeded best in

The Bride of Messina. But in *William Tell*, the scene between Rudenz and Bertha is without life; and even in *Wallenstein*, when such a scene was quite necessary, he has through the absence of Countess Terzky put a damper on it; Thekla must keep the loved one from the camp and from the astrologer's room, till finally by herself for a brief time, she can utter the significant warning.

The brilliant examples of Shakespeare and Goethe show, also, the danger of these scenes. This, too, must be discussed. The utterance of lyric emotions on the stage, if it is at all continued, will, in spite of all poetic art, certainly weary the hearer; it becomes the dramatic poet's profitable task then, to invent a little occurrence in which the ardent feeling of the loving pair can express itself by mutual participation in a moment of the action; in this way he possesses the dramatic thread on which to string his pearls. The sweet love chatter which has no purpose beyond itself, he will rightly avoid; and where it is inevitable, he will replace with the beauty of poetry what he, as a conscientious man, must take from the length of such scenes.

The entrance of a third person into the dialogue gives it a different character. As through the third man the stage picture receives a middle point, and the setting up of a group, so the third man often becomes, in import, an arbitrator or judge before whom the two parties lay the reasons they have at heart. These reasons of the two parties are, in such a case, arranged directly for him, according to his disposition, and thereby take on the nature of something that is known. The course of the scene becomes slower; between speech and response, a judgment enters which must, also, present itself to the hearer with some significance. Or the third player is himself a party and associate of one side. In this case, the utterances of one party will become more rapid, must break out with more feeling, because from the interested hearer, greater intensity of attention is exacted, while he must put the character and import of two persons in one scale.

Finally, the third and most infrequent case is that each of the three sets up his will against the other two. Such scenes are sometimes serviceable as the last notes of a relieved suspense. They have but a brief service to render; for the three speakers utter themselves really in monologues: thus the scene with Margaret in *Richard III.*, where one character gives the melody, both the other characters in contrasts give the accompaniment. But such scenes with three players rarely gain significance in greater elaboration, except when at least one of the players goes over to the point of view of another in simulated play.

Scenes which collect more than three persons for active participation in the action, the so-called *ensemble* scenes, have become an indispensable element in our drama. They were unknown to the old tragedy; a part of their service was replaced by a union of a solo actor and the chorus. They do not comprise, in the newer drama, specially, the highest tragic effects, although a greater part of the most animated action is executed in them. For it is a truth not sufficiently regarded, that what originates from many, or consists of many things, excites and holds attention less than what receives its vividness or comes alive from the soul of the chief figures. The interest in the dramatic life of the subordinate characters is less, and the remaining of many participants on the stage may easily distract the eye or the curiosity, rather than attract and arouse. On the whole, the nature of these scenes is that by good management on the part of the poet, they keep the audience busily occupied and relieve the suspense created by the chief heroes ; or they help to call forth such a suspense in the souls of the chief figures. They have, therefore, the character of preparatory, or of closing scenes.

It hardly need be mentioned that their peculiarities do not always become apparent when more than three persons are on the stage. For when a few chief rôles alone, or almost exclusively, present the action, accessory figures may be desirable in considerable number. A council scene or parade scene may easily collect a multitude of actors on the stage, without their coming forward actively in the action.

The first direction for the construction of the *ensemble* scene is, the whole company must be occupied in a manner characteristic of the persons and as the action demands. They are like invited guests, for whose mental activity the poet must, as invisible host, have incessant care. During the progress of the action, he must perceive clearly the effects which the individual processes, speech, response, produce on each of the participants in the play.

It is evident that one person must not express in the presence of another person on the stage, what this one is not to hear; the usual device of an *aside* must be used only in extreme cases, and for a few words. But there is a greater difficulty. A rôle must also not express anything to which another person present is to give an answer which, according to his character, is necessary, but which would be useless and clogging to the action. In order to be just to all characters in a scene full of persons, the poet must have unrestricted mastery of his heroes, and a clear vision for stage pictures. For every individual rôle influences the mood and bearing of every other, and has a tendency, besides, to limit the freedom of expression of the others. In such scenes, therefore, the art of the poet will specially show itself by setting the characters in contrast, through sharp little strokes. And it is well to observe that suitably to occupy all of the collected persons is rendered difficult by the nature of our stage, which incloses the actors by its curtains as in a hall; and if the poet does not take definite precautions, as it is often impossible to do, this makes the separation of individuals difficult.

But further, the more numerous the actors invited into a scene, the less space individuals have to express themselves in their own way. The poet must also see to it that the respective parts of the action are not broken up into fragments by the greater number of participants and made to move forward monotonously in little waves; and as he arranges the persons in groups, he must likewise arrange the action of the scene so that the movement of subordinate rôles does not excessively limit the movement of the leading characters. Hence the value of the principle: the greater the number of persons in a scene, the stronger must be the organization of the structure. The chief parts must then be so much the more prominent, now the individual leading moods in contrast with the majority, now the coöperation of the whole stand in the foreground.

Since with a greater number of players, the individual is easily concealed, those places in the *ensemble* scene are specially difficult in which the effect of any thing done is made to appear upon individual participants. When in such a case, a single brief word thrown in does not suffice to inform the spectator, some contrivance is needed which, without appearing to do so, separates the individual from the group and brings him to the front. It is entirely impracticable in such a case suddenly to interrupt the dramatic movement of the majority, and convert all the others into silent and inactive spectators of the private revelations of an individual.

The more rapidly the action moves forward in ...erted play, the more difficult the isolation of the individual becomes. When the action has attained a certain height and momentum, it is not always possible even with the greatest art, to afford the chief actor room for a desirable exhibition of his inmost mood. Hence for such scenes, the value of the third law: the poet will not have his persons say all that is characteristic of them, and that would be necessary in itself for their rôles. For here arises an inner opposition between the requisites of single rôles and the advantage of the whole. Every person on the stage demands a share for himself in the progress of the action, so far as his associated relation with the other characters of the scene allows it. The poet is under the necessity, however, of limiting this share. Even chief characters must sometimes accompany with dumb play, when in real life opportunity would be given to engage in the conversation. On the other hand, a long silence is embarrassing to a player, the subordinate character becomes wearied and sinks into a stage walker, the chief character feels keenly the wrong which is done to his part; far less, he feels its higher necessity. It does not always suffice for the right aggregate effect, that the poet have regard to the activity of the rôles not standing entirely in the foreground, and by means of a few words, or by means of a not unknown employment, afford to the actor a certain direction for his dumb play, and at the same time a transition to the place where he shall again participate in the action. There are extreme cases where the same thing is valuable in a scene, that is allowed in a great painting showing numerous figures in vigorous action and complication. Just as in the picture, the swing of the chief lines is so important that the right foreshortening of an arm or a foot must be sacrificed to it, so in the strong current of a scene rich in figures, the representation necessary for individual characters must be given up for the sake of the course, and the aggregate effect of the scene. In order that the poet may be able to practice attractively such offered deceptions, his understanding must be clear that in themselves they are blemishes.

It is really to the advantage of a piece, to limit the number of players as much as possible. Every additional rôle makes the setting more difficult, and renders the repetition of the piece inconvenient, in case of the illness or withdrawal of an actor. These external considerations alone will determine the poet to weigh well, in composing his *ensemble* scenes, what figures are absolutely indispensable. Here comes an internal consideration: the greater the number of accessory persons in a scene, so much the more time it claims.

The *ensemble* scenes are, of course, an essential help to give to the piece color and brilliancy. They can hardly be spared in using historical subjects. But they must be used in such pieces with moderation, because more than the others they make success depend on the skill of the manager, and because in them, the elaborate representation of the inner life of the chief figures, a minute portrayal of the mental processes, which claim the highest dramatic interest, is much more difficult. The second half of the piece will demand them most urgently, because here the activity of the counter-players comes forward more powerfully, tolerated, however, without injury, only when in this division of the action, the ardent sympathy of the spectators has already been immovably fixed with the chief characters. Here, too, the poet must take care not to keep the inner life of the hero too long concealed.

One of the most beautiful *ensemble* scenes of Shakespeare is the banquet scene in Pompey's galley, in *Antony and Cleopatra*. It contains no chief part of the action, and is essentially a situation scene, a thing not occurring frequently in the tragic part of the action in Shakespeare. But it receives a certain significance, because it is at the close of the second act, and also stands in a place demanding eminence, especially in this piece, in which the preceding political explanations make a variegated and animated picture very desirable. The abundance of little characterizing traits which are united in this scene, their close condensation, above all, the technical arrangement, are admirable. The scene is introduced by a short conversation among servants, as is frequently the case in Shakespeare, in order to provide for the setting of the tables and the arrangement of the furniture on the stage. The scene itself is in three parts. The first part presents the haughty utterances of the reconciled triumvirs, and the pedantry of the drunken simpleton, Lepidus, to whom the servants have already referred; the second, in terrible contrast, is the secret interview of Pompey and Menas; the third, introduced by the bearing out of the drunken Lepidus, is the climax of the wild Bacchanalia and rampant drunkenness. The connecting of the three parts, as Menas draws Pompey aside, as Pompey again in the company of Lepidus, resuming, continues the carouse, is quite worthy of notice. Not a word in the whole scene is without its use and significance; the poet perceives every moment the condition of the individual figures, and of the accessory persons; each takes hold of the action effectively; for the manager, as well as for the rôles, the whole is adapted in a masterly way. From the first news of Antony across the Nile,— through which the image of Cleopatra is introduced even into this scene,—and the simple remark of Lepidus, "You have strange serpents there," through which an impression is made on the mind of the hearer, that prepares for Cleopatra's death by a serpent's sting, to the last words of Antony, "Good; give me your hand, sir," in which the intoxicated man involuntarily recognizes the superiority of Augustus Cæsar, and even to the following drunken speeches of Pompey and Enobarbus, everything is like fine chiseled work on a firmly articulated metal frame.

A comparison of this scene with the close of the banquet act in *The Piccolomini*, is instructive. The internal similarity is so great that one is obliged to think Schiller had the Shakespearean performance before his eyes. Here also, a poetic power is to be admired, which can conduct a great number of figures with absolute certainty; and here is a great wealth of significant forces, and a powerful climax in the structure. But what is characteristic of Schiller, these forces are partly of an episodical nature; the whole is planned more broadly and extensively. This last has its justification. For the scene stands at the end, not of the second, but of the fourth act, and it contains an essential part of the action, the acquisition of the portentous signature; it would have had a still greater place if the banquet did not fill the entire act. The connection of parts is exactly as in Shakespeare.[21] First comes an introductory conversation between servants, which is spun out in disproportionate dimensions; the description of the drinking cup has no right to take our attention, because the cup itself has nothing further to do with the action, and the numerous side lights which fall from this description upon the general situation are no longer strong enough. Then comes an action, also in three parts: first, Terzky's endeavor to get the signature from accessory persons; second, in sharp contrast with the first, the brief conversation of the Piccolomini; third, the decision, as a strife of the drunken Illo with Max. Here the union of the individual parts of the scene is very careful. Octavio, through Buttler's cautious investigation, quietly calls attention away from the excited group of generals toward his son; through the search for the wanting name, attention is completely turned to Max. Hereupon the intoxicated Illo turns first with great significance to Octavio before his collision with Max. The uniting and separating of the different groups, the bringing into prominence the Piccolomini, the excited side-play of the accessory characters, even to the powerful close, are very beautiful.

Besides, we possess two powerful mass scenes of Schiller, the greatest out of the greatest time of our poetic art; the Rütli scene, and the first act of *Demetrius*. Both are models which the beginner in dramatic work may not imitate, but may study carefully, in their sublime beauty. Whatever must be said against the dramatic construction of *William Tell*, upon single scenes there rests a charm, which continually carries one away with new admiration. In the Rütli scene, the dramatic movement is a moderately restrained one, the execution broad, splendid, full of beautiful local color. First, there is an introduction, the mood. It consists of three parts: arrival of the under forester, interview of Melchthal and Stauffacher, greeting of the cantons. Let it be noted that the poet has avoided wearying by a triple emphasizing of the entrance of the three cantons. Two chief figures here bring themselves into powerful contrast with the subordinate figures, and form a little climax for the introduction; and distraction through several forces of equal impulse, is avoided. With the entrance of the Urians, through whose horn the descent from the mountain, and the discourse of those present is sufficiently emphasized, the action begins. This action runs along in five parts. First, appointment for public meeting, with short speeches and hearty participation of the subordinate persons; second, after this, Stauffacher's magnificent representation of the nature and aim of the confederation; third, after this powerful address of the individual, excited conflict of opinions and parties concerning the position of the confederation with reference to the emperor; fourth, high degree of opposition, even to an outbreaking strife over the means of release from the despotism of the governors, and disagreement over the conclusions. Finally, fifth, the solemn oath. After such a conclusion of the action, there is the dying away of the mood which takes its tone from the surrounding nature, and the rising sun. With this rich organization, the beauty in the relations of the single parts is especially attractive. The middle point of this whole group of dramatic incidents or forces, Stauffacher's address, comes out as climax; after this as contrast, the restless commotion in the masses, the dawning satisfaction, and the lofty exaltation. Not less beautiful is the treatment of the numerous accessory figures, the independent seizing upon the action by single little rôles, which in their significance for the scene stand near each other with a certain republican equality of justification.

The greatest model for political action is the opening scene in *Demetrius*, the Polish parliament.

The subject of this drama makes the communication of many presupposed conditions necessary; the peculiar adventures of the boy, Demetrius, demanded a vigorous use of peculiar colors, in order to bring that strange world poetically near. Schiller, with the bold majesty peculiar to himself, made the epic narrative the center of a richly adorned spectacular scene, and surrounded the long recital of the individual, with the impassioned movements of the masses. After a short introduction follows, with the entrance of Demetrius, a scene in four parts, (1) the narrative of Demetrius, (2) the short, condensed repetition of the same by the archbishop, and the first waves which are thereby excited in the gathering, (3) the entreaty of Demetrius for support, and the increase of the agitation, (4) counter argument and protest of Sapieha. The scene ends with tumult and a sudden breaking off. By means of a slight dramatic force, it is connected with the following dialogue between Demetrius and the king. The excitement of the subordinate characters is brief but violent, the leaders of opinion few; except Demetrius, there is only one raising strong opposition, from all the mass. It is perceived and felt that the masses have been given their mood in advance; the narrative of Demetrius, in its elegant elaboration forms the chief part of the scene, as was befitting for the first act.

Goethe has left us no mass scene of great dramatic effect unless we are to consider some short scenes in *Götz* as such. The populace scenes in

Egmont lack in powerful commotion; the beautiful promenade in *Faust* is composed of little dramatic pictures; the student scene in Auerbach's cellar proposes no tragic effect, and presents to the actor of Faust, the disadvantage that it leaves him idle, unoccupied on the stage.

The action scenes in which great masses work, demand the special support of the manager. If our stages have already, in the chorus personnel of the opera, a tolerable number of players, and these are accustomed to render service as stage-walkers, yet the number of persons who can be collected on the stage is often so small as to be lost sight of, when compared with the multitude which in real life participate in a populace scene, in a fight, in a great uproar.

The auditor, therefore, easily feels the emptiness and scantiness as he sits before the little crowd that is led in. It is also a disadvantage that the modern stage is little adapted to the disposition of great masses. Now, of course, the external arrangement of such scenes is for the most part in the hands of the manager; but it is the poet's task through his art, to make it easy for the manager to produce the appearance of a lively multitude on the stage.

Since the entrance and exit of a great number of persons requires considerable time and distracts attention, this must be attracted and retained by suggestive little contrivances, and through the distribution of the masses in groups.

The space of the stage must be so arranged, that the comparatively small number of really available players can not be overlooked,—by shifting side-scenes, good perspective, an arrangement along the sides that shall suggest to the fancy greater invisible multitudes which make themselves noticeable by signs and calls to each other behind the scenes.

Brilliant spectacular pageants, such as Iffland arranged for *The Maid of Orleans*, the composer of a tragedy will deny himself with right; he will avoid as much as possible, the opportunity for this.

On the other hand, mass effects in which the multitude surges in violent commotion, populace-scenes, great council assemblies, camps, battles, are sometimes desirable.

For populace scenes, the beautiful treatment of Shakespeare has become a model often patterned after,—short, forcible speeches of individual figures, almost always in prose, interrupting and enlivening cries of the crowd, which receives its incitement from individual leaders. By means of a populace scene on the stage, other effects may be produced, not the highest dramatic effects, but yet significant, which till the present time have been little esteemed by our poets. Since we should not give up verse in populace scenes, another treatment of the crowd is offered than that which Shakespeare loved. Now the introduction of the old chorus is impossible. The new animation which Schiller attempted, dare not find imitation, in spite of the fulness of poetic beauty which is so enchanting in the choruses of the *Bride of Messina.* But between the chief actors and a great number of subordinate actors, there is still another, dramatic, animated, concerted play conceivable, which connects the leader with the multitude as well as places him over against it. Not only short cries, but also speeches which require several verses, receive an increased power through the concert recitation of several with well practiced inflection and in measured time. With the multitude introduced in this way, the poet will be put in a position to give it a more worthy share in the action; in the change from single voices to three, or four, and to the whole together, between the clear tenor and powerful bass, he will be able to produce numerous shades, modulations, and colors. With this concert speech of great masses, he must take care that the meaning of the sentence, and the weight and energy of the expression correspond; that the words are easily understood and without discord; that the individual parts of the sentence form a pleasing contrast.

It is not true that this treatment puts on the stage an artificial instead of a varied and natural movement; for the usual manner of arranging populace scenes is an accepted artistic one, which transforms the course of the action according to a scheme. The way proposed here is only more effective. In making use of it, the poet may conceal his art, and by alternating in the use of the concert speech and counter-speech, produce variety. The sonorous speech in many voices is adapted not only to animated quarrels and discussions, it is available for every mood which effervesces in a popular tumult. On our stage up to the present time, the practice of concert speech has been unaccountably neglected; it is often only an unintelligible scream. The poet will do well, therefore, to indicate specifically in the stage copies of his plays, how the voice groups are to be divided. In order to indicate this properly, he must have first felt the effects distinctly in advance.

Battle scenes are in bad repute on the German stage, and are avoided by the poet with foresight. The reason is, again, that our theaters do such things badly. Shakespeare has an undeniable fondness for martial movements of masses. He has not at all lessened them in his later pieces; and since he occasionally speaks with little respect of the means by which fights are represented in his theater, one is justified in believing that he would willingly have kept away from them if his audiences had not liked them so well. But upon such a martial-spirited people, who passionately cultivated all manner of physical exercise, such an impression was possible only when in these scenes a certain art and technique were evident, and when the conventionalities of the stage did not make them deplorable. Scenes like the fight of Coriolanus and Aufidius, Macbeth and Macduff, the camp scenes in *Richard III.* and *Julius Cæsar*, have such weight and significance that it is evident with what confidence Shakespeare trusted in their effects. In more recent times, on the English stage, these martial scenes have been embellished with a profusion of accessories, and their effects wonderfully enhanced; the audience has been only too much occupied with them. If in Germany there is too little of this occurring, this negligence can afford the poet no grounds to keep himself anxiously free from battle scenes. There are accessory effects which can render him acceptable service. He must take a little pains, himself, to find out how they may be best arranged, and see to it that the stage does its duty.

CHAPTER IV.

THE CHARACTERS.

I.

THE PEOPLE AND POETS.

The fashioning of the dramatic characters, among the Germanic peoples, shows more distinctly than the construction of the dramatic action the progress which the human race has made since the appearance of dramatic art among the Greeks. Not only the natural disposition of our people, but its altitude above the historic periods of a world spread out to full view, and the consequent development of an historic sense, declare and explain this difference. Since it has been the task of the new drama, by means of the poetic and histrionic arts to represent upon the stage the appearance of an individual life, even to illusion, the delineation of character has won a significance for the art, which was unknown to the ancient world.

The poetic power of the dramatic poet displays itself most immediately in the invention of dramatic characters. In the construction of the action, in the adaptation to the stage, other characteristics help him : a true culture, manly traits of character, good training, experience ; but when the capability for a sharp defining of characters is small, a work, perhaps correct from the point of view of the stage, may be created, but never one of real significance. If, on the other hand, peculiar power of invention makes the individual rôles attractive, a good hope may be cherished, even if the coöperation of the figures for a collective picture is quite lacking. Right here, then, in this part of artistic creation, less help is gained from instruction than in any other part. The poetics of the Greek thinkers, as we have received it, contains only a few lines on the characters. In our time, too, the technique is able to set up nothing but a few bare directions, which do not essentially advance the creating poet. What the rules for work can give, the poet carries, on the whole, securely in his own breast; and what he does not possess, they are not able to give.

The poet's characterization rests on the old peculiarity of man, to perceive in every living being a complete personality, in which a soul like that of the observer's is supposed as animating principle; and beyond this, what is peculiar to this being, what is characteristic of it, is received as affording enjoyment. With this tendency, long before his power of poetic creation becomes an art, man transforms all that surrounds him into personalities, to which, with busied imagination, he attributes much of the character peculiar to human beings. In thunder and lightning, he perceives the form of a god, traversing the concave heaven in a war chariot, and scattering fiery darts; the clouds are changed into celestial cows and sheep, from which a divine figure pours the milk upon the earth. Also the creatures which inhabit the earth with man, he perceives as possessed with a personality similar to that of man himself — thus bears, foxes, wolves. Every one of us imputes to the dog and to the cat ideas and emotions which are familiar to us; and only because such a conception is everywhere a necessity and a pleasure, are animals so domesticated. This tendency to personify expresses itself incessantly: in intercourse with our fellow men, daily; at our first meeting with a stranger; from the few vital expressions which come to us from him; from single words, from the tone of his voice, from the expression of his countenance, we form the picture of his complete personality; we do this especially by completing with lightning rapidity the imperfect impressions, from the stock of our phantasy, according to their similarity with previous impressions, or what has been previously observed. Later observation of the same person may modify the image which has fallen upon the soul, may give it a richer and deeper development; but already, at the first impression, however small the number of characteristic traits may be, we perceive these as a logical, strictly computed whole, in which we recognize what is peculiar to this man, upon the background of what is common to all men. This creating of a form is common to all men, to all times; it works in every one of us with the necessity and the rapidity of an original power; it is to each one a stronger or a weaker capability; it is to each a rapturous necessity.

Upon this fact rests the efficacy of dramatic characterization. The inventive power of the poet produces the artistic appearance of a rich individual life, because he has so put together a few vital expressions of a person — comparatively few — that the person, understood and felt by him as a unity, is intelligible to the actor and to the spectator as a characteristic being. Even in the case of the chief heroes of a drama, the number of vital expressions which the poet, limited in time and space, is able to give, the aggregate number of characterizing traits, is much too small; while in the case of accessory figures, perhaps two or three indications, a few words, must produce the appearance of an independent, highly characteristic life. How is this possible? For this reason: the poet understands the secret of suggesting; of inciting the hearer, through his work, to follow the poet's processes and create after him. For the power to understand and enjoy a character is attained only by the self-activity of the receptive spectator, meeting the creating artist helpfully and vigorously. What the poet and the actor actually give is, in itself, only single strokes; but out of these grows an apparently richly gotten-up picture, in which we divine and suppose a fulness of characteristic life, because the poet and the actor compel the excited imagination of the hearer to coöperate with them, creating for itself.

The method of fashioning characters, by different poets, is of the greatest variety. It varies with different times and different peoples. The method of the Latin races is very different from that of the Germanic races. With the early Germans, the enjoyment has always, from the first, been greater in the invention of characterizing details; with the Latins, the joy has been greater in compactly uniting, for a special purpose, the men represented, in an artistically interwoven action. The modern German reaches more deeply into his artistic product; he seeks to put upon exhibition a richer inner life; what is peculiar, indeed what is specially rare, has the greatest charm for him. But the Latin perceives what is restricted to the individual, specially from the point of view of convenience and adaptability to purpose; he makes society the center, not the inner life of the hero, as the German does; he is glad to set over against each other, persons fully developed, often with only hasty outlines of character. It is their diverse tendencies that make them interesting to each other in the counterplay. Where the special task is the accurate representation of a character, as in Molière, and where characteristic details elicit special admiration, these characters, the miser and the hypocrite, are inwardly most nearly complete; they are exhibited with a monotony at last wearisome, in different social relations; in spite of the excellence in delineation on our stage, they become more and more foreign to us, because the highest dramatic life is lacking to them — the processes of coming into being, the growth of character. We prefer to recognize on the stage how one *becomes* a miser, rather than see how he *is* one.

What fills the soul of a German, then, and makes a subject of value, what stimulates to creative activity, is especially the peculiar transformations of character in the chief persons; the characters blossom first in his creating mind; for these he invents the action; from them beams the color, the warmth, the light, upon the accessory figures: the Latin has been more strongly attracted by the combinations of the action, the subordination of individual elements to the dominion of the whole, suspense, intrigue. This contrast is old, but it comes down to the present time. It is more difficult for the German to construct an action for his clearly conceived characters; for the Latin, the threads interlace easily and spiritedly into an artistic web. This peculiarity occasions a difference in the productiveness and the value of the dramas. The literature of the Latins has little that can be compared with the highest products of the German mind; but frequently, in the condition of our people, no piece available for the stage comes from their weaker talents. Single scenes, single characters, command attention and admiration; but they lack, as a whole, in neat elaboration and power to excite feeling. Mediocrity succeeds better outside of Germany; and where neither the poetic idea nor the characters lay claim to poetic value, the shrewd invention of intrigue, the artistic combination of persons for animated life, is found entertaining. While with the Germans, that which is most highly dramatic,— the working out of the perceptions and feelings in the soul, into a deed,— comes to light more seldom, yet once in a while, in irresistible power and beauty in art, with the Latins is found more frequently and more productive the second characteristic of dramatic creation,— the invention of the counter-play, the effective representation of the conflict which the environment of the hero wages against his weaknesses.

But further, in the work of every individual poet, the method of characterization is diverse; very different is the wealth of figures, and the pains and distinctness with which their essential nature is presented to the hearer. Here Shakespeare is the deepest and richest of creative geniuses, not without a peculiarity, however, which often challenges our admiration. We are inclined to accept it, and we learn it from many sources, that his audience did not consist entirely of the most intelligent and cultured people of old England; we are also justified in supposing that he would give to his characters a simple texture, and accurately expose their relation to the idea of the drama, from all sides. This does not always occur. The spectator, in the case of Shakespeare's heroes, does not remain in uncertainty as to the chief motive of their actions; indeed the full power of his poetic greatness is evident just in this, that he understands, as no other poet does, how to express the mental processes of the chief characters, from the first rising perception to the climax of passion, with extremely affecting power and truth. The propelling counter-players in his dramas, Iago and Shylock, for instance, do not fail to make the spectator a confidant in what they wish. And it may be well said that the characters of Shakespeare, whose passion beats in the highest waves, allow the spectator to look into the depths of their hearts, more than the characters of any other poet. But this depth is sometimes unfathomable to the eyes of the histrionic artist, as well as to the sight of the audience; and his characters are by no means always so transparent and simple as they appear at a casual glance. Indeed, many of them have something about them peculiarly enigmatical, and difficult to understand, which perpetually allures toward an interpretation, but is never entirely comprehended.

Not only such persons as Hamlet, Richard III., Iago, in whom peculiar thoughtfulness, or an essential characteristic not easily understood, and single real or apparent contradictions are striking, come into this list, but such as, with superficial observation, stride away down the straight street, stage fashion.

Let the judgments be tested which for a hundred years have been pronounced in Germany on the characters in *Julius Cæsar*, and the glad approval with which our contemporaries accept the noble effects of this piece. To the warm-hearted youth,

Brutus is the noble, patriotic hero. An honest commentator sees in Cæsar, the great, the immovable character, superior to all; a politician by profession rejoices in the ironical, inconsiderate severity with which, from the introduction forward, the poet has treated Brutus and Cassius as impractical fools, and their conspiracy as a silly venture of incapable aristocrats. The actor of judgment, at length, finds in the same Cæsar whom his commentator has held up to him as a pattern of the possessor of power, a hero inwardly wounded to death, a soul in which the illusion of greatness has devoured the very joints and marrow. Who is right? Each of them. And yet each of them has the notion that the characters are not entirely a mixture of incongruous elements, artfully composed, or in any way untrue. Each of them feels distinctly that they are excellently created, live on the stage most effectively; and the actor himself feels this most strongly, even if the secret of Shakespeare's poetic power should not be entirely understood.

Shakespeare's art of character building represents to an unusual extent and perfection, what is peculiar to the Germanic method of creation, as opposed to that of the old world, and that of those peoples of culture, not pervaded with German life. What is German is the fulness, and affectionate fervor which forms every single figure carefully, accurately, according to the needs of each individual masterpiece of art, but considers the entire life of the figure, lying outside of the piece, and seeks to seize upon its peculiarity. While the German conveniently casts upon the pictures of reality, the variegated threads spun by his teeming fancy, he conceives the real foundations of his characters, the actual counterpart, with philanthropic regard, and with the most exact understanding of its combined contents. This thoughtfulness, this fond devotion to the individual, and again the perfect freedom which has intercourse, for a purpose, with this image as with an esteemed friend, have, since the old times, given a peculiarly rich import to the successful figures in German dramatic art; therefore, there is in them, a wealth of single traits, a spiritual charm, a many-sidedness, through which the compactness, necessary to dramatic characters, is not destroyed, but in its effects, is greatly enhanced.

The Brutus of Shakespeare is a high-minded gentleman, but he has been reared an aristocrat; he is accustomed to read and to think; he has the enthusiasm to venture great things, but not the circumspection and prudence to put them through. Cæsar is a majestic hero who has passed a victorious, a great life, and who has proved his own excellence in a time of selfishness and pretentious weakness; but with the lofty position, which he has given himself above the heads of his contemporaries, ambition has come upon him, simulation and secret fear. The fearless man who has risked his life a hundred times and feared nothing but the appearance of being afraid, is secretly superstitious, variable, exposed to the influence of weaker men.

The poet does not hide this; he lets his characters, in every place, say exactly what occurs to them in such a business; but he treats their nature as in itself intelligible, and explains nothing; not because it has become distinct to him through cool calculation, but because it has arisen with a natural force from all the presupposed conditions.

To the admirer of Shakespeare, this greatness of his poetical vision presents here and there difficulties. In the first part of *Julius Cæsar*, Casca comes prominently into the foreground; in the following action of the piece, not a word is heard about him; he and the other conspirators are apparently of less consequence to Shakespeare than to the audience. But he who observes more carefully, sees the reason for this, and perceives that this figure which he made so benevolently prominent at first, the poet throws aside immediately without ado. Indeed, he indicates this in the judgment which, by way of exception this time, Brutus and Cassius let fall concerning Casca. To him and to the piece, the man is an insignificant tool.

In many subordinate rôles, the great poet stands strikingly silent; with simple strokes, he moves them forward in their embarrassment. The understanding of their nature, which we occasionally seek, does not at last remain doubtful, but it is clear only by streaks of light falling upon it from without. Anne's changes of mind, in *Richard III.*, in the celebrated scene at the bier, are, in a manner, concealed. No other poet would dare venture these; and the rôle, otherwise brief and scanty, would have been one of the most difficult. The same thing holds good of many figures which, composed of good and evil, appear to help forward the action. In the case of such rôles, the poet trusts much to the actor. Through suitable representation, the artist is able to transform many apparent and real harshnesses into new beauty. Indeed, one often has the feeling, that the poet omitted some explanatory accompaniments, because he wrote for a definite actor, whose personality was specially adapted to fill the rôle. In other cases, a man is distinctly seen, who, more than any other dramatic author, is accustomed as actor and spectator to observe men in the better society, and who understands how to conceal or let peep through, the characteristic weaknesses which are behind the forms of good manners. In this style, most of his courtiers are fashioned. Through such silence, through such abrupt transitions, he affords the actor more gaps to fill than any other dramatist does. Sometimes his words are merely like the punctured background of embroidery; but everything lies in them exactly indicated, felt to be adapted to the highest stage effects. Then the spectator, surprised by good acting, beholds a rich, well-rounded life, where in reading, he saw only barren flatness. It once in a while happens to a poet, that he really does too little for a character. Thus the little rôle of Cordelia, even with good acting, does not come into the proportion which it should bear toward the rest of the piece. Much in some characters appears strange to us, and in need of explanation, which was transparent and easily understood by the writer's contemporaries, as a reflection of their life and their culture.

What is greatest in this part, however, is, as has already been said, the tremendous impelling force which operates in his chief characters. The power with which they storm upward toward their fate, as far as the climax of the drama, is irresistible—in almost every one a vigorous life and strong energy of passion. And when they have attained the height, from which by an overpowering might they are drawn downward in confusion, the suspense has been relieved for a moment in a portentous deed; then come in several passages, finished situations and individual portrayals, the most sublime that the new drama has produced. The dagger scene and banquet scene in *Macbeth*, the bridal night in *Romeo and Juliet*, the hovel scene in *Lear*, the visit to the mother in *Hamlet*, Coriolanus at the altar of Aufidius, are examples. Sometimes, the interest of the poet in the characters appears to become less from this moment; even in *Hamlet*, in which the graveyard scene — however celebrated its melancholy observations are — and the close decline, when compared to the tension of the first half. In *Coriolanus*, the two most beautiful scenes lie in the second half of the play; in *Othello*, the most powerful. This last piece, however, has other technical peculiarities.

If Shakespeare's art of characterization was sometimes dark and difficult for the actors of his time, it is natural that we perceive his peculiarities very clearly. For no greater contrast is conceivable than his treatment of characters, and that of the German tragic poets, Lessing, Goethe, and Schiller. While in Shakespeare we are reminded through the reservedness of many accessory characters, that he still stood near the epic time of the middle ages, our dramatic characters have, even to superfluity, the qualities of a period of lyric culture, a continual, broad and agreeable presentation of internal conditions upon which the heroes reflect with an introspection sometimes dismal; and they use sentences which doubtless make clear the shifting point of view of the characters in relation to the moral order of things. In the German dramas, there is nothing dark, and, Kleist excepted, nothing violent.

Of all the great German poets, Lessing has best understood how to represent his characters in the surge of intense dramatic excitement. Among his contemporaries in art, the poetic power of the individual is most esteemed according to his characters; and in just this matter of characterization, Lessing is great and admirable; the wealth of details, the effect of telling, vital expressions, which surprise by their beauty as well as by their truth, is, in his works, in the limited circle of his tragic figures, greater than in Goethe, more frequent than in Schiller. The number of his dramatic types is not great. About the tender, noble, resolute maiden, Sara, Emilia, Minna, Recha, and her vacillating lover, Melfort, Prince, Tellheim, Templer, the serving confidants range themselves; the dignified father, the rival, the intriguer, are all written according to the craft of the troops of players of that time. And yet in these very types, the multiformity of the variations is wonderful. He is a master in the representation of such passions as express themselves in the life of the middle classes, where the struggle toward beauty and nobility of soul stands so marvellously near crude desire. And how conveniently all is thought out for the actor! No one else has so worked out of his very soul for him; what seems, in reading, so restless and theatrically excited, comes into its right proportion only through representation on the stage.

Only at single moments, his dialectic of passion fails to give the impression of truth, because he over-refines it and yields to a pleasure in hair-splitting quibbles. In a few places, his reflections expand to where they do not belong; and sometimes in the midst of a profound poetic invention, there is an artificial stroke which cools instead of strengthening the impression. Besides much in *Nathan the Wise*, there is an example of this in *Sara Sampson*, III. 3, the passage in which Sara discusses passionately with herself whether she shall receive her father's letter. This stroke is specially to be made use of as a brief detail in characterization; for this purpose, also, it is to be treated as a suggestion; in broad elaboration, it would be painful.

For a long time yet, Lessing's pieces will be a

fine school for the German actor; and they will still preserve the fond respect of the artist on our stage, if only a more manly culture shall make the spectator more sensitive to the weakness of the return action in *Minna von Barnhelm*, and *Emilia Galotti*. For the great man erred in this, that violent passion suffices to make a poetic character dramatic, since it depends much more on the relation in which the passion stands to power of will. His passion creates sorrow and excites sometimes in the spectator a protesting pity. Still his chief characters vacillate — though this is not his badge, but that of his time — driven hither and thither by strong emotion; and when they are brought to commit an ominous deed, this often lacks the highest justification. The tragic development in *Sara Sampson* rests upon this: Melfort perpetrates the indignity of appointing a rendezvous between his former mistress and Miss Sara; in *Emilia Galotti*, the maiden is stabbed by her father, out of caution.

The freedom and the nobility with which the poetic characters of the last century express their spiritual moods, is not accompanied with a corresponding mastery of performance; only too frequently a time is perceived in which the character, even the best, was not firmly drawn out, and hardened to steel by a strong public opinion, by the strong, certain import which public political life gives one. Arbitrariness in the moral point of view, and sensitive uncertainty, disturb the highest artistic effects of even the power of genius. The reproach has often been made against Goethe's plays that here is only indicated the progress that was introduced with dramatic effects by him and Schiller.

In the characterizing details of his rôles, Goethe is not more abundant than Lessing, — Weislingen, Clavigo, Egmont, are dramatically even more scanty than Melfort, Prince, Tellheim ; — his figures have nothing of the violently pulsating life, of the restless, feverish element, which vibrates in the emotions of Lessing's characters ; nothing artificial disturbs ; the inexhaustible charm of his spirit ennobles even what is lacking. In the first place, Goethe and Schiller have opened up to the Germans the historical drama, the more elevated style of treating characters, which is indispensable to great tragic effects, even if Goethe did not attain these effects particularly by the power of his characters, not by the action, but by the unsurpassable beauty and sublimity with which he made the spirit of his heroes ring out in words. There especially, where from his dramatic persons the hearty sincerity of lyric feeling could ring through, is seen, in little traits, a magic of poetry which no other German has even approximately attained. Thus operates the rôle of Gretchen.

It is not by chance that such supreme beauty in Goethe's female characters is effective ; the men do not, as a rule, drive forward ; they are driven ; indeed, they sometimes claim a sympathy on the stage, which they do not merit, and appear as good friends of the poet himself; and their good qualities are known only to him, because they do not turn their good side to the society into which he has invited them. What makes *Faust* our greatest poetic masterpiece is not its fulness of dramatic life, least of all, in the rôle of Faust himself. If, however, the impelling force of Goethe's heroes is not powerful enough to make sublime effects and mighty conflicts possible, their dramatic movement in single scenes is compact, skilful and adapted to the stage; and the connection of the dialogue is admirable. For the greatest beauty of Goethe's plays is the scenes which have their course between two persons. Lessing understands how to occupy three persons on the stage, with great effect, in passionate counter-play; but Schiller directs a great number with firmness, and superior certainty. Schiller's method of delineating character in his youth is very different from the method of his riper years. He shows great progress, but not entirely without loss. What a transformation from his conception of beautiful souls which in *The Robbers* he erected into something monstrous, and later into the heroic, and at last in *Demetrius*, into the firm compactness of character similar to that of Shakespeare's persons!

During more than half a century, the splendor and nobility of Schiller's characters have ruled the German stage; and the weak imitators of his style have not long understood that the fulness of his diction produced so great an effect only because beneath it there lies a wealth of dramatic life, covered as by a plating of gold. This dramatic life of his persons is already very striking in his earliest plays. In *Love and Intrigue*, it won such significant expression, that in this direction in later works, an advance is not always visible. To verse and the more elevated style, he has added at least pithy brevity, an expression of passion suitable to the stage, and many a consideration for the actor. His expression of feelings and perceptions becomes continually fuller in speech and more eloquent. His characters, also,—specially the fully elaborated ones,—have that peculiar quality of his time, impressively to enunciate to the hearer their thought and feeling at many moments in the action. And they do it in the manner of highly cultured and contemplative men; for a beautiful, and often a finished picture, depends for them on passionate feeling; and the mood which sounds forth from their souls is followed by a meditation, an observation,—as we all know, often of highest beauty,—through which the moral grounds of the excited feeling is made clear, and the confusion, the embarrassment of the situation, through an elevation to a higher standpoint, appears for the moment cleared away. It is evident that such a method of dramatic creation, of the representation of strong passion, is in general not favorable, and will certainly in some future period cease to appear among our successors. But it is just as certain that it perfectly repeats the manner of feeling and perceiving which was peculiar to the cultured Germans at the end of the last century, as no other poetic method does, and that upon it rests a part of the effect which Schiller's dramas produce to-day upon the people; certainly only a part, for the greatness of the poet lies in this, that he who accords to his characters so many resting places, even in excited movements, knows how to keep these in extreme tension; almost all have a strong, inspired, inner life, a content with which they stand securely against the outer world. In this embarrassment, they sometimes give the impression of somnambulists, to whom a disturbance from the outer world becomes fatal; thus the Maid, Wallenstein, Max, Thekla; or who at least need a strong shock to their inner life, to be brought to a deed, like Tell, even Cæsar and Manuel. Therefore, the impassioned agitation of Schiller's chief characters, is in the last analysis, not always dramatic; but this imperfection is often covered by the rich detail and beautiful characterization with which he equips the accessory figures. Finally, the greatest advance which German art has made through him, is that in a powerful tragic material, he makes his persons participants in an action which has for its background, not the relations of private life, but the highest interests of man, of the state, of faith. His beauty and power will always be dangerous to young poets and actors, because the inner life of his characters streams forth richly in speech. In this, he does so much that there remains, often, little for the actor to do; his plays need less from the stage than those of any other poet.

II.

THE CHARACTERS IN THE MATERIAL, AND ON THE STAGE.

Both the rights and the duty of the poet compel him, during his labor, to an incessant conflict with the pictures which history, the epic, and his own life offer him. .

It is undeniable that ardor and the charm of invention, are frequently first given to the German poet by his characters. Such a method of creation appears irreconcilable with the old fundamental law for the forming of the action, that the action must be the first, the characters second. If pleasure in the characteristic nature of the hero can cause the poet to compose an action for it, the action stands under the dominion of the character, is fashioned through it, is invented for it. The contradiction is only an apparent one; for to the creating genius, the disposition and character of a hero do not appear as they do to the historian, who at the end of his work draws the results of a life, or as they appear to a reader of history, who from the impressions of different adventures and deeds, gradually paints for himself the portrait of a man. The creative power comes into the ardent mind of the poet more in such a way, that it brings out vividly and with charm, the character of a hero, in single moments of its relations to other men. These moments in which the character becomes a living thing, are in the work of the epic poet, situations; in the work of the dramatist, actions in which the hero proceeds with some commotion; they are the foundations of the action, not yet connected and full of life; in them, already the idea of the piece lies, probably not yet clarified and separate. But it is always a presumption of this first beginning of poetic work, that the character becomes a living, animated thing under the compulsion of some part of the action. Only under such a presumption is a poetic conception of it possible.

But the process of idealization begins in this way: the outlines of the historic character, or character otherwise deemed of worth, fashion themselves according to the demands of the situation which has appeared in the soul of the poet. The trait of character which is useful to the invented moments of the action, becomes a fundamental trait of the being, to which all the remaining characteristic peculiarities are subordinated as supplementary adjuncts. Suppose the poet is to grasp the character of Emperor Charles V.; he is able to perceive him poetically only when he makes him pass through a definite action. The emperor at the parliament of Worms, or standing over against the captive king, Francis, or in the scene in which the Landgrave of Hesse prostrates himself at Halle, or at the moment when he receives the news of the threatened incursion of the elector Moritz,—the emperor under the pressure of each of these situations, is every time quite a different person; he retains all the features of the historical Charles; but his expression becomes a peculiar one, and so dominates the entire picture that it cannot pass for a historic portrait. Yet the transformation quickly goes further. To the first poetic vision others are joined; there is a struggle to become a whole, it contains beginning and end. And each new member of the action, which develops itself, forces upon the character something of color and motive, which are necessary to its understanding. If the action is directed in this way, the real character is fully transformed under the hand of the poet, according to the needs of his idea. Of course the creative artist, all this time, during his entire work, carries in his soul the features of the real person, as an accessory picture or counter-portrait. He takes from this what he can use in details; but what he creates from this, is brought out freely according to the demands of his action, and with additions of its own is molten to a new mass.

A striking example is the character of Wallenstein in Schiller's double drama. It is no accident that the figure in the poem was fashioned so different from that of the historical picture of the imperial general. The demands of the action have given him his appearance. The poet is interested in the historical Wallenstein; since the death of Gustavus Adolphus, this man has become enchanting. He has great plans, is a magnificent egotist, and has an unclouded conception of the political situation. Now a drama the business of which was to portray the end of his career, had the fewest possible pre-supposed conditions to represent, as the hero becomes a traitor by degrees, through his own guilt, and under the stress of his relations. Schiller saw in his mind's eye the figure of Wallenstein, as from premonitions it seeks to learn its fate (probably the first vision), then as it comes in contact with Questenberg, then with Wrangel, then as the loyal men free themselves from him. These were the first moments of action. Now it was conceivable that such a criminal beginning, if the plans miscarried, would show the hero actually weaker, more short-sighted, smaller, than the opposing powers. Therefore, in order to preserve his greatness and maintain interest in him, a leading, .fundamental trait of character must be invented for him, which should elevate him, and prove him free and independent, self-active before what allured him to treason, and which should explain how an eminent and superior man could be more short-sighted than those about him. In the real Wallenstein, there was something of this kind to be found; he was superstitious, believed in astrology—but not more than his contemporaries. This trait could be made poetically useful. But as a little motive, as a thing to wonder at in his character, it would have been of little use; it had to be ennobled, spiritually refined. So there arose the image of a thoughtful, inspired, elevated man, who in a time of carnage, strides over human life and human rights, his eye turned fixedly toward the heights where he believes he sees the silent rulers of his destiny. And the same sad, dreary playing with the inconceivably great, could exalt him out of, and above external relations; for the same fundamental characteristic of his being, a certain inclination to equivocal and underhand dealing, groping attempts and a feeling about, might gradually entangle him, the freeman, in the net of treason. Thus a dramatic movement of its own kind was found for his inward being. But this characteristic of his being was, in its essential nature, yet an irrational force; it held spell-bound; it placed him, for us, near the supernatural; it remained a great anomaly. In order to work tragically, the same characteristic must be brought into relation with the best and most amiable feelings of his heart. That belief in the revelations of powers incomprehensible to the hero, consecrates the friendly relations to the Piccolomini; that this same belief is not called out, but ominously advanced, by a secret need of something to honor, something to trust, and that this trust in men, which Wallenstein has confidently made clear through his faith; that this faith must destroy him,—this brings the strange figure very near to our hearts; it gives the action inner unity; it gives the character greater intensity. In such a way, the first-found situations, and the necessity of bringing them into an established connection of cause and effect, and to round them out to a dramatically effective action, have transformed the historical character feature by feature. So his adversary, Octavio, too, has been transformed by the tendency to give an inner connection with Wallenstein, of course in dependence on his character. A cold intriguer, who draws together the net over those who trust him, would not have sufficed; he must be exalted, and be placed intellectually near the chief hero; and if he were conceived as friend of the deluded one, who,—no matter from what sense of duty,—surrenders the friend, so it would be to the purpose to invent a trait of character in his life, which should weave his destiny with that of Wallenstein. Since there was needed in this gloomy material, a warmer life, brighter colors, a succession of gentle and touching feelings, the author created Max. This poor, unsuspecting child of the camp, was at once the opposite of his father and of his general. The poet cared too little, with respect to this figure, that it stood a fresh, harmless, unspotted nature, in contradiction to its own presupposed conditions, and to the unbridled life of a soldier, in which it had grown up; for Schiller was not at all careful to give motive to anything, if it only served his purpose. It satisfied him that this being, through character and aptness, could come into a noble and sharply-cut contrast with the hero and his opponent; and so him, and the corresponding figure of his beloved, the poet produced with a fondness which determined even the form of the drama.

Considered on the whole, then, it was not a freak, a chance discovery of the poet, which formed the character of Wallenstein and his counter-player. But of course, these persons, like every poetic image, are colored by the personality of the poet. And it is characteristic of Schiller to imbue all his heroes visibly with the thoughts which fill his own soul. This spirited contemplation, as well as the great, simple lines of a broad design, we perceive already as his peculiarity. The characteristic of his age was quite otherwise. Mastery in meditation and pondering is not, in Wallenstein, brought into equilibrium by a decisive power of will. That he listened to the voice of the stars, which at last becomes the voice of his own heart, would be expected. But he is represented as dependent on his environment. The Countess Terzky directs him; Max re-directs him; and the accident that Wrangel has disappeared, hinders, possibly, a reverse of results. Surely it was Schiller's purpose to make prominent Wallenstein's lack of resolution; but vacillation is, with us, a disadvantage, to be used for every hero of a play, only as a sharp contrast to a sustained power of action.

If this process of deriving the character from the internal necessity of the action seems a result of intelligent consideration, it is hardly necessary to confess that it does not thus perfect itself in the warm soul of the poet. Indeed, here enters during many hours, a cool weighing, a supervision, a supplementing, of creative invention; but the process of creation goes on still, in essentials, with a natural force in which the same thought is unconsciously active with the poet, the same thought which we in presence of the completed masterpiece, recognize through reflection as the indwelling law of intellectual production. Not only is the transformation of historical characters according to the demands of the action, specially shown to be different in different authors ; but the same poetic mind does not always appear equally free and unembarrassed before all its heroes. It is possible that a strong poetic power may seek, for some purpose, to represent with special care, single historical traits in the life of a hero. In the completed work, then, this care is recognized in a peculiar wealth of appropriate features, which are valuable for purposes of characterization. Shakespeare's Henry VIII. shows a fuller portraiture than any other heroic figure of that poet's plays. This figure is entirely transformed in essentials, to conform to the needs of the action, and is separated by a wide gulf, from the historic Henry. But what is valuable for portraiture in the sketching, as well as the numerous considerations which the poet had for real history, in constructing the action, give to the drama a strange coloring. However numerous the traits in this richly endowed character are, it will seldom appear to an actor as the most remunerative rôle to study.

For similar reasons, the introduction and use of historical heroes whose portraits have become specially popular, for example Luther, and Frederick the Great, is very difficult. The temptation is too strong to bring out such well-known traits of the historical figure as are not essential to the action of the play, and therefore appear accidental. This addition to a single figure taken from reality, gives it in the midst of persons, the product of unfettered invention, a remarkable, a painfully pretentious, a repulsive appearance. The desire to present the most accurate reflection of the real being, will too strongly allure the actor to petty delineation. Even the spectator wants an accurate portrait, and is perhaps surprised if the other characters and the action are less effective, because he is so strongly reminded of an esteemed friend in history.

The requirement is easily given that the dramatic character must be true; that especially the life forces must be in unison with each other, and must be felt as belonging together, and that the characters must exactly correspond to the whole of the action, in respect to coloring and spiritual import. But such a rule, so generally expressed, will, in many cases, afford the beginning poet no aid, where the discord between the ultimate demands of his art, and of the historian's art, and even of many a poetic truth, prepares secret difficulties.

It is understood that the poet will faithfully preserve the deliverances of history, where they are of service to him and cause no derangement. For our time, so advanced in historical culture and in the knowledge of the earlier relations of civilization, keeps an eye upon the historical culture of its dramatists. The poet must have care that he do not give his heroes too little of the import of their own time, and that a modern perception and feeling in the characters do not appear to the educated spectator in contradiction to the well-known embarrassments and peculiarities of the life of the soul in older times. The young poets easily lend to their heroes a knowledge of their own times, a certain skill in philosophizing upon the most important occurrences, and in finding such points of view for their deeds as are current in historical works of modern times. It is uncomfortable to hear an old emperor of the Franconian or Hohenstaufen line express the tendencies of his time, so self-consciously, so for a purpose, so very shrewdly as, for instance, Stenzel and Raumer have represented. But not less dangerous is the opposite temptation into which poets come through the effort vividly to set forth the peculiarities of the past. The remarkable, that which deflects from our own nature toward older times, easily seems to them as characteristic and effective for their purpose. Then the poet is in danger of smothering the immediate interest which we take in the easily intelligible, the universally human, and in still greater danger of building the course of his action upon singularities of that past, on the transitory, which in art gives the impression of the accidental and arbitrary.

And yet there often remains, in an historical piece, an inevitable opposition between the dramatically arranged characters and the dramatically arranged action. At this dangerous point, it is profitable to tarry a little. Since it is a duty of the poet who uses historical material, to give special attention to what we call the color and costume of the time, and since not only the characters but the action, too, is taken from a distant age, there will certainly be, in the idea of the piece and of the action, in the motives and situations, much that is not universally human and intelligible to every one, but that is explained through what is remarkable and characteristic of that time. When, for instance, the murder of a king is committed by ambitious heroes, as in *Macbeth* or *Richard*, where the intriguer attacks his rival with poison or dagger, where the wife of a prince is thrown into water because she springs from the middle class, — in these and innumerable other cases, the embarrassment and the destiny of the heroes must be derived from the represented event, from the peculiarities and customs of their times.

If these figures belong to a time which has here been called the epic, in which man's inward freedom has been in reality little developed, in which the dependence of the individual upon the example of others, upon custom and usage, is much greater, in which man's inner being is not poorer in strong feeling, but is much poorer in the ability to express it by means of speech, then the characters of the drama can not at all represent, in the essential thing, such an embarrassment. For since upon the stage, the effect is produced not by deeds, not by beautiful discourse, but by the exhibition of mental processes, through which feeling and volition are concentrated into a deed, the dramatic chief characters must show a degree of freedom of will, a refinement and a dialectic of passion, which stand in the most essential contrast with the actual embarrassment and naïvetè of their old prototypes in reality.

Now the artist would, of course, be easily forgiven for endowing his people with a fuller, stronger, and richer life than they had in the real world, if only this richer fulness did not give the impression of untruth, because individual conditions presupposed for the action, do not tolerate a character so constructed. For the action which is derived from history or from legend, and which everywhere betrays the social features, the degree of culture, the peculiarities of its time, the poet cannot always so easily imbue with a deeper import as he can individual characters. The poet may, for example, put into the mouth of an oriental the finest thoughts, the tenderest feelings of the sweetest passion, and yet so color the character that it contains the beautiful appearance of poetic truth. But now, perhaps the action makes it necessary that this same character have the women of his harem drowned in sacks, or have them beheaded. Then the contradiction between action and character crops out inevitably. This is, indeed, a difficulty of dramatic creation which cannot always be met, even by the greatest talent in that direction. Then it requires all art to conceal from the spectator the latent contradiction between the material and the vital needs of the action. For this reason, all love scenes in historic pieces present peculiar difficulties. Here, where we demand the most direct expression of a lovely passion, it is a difficult task to give at the same time the local color. The poet is most likely to succeed if, as in the case of Goethe and Gretchen, he can, in such a situation, paint peculiarities of character in a stronger color, and even approach the borders of *genre* painting. The quiet struggle of the poet with the assumptions of his subject-matter, which are undramatic and yet not to be dispensed with, occurs in almost every action taken from heroic legend or the older histories.

In the epic material which the heroic legends of the great civilized races offer, the action is already artistically arranged, even if according to other than dramatic requirements. The life and adventures of heroes appear complete, determined by momentous deeds; usually, the sequence of events in which they appear acting or enduring, forms a chain of considerable length; but it is possible to detach single links for the use of the drama. The heroes themselves float indistinctly in great outlines, while single characteristic peculiarities are powerfully developed. They stand upon the heights of their nationality, and display a power and greatness as sublime and peculiar as the creative phantasy of a people can invent; and the momentous results of their lives are frequently just what the dramatic poet seeks,—love and hate, selfish desire, conflict and destruction.

Such materials are further consecrated through the fondest recollections of a people; they were once the pride, joy, entertainment of millions. After their transformation through a creative popular spirit, which lasted for centuries, they were still flexible enough to afford to the invention of the dramatic poet opportunity for the intensification of character, as well as for alterations in the connection of the action. Many of them have come to us with the elaboration which they underwent in a great epic; the most of them, in their essential contents, are not, even according to our culture, entirely strange to us. What is here said is more or less applicable to the great cycles of Greek legends, of the legendary traditions which are interwoven with the earliest history of the Romans, of the heroic tales of the Germans, and Latins of the Middle Ages.

Indeed, upon a closer inspection, the characters of the epic tradition differ much from the persons necessary to the drama. It is true, the heroes of Homer and of the *Nibelungen Lied* are quite distinct personalities. A glance into the interior of a human soul, into the surging feeling, is not entirely forbidden to epic poets; indeed they often derive the fate of the hero from his character; they derive his ominous deeds from his passions. In the poetry of early times, the knowledge of the human heart, and the sane judgment which might explain a man's destiny from his virtues, faults, and passions, are admirable. Not so well developed is the capability of representing the details of mental processes. The life of the persons expresses itself in little anecdotal traits which are often perceived with a surprising fineness: what lies before, the quiet labor within, what follows after such a deed, the quiet effect on the soul, is passed over or quickly disposed of.

How a man asserts himself among strangers, is victorious, or perishes in a strife with stronger powers which stand against him,—to relate this is the chief charm; also, describing high festivals, duels, battles, adventures of travel. The expression of feeling is most animated where the suffering man rebels against the unendurable; but here, too, the expression becomes rigid, relatively unanimated, in frequently recurring forms, complaints, prayer to the gods, perhaps so that the speaker holds up another's fate in contrast with his own, or mirrors his situation in an elaborate picture. The speech of the hero is almost always scanty, simple, monotonous, with the same recurring notes of feeling. Thus the soliloquies of Odysseus and of Penelope are made in the poem, in which the peculiar life is most richly represented, and with the best individual traits. Where the inner connection of events rests upon the secret plots and the peculiar passion of a single person, also where a momentous action is developed from the inward being of a character, the analysis of the passion is scarcely at hand. Kriemhild's plan to take revenge for the murder of her husband, all the emotions of soul of this most enchanting person, who lives so powerfully in the poet's heart,—how brief, and concealed they are in the narrative! It is characteristic that in these German poems, the lyric accompaniments, monologues, complaints, genial observations, are much less numerous than in the *Odyssey;* on the other hand, every peculiarity of the chief characters, which determines their friendship or hostility to others, is elaborated with special vividness and beauty.

But as soon as one conceives of these powerful, shadowy forms of legend as human beings, and represented to human beings by human beings on the stage, they lose the dignity and magnitude of outline, with which the busied imagination has clothed them. Their speeches, which within epic narrative produce the most powerful effects, are in the iambics of the stage, circumscribed, heavy, commonplace. Their deeds seem to us crude, barbarous, dreary, indeed quite impossible; they seem sometimes like the old water sprites and goblins of ancient folk-lore, with no human and rational soul. The first work of the poet must be a transformation and intensifying of characters, by which they may become human and intelligible to us. We know how attractive such labor was to the Greeks.

Their relation to the material in their old heroic tales was peculiarly favorable. It was bound to the life of their present by a thousand threads, by local traditions, divine service, and the plastic arts. The more liberal culture of their times allowed important changes to be made; allowed what was transferred to them to be treated with the utmost freedom as raw material. And yet, the history of the Attic tragedy is the history of an inward warfare, which great poets waged with a realm of material that so much the more violently resisted the fundamental laws of dramatic creation, as the actor's art developed, and the demand of the audience for a richer fulness of character increased.

Euripides is our most instructive example of how the Greek tragedy was disorganized by the internal opposition between its field of material and the greater requisites which the art of representation gradually brought into operation. None of his great predecessors understands better than he, how to imbue the persons of the epic legend with burning, soul-devouring passion. None has ventured to bring dramatic characters so realistically near the sensibility and the understanding of his audience; none has done so much to aid the actor's art. Everywhere in his pieces, it is perceived distinctly that the actor and the needs of the stage have won significance.

But the treatment of his rôles, effective from the actor's point of view, an advance in itself, the undeniable right of the acting drama, yet contributed in this way to depreciate his pieces. What was wild and barbarous in the action must strike as repulsive, if persons like the Athenians of the poet's own time, were made to think and feel and act like ungovernable Scythians. His Electra is an oppressed woman from a noble house, who in need, has married a poor but worthy peasant, and perceives with astonishment that beneath his tunic, a brave heart beats; but we can scarcely believe her assurance that she is the daughter of the dead Agamemnon. When in *Iphigenia in Aulis*, mother and daughter, entreating aid, place their hands on the chins of Achilles and Agamemnon, and taking an oath, according to the custom of their people, seek to soften these men; and when Achilles refuses his hand to Clytemnestra, who greets him, —this imitative invention was in itself an excellent histrionic motive; but it stood in striking contrast to the customary movement of the masked and draped persons; and while this advance of the actor's art no doubt powerfully enhanced the effects of the scenes, in the eyes of the audience, it reduced Iphigenia at the same time to an oppressed Athenian woman, and made the proposed slaughtering of her more strange and untrue.

In many other cases, the poet yields so far to the desire of his player of pathos parts, for great song effects, that suddenly and without motive, he interrupts the intelligible and agreeable course of his action, by illuminating some old heroic trait, by ragings, by child murder and the like. With this intrusion of opera-like and spectacular effects, the causative connection of events becomes a subordinate matter, the tragic momentum is lost, the persons become vessels for different kinds of feeling; and sportive and sophistical, they are freed from any pressure from their past lives. In almost every piece, it can be felt that the poet finds his material from old legends, torn into fragments like a rotten web, through a well justified climax of stage effects, and entirely unserviceable for the establishing of a unified dramatic action. If pieces from other contemporaries had been preserved for us, we should probably recognize how others have struggled to secure a reconciliation between the given material and the vital requisites of their art. It must be repeated: what detracts from the poetic greatness of Euripides is not specially the lack of *morale*, of the manners and habits of the time, so peculiar to him; but it is the natural and inevitable disorganization which must come into the material used in a drama, but not essentially dramatic. Of course, the repeated use of the same material contributed to bring the disadvantage to light; for the later poets, who came upon great dramatic treatment of almost all the legends, had pressing occasion to win their audiences by something new, something charming, and they found this in setting a new and higher task for the art of the actor; but this adequate advance hastened the destruction of the action, and thereby, of the rôles.

We Germans are far more unfavorable to the epic legend; it is for us a world in ruins. Even where our science has spread knowledge of it, throughout broad circles, as of Homer and *The Nibelungen*, the knowledge and the enjoyment of it are the prerogative of the learned. Our stage has become much more realistic than that of the Greeks, and demands in the characters far richer individual traits, an import not painfully wounding to our sensibilities. If upon our stage, Tristan had married one woman to conceal his relations with another woman, the actor of his part would incur the danger of being pelted with apples from the gallery, as a low-lived monster; and the bridal night of Brunhild, so effectively portrayed in the epic, will always awaken on the stage a dangerous mood in the minds of the spectators. To us Germans, history has become a more important source of dramatic subjects than the legend. For a majority of the younger poets, the history of the Middle Ages is the magic fountain from which they draw their plays. And yet, in the life of our German ancestors, there lies something difficult to understand, something that hides the heroes of the Middle Ages as with a mist, — indeed still more the circumstances of the people,— and that makes a princely scion in the time of Otto the Great, less transparent than a Roman prince in the time of the Second Punic War. The lack of independence of the man is far greater; every individual is more strongly influenced by the views and customs of the circle in which he moves. The impressions that fall upon the soul from without, are quickly covered with a new tissue, given a new shape, receive a new color, by the exercise of an active imagination. Indeed, the activity of sense is incisive, energetic;

but the life of nature, the person's own life and the impulse from others, are conceived far less according to an intelligible consistency of appearances, than transformed according to the intellectual demands. The egotism of the individual easily rears itself, and assumes the attitude of battle; just as ready is its submission to a superior force. The original simplicity of a child may be combined in the same man with effective cunning and with vices which we are accustomed to consider the outgrowth of a corrupt civilization. And this combination as well as the union of the — apparently — strongest contradictions in feeling and way of dealing, are found in the leaders of the people as well as among ordinary men and women. It is evident that in this way, the judgment concerning characters, their worth or worthlessness, their individual actions, concerning moods and motives of actions, is rendered difficult. We are to judge the man according to the civilization and moral feeling of his time, and judge his time according to the civilization and morals of our own.

Let it be tried to make a mental picture of the average morality among the people in any one of the earlier centuries of the Middle Ages, and it will be perceived how difficult this is. Could we judge from the penalties which the oldest popular justice inflicted upon all kinds of abominable crimes, or from the horrible practices at the Court of the Merovingians? There was still almost nothing of what we call public opinion, and we can say with positiveness that the historians give us the impression of men who merit confidence. When a royal scion arose in repeated rebellion against his father, to what extent was he justified or pardoned because of the notions of his time, or his own inmost motives? Even in the case of events which seem very clear and are received by us in a dazzling light, we perceive a lack in our comprehension, not only because we know too little of that time, but also because we do not always understand what has come down to us, as the dramatic poet must understand it, in its causative connections and in its origin in the germ of a human life.

Whoever would not more carefully investigate the real relations and the historical character of his hero, but would only make use of his name, in order to provide some events of his time, with bold observations on the stage, according to the report of a convenient historical work, would avoid every difficulty. But he would, in fact, hardly find a dramatic material. For this noble mass of dramatic material is embedded in the rock of history, and almost always only where the private, familiar life of the heroic character begins; there one must know how to look for it.

If one really takes pains to become acquainted as well as possible with the heroes of the distant past, one discovers in their nature something very undramatic. For as it is characteristic of those epic poems, it is characteristic also of historical life, that the inward struggle of man, his feelings, his thoughts, the existence of his will, have found from the hero himself no expression; nor have they found expression from an observer. The people, its poets, its historians, see the man sharply and well at the moment of his deed; they perceive — at least the Germans — with great penetration, what is characteristic of the expressions of his life, as connected with emotion, with exaltation, with caprice, with disinclination. But only the moments in which his life turns toward the external, are attractive, enchanting, intelligible, to that time. Even speech has but a meager expression for the inner processes up to the deed; even passionate excitement is best enjoyed in the effect which it has upon others, and in the light which it throws upon the environment. For the intellectual conditions, and the reaction which the occurrences have upon the sensibilities and character of the man, every technique of representation fails, interest fails. Even the depiction of apparent characteristic peculiarities, as well as a full elaboration of the occurrence, is not frequent in the narrative; a comparatively dry rehearsal of events is interrupted more or less by anecdotes, in which a single vital trait of importance to a contemporary, comes to view,— here a striking word, there a mighty deed. Preferably in such legends, remain the recollections which the people preserve of their leader and his deeds. We know that till after the Reformation, indeed, till after the middle of the last century, this same notion was not infrequent among educated people, and that it has not disappeared yet from among our people.

The poverty of dramatic life makes difficult to the poet the understanding and the portrayal of every hero. But in the temper of our ancestors, there was something very peculiar, something which made their character at times quite mysterious. Already in the most ancient heroic times, they evince in character, in speech, in poetry, in customs, the inclination to make prevalent a peculiar subtle introspection and interpretation. Not the things themselves, but what they signify, was the chief thing to the ancestors of our thinkers. The images of the external world press multitudinously into the soul of the old Germans, who are more versatile, quicker to recognize, endowed with greater receptivity, than any other people on earth. But not in the beautiful, quiet, clear manner of the Greeks, nor with the sure, practical, limited one-sidedness of the Romans, did what was received mirror itself again in speech and action; they worked it over slowly and quietly; and what flowed from them had a strong subjective coloring, and an addition from their own spirit, which we might, in the earliest times, call lyric.

Therefore the oldest poetry of the Germans stands in most striking contrast to the epic of the Greeks; its chief affair is not the rich, full narrative of the action, but a sharp relief of single, brilliant traits, the connecting of the force to an elaborate image, a representation in short, abrupt waves, upon which is recognized the excited mind of the narrator. So in the characters, the defiant self-seeking, combined with a surrender to ideal perceptions, has given to the Germans since prehistoric time, a striking imprint, and has made themselves, rather than their physical power and martial rage, a terror to the Romans. No other popular morality has conceived of woman so chastely and nobly; no pagan faith has overcome the fear of death, as the German faith has; for to die on the battlefield is the German hero's honor and joy. Through this prominence of spirit and courage, of ideal perception and feeling, the characters of German heroes very early receive in life, as in the epic, a less simple composition, an original, sometimes a wonderful stamp, which lends them, now a remarkable greatness and depth, now an adventurous and unreasonable appearance.

Let no one compare the poetic value of delineation, but the foundations of character, in the heroes of the *Iliad* and the *Odyssey*, with the heroes in the *Nibelungen Lied.* To the bravest Greek, death remained a terror; the danger of battle weighed him down; it was not dishonorable to him, in one sense, to slay a sleeping or unarmed foe; it was by no means the least renown prudently to avoid the danger of conflict, and strike from behind an unsuspecting victim. The German hero, on the contrary, the same one who from fidelity to his commander performs the most atrocious act which a German can, and cunningly hits an unarmed man from behind,— just such a one can avoid death and destruction for himself, for his lord and for his posterity, if he only announces at the right time that danger is at hand. Supernatural beings have prophesied destruction for him and his friends, if the momentous journey is continued ; yet he thrusts back into the stream the boats which make a return possible ; again, at the king's court, where death threatens him, a word to the benevolent king, an honest answer to a serious question, may divert the worst from him, but he keeps silent. Still more : he and his friends deride and enrage his embittered enemies ; and with the certain prospect of death, they playfully challenge and incite to bloody strife.

To the Greek, to every other people of antiquity, possibly with the exception of the Gauls, such a kind of heroism would appear thoroughly unearthly and unreasonable ; but it was true German, the wild, dark expression, the character of a nation in which to the individual, his honor and his pride were of more account than his life. Not otherwise is this consideration with historical heroes. The ideals which rule their lives, however unreasonable they were long before the development of chivalry, the duty of honor, of fidelity, the feeling of manly pride and of one's own dignity, contempt for death, and love for individual men, often had a strength and power which we can scarcely appreciate, and do not always recognize as the governing motive.

Thus swings the soul of the German in the ancient times, in a bondage which to us is often no longer recognizable; pious surrender and longing, superstition, and fidelity to duty, a secret magic word, or secret oath, advanced his resolution to deeds which we try vainly to explain on reasonable grounds taken from our civilization.

And into such a disposition eventuated, in the Middle Ages, the great cycle of moods, laws, and fantastic reveries, which surged in with Christendom. While on one side, the incisive contrast in which the gentle faith of renunciation stood to the rude inclinations of a victorious, war-like people, the contradiction between duty and inclination, between external and internal life, increased greatly, it corresponded on the other side in a striking manner, to the necessity of giving one's self entirely to great ideas, which the German had long practiced. When instead of Wuotan and the slain Ase-god, the Father of the Christians and his only begotten Son came; when in place of the battle-virgins the hosts of The Holy One came, the life after death received a new consecration and a more sincere significance. And to the old powers, which in quietness had controlled human volition, to the magic word, to the approaching animal, to the drinking-bout, to the premonitions of heathen priests, and the prophesies of wise women, came the demands of the new church, its blessing and its curse, its vows and its shrifts, the priests and the monks. Following close on rude, reckless dissipation, came passionate repentance, and the strictest asceticism. Near the houses of beautiful women, were reared the cloisters of the nuns. How, since the dominion of the Christian faith, characters have been drawn in their deepest principles; how perception and motives of action have become more manifold, more profound and artistic, is shown, for instance, by the numerous figures from the time of the Saxon Emperor, where pious devotion was practiced by the most distinguished persons, and men and women were driven hither and thither, now by efforts to win the world for themselves, now by the penitent wish to reconcile heaven to themselves.

Any one who has ever felt the difficulty of understanding the men of the Middle Ages, who were formed by the thoughtful nature of the Germans and by the old church, will complete these brief suggestions in every direction.

Here, therefore, a former example is repeated, but from another point of view. What was working in the soul of Henry IV. as he stood in the penitent's frock by the castle wall of Canossa? In order that the poet may answer this question by a noble art effect, he will first let the historian tell what he knows about it; and he will learn with astonishment how different the conception of the situation, how uncertain and scanty the received account, and how troublesome and difficult it is to sound the heart of his hero.

That he did not go to the pope with inward contrition, this haughty powerful man, who hated, in the Romish priest, his most dangerous opponent, is easy to comprehend. That he had long revolved, in his rebellious mind the bitter necessity of this step, and had not put on the penitent's garment without a grim mental reservation, is to be assumed. But he came just as little as a crafty politician, who humiliated himself by a cool calculation, because he perceived a false step of his opponent, and saw growing from this surrender, the fruits of future victory. For Henry was a Christian of the Middle Ages. However intensely he hated Gregory, the curse of the church certainly had in it something uncomfortable, something frightful; to his God, and to the heaven of the Christian, there was no other way than through the church. Gregory sat on the bridge to heaven; and if he forbade, the angels, the new battle-virgins of the Christian, would not lead the dead warrior before the throne of the Father, but would thrust him into the abyss of the old dragon. The pope writes that the emperor has wept much, and besought his mercy, and that the attendants of the pope have with sobs and tears witnessed the emperor's penance. Was the emperor firm in the faith that the pope had the right thus to torment him? This influence of the ecclesiastical conscience upon worldly aims, this adventurous and uncertain mingling of opposites, now pride, higher thought, enduring, imperturbable power, which we consider almost superhuman, and again a lamentable emptiness and weakness, which seems contemptible to us,—this offers the poet no easily accomplished task. Of course he is master of his subject; he can transform the historical character at will, according to the needs of his work. It is possible that the real Henry stood before the wall of Canossa, like an ungoverned and vicious knave, who was to undergo a severe chastising. What did the poet care for that? But just as binding as possible, is his duty to fathom to its deepest recesses the real nature of the emperor. Not only the sad penitent, but the cold politician, will become falsities under such an examination. The poet has to form the character of the prince out of component parts, for which he does not find in his own mind the corresponding intuitions, and which he has to convert into intuitions and warm perceptions through reflection. There are few princes of the Middle Ages who do not appear, in the essential occurrences of their lives, and measured by the standard of our civilization and habits, either as short-sighted dunces, or conscienceless scoundrels—not seldom as both. The historian performs his difficult task in his unpretentious manner; he seeks to understand the connections of their time, and tells us honestly where his understanding ceases. The poet draws these adventurous persons imperatively into the clear light of our day; he fills their being with warm life; he endows them with modern speech, with a good share of reason and of the culture of our times; and he forgets that the action in which he has them move, is taken from a former age and can not be so much transformed, and that it accords extremely ill with the higher human endowments given his characters.

The historical materials from the dim past, and from the little known periods of our national existence, allure our young poets, as once the epic materials allured Euripides: they mislead to the spectacular, as the epic did to declamation. Now their figures are not for this reason to be laid aside as useless ; but the poet will ask whether the transformation which he is bound to undertake with every character of former times, is not possibly so great that all similarity to the historical person disappears, and whether the irrepressible presumptions of the action are not inconsistent with his free creation of character. This will certainly be sometimes the case.

Not less worthy of note is the conflict which the poet must wage in his rôles, with what as nature, he has to idealize. His task is to give greater expression to greater passion; as an adjunct in this, he has the actor, — the passionate emphasis of the voice, of figure, of pantomime, of gesture. Despite all this abundant means, he may almost never, and just in the more exalted moments of passion, use the corresponding appearances of real life without great changes, however strongly and beautifully and effectively, in powerful natures, a natural passion expresses itself, and however great an impression it may make on the accidental observer. On the stage, the appearance is to have its effect in the distance. Even in a little theater, a comparatively large auditorium is to be filled with the expression of passion. Just the finest accents, but of real feeling in the voice, glance, even in carriage, are, on account of the distance, not at all so distinct to the audience and enchanting as they are in real life. And further, it is the task of the drama to make such laboring of passion intelligible and impressive at every moment; for it is not the passion itself which produces the effect, but the dramatic portrayal of it by means of speech and action; it must always be the endeavor of the characters on the stage to turn their inward being toward the spectator. The poet must then make choice for effects. The transient thoughts that flit through the mind of the impassioned one, conclusions arrived at with the rapidity of lightning, the varying emotions of the soul in great numbers, which now less distinctly, now more animatedly, come into view,—to all these in their disordered fulness, their rapid course, art can not often afford even imperfect expression. For every idea, for every strong emotion, there is needed a certain number of words and gestures; their union by means of transition or sharp contrast demands a purposed play; every single moment presents itself more broadly, a careful progressive rise must take place,—in order that the highest effect be attained. Thus dramatic art must constantly listen to nature, but must by no means copy; nay, it must mingle with the single features which nature affords, something else that nature does not offer, and this as well in the speeches as in the acting. For poetic composition, one of the most ready helps is the wit of comparison, the color of the picture. This oldest ornament of speech comes by natural necessity, everywhere, into the discourse of men, where the soul, in a lofty mood freely raises her wing. To the inspired orator, as to the poet, to every people, to every civilization, comparison and imagery are the immediate expressions of excited feeling, of powerful, spirited creation. But now it is the duty of the poet to represent with the greatest freedom and elevation the greatest embarrassment of his persons in their passions. It will also be inevitable that his characters, even in the moments of highest passion, evince far more of this inward creative power of speech, of unrestrained power and mastery of language, expression, and gesture, than they ever do in natural circumstances. This freedom of soul is necessary to them, and the spectator demands it. And yet here lies the great danger to the poet, that his style may seem too artificial for the passion. Our greatest poets have often used poetic means and devices with such lavishness in moments of intense passion, as to offend good taste. It is well known that Shakespeare yields too often to the inclination of his time, and in his pathetic passages makes use of mythological comparisons and splendid imagery; on this account, there often appears in the language of his characters a bombast which we have to forget in the multitude of beautiful significant features, idealized from nature. The great poets stand nearer German culture; but even in their works, — among others Schiller's, — a fine rhetoric intrudes upon pathos, which is not propitious to an unbiased apprehension.

If in every expression of passion, there is perceptible a contradiction between nature and art, this occurs most in the case of the most secret and genuine feelings. Here again, the love scene must be once more recalled. In real life, the expression of this sweet passion which presses from one soul to another, is so tender, is in so few words, is so modest, that in art it brings one into despair. A quick gleam from the eye, a soft tone of the voice, may express more to the loved one than all speech. Just the immediate expression of tender feeling needs words only as an accessory; the moments of the so-called declaration of love, frequently almost without words and with action scarcely visible, will escape the notice of one standing at a distance. Only through numerous devices can the highest skill of the poet and the actor replace for the spectator the eloquent silence and the beautiful secret vibrations of passion. Right here, indeed, poets and actors must use an abundance of speech and action which is improbable in nature. The actor may, of course, enhance and supplement the language of the poet, through tone and gesture; but that he secure these enhancing effects, the language of the poet must lead him, and to a high degree in conformity with a purpose, furnish the motive for the effects of the actor's art; and therefore the actor requires also the creative activity of the poet, which gives, not an imitation of reality, but something quite different,— the artistic.

In the face of these difficulties which the expression of higher passion offers, if one dared to advise the poet, the best advice would be, to remain as exact and true to life as his talents would allow, to compress the single moments to a strong climax, and to expand as little as possible the embellishments of reflection, comparison, imagery. For while these give fulness to the lines, they too easily cover up desultoriness and poverty of invention. If everywhere, constant and exact observation of nature is indispensable to the dramatic poet, it is most indispensable in the delineation of violent emotion; but the poet must know most surely that he is here least of all to imitate nature.

Another difficulty arises for the poet through the inner contrast into which his art of creation comes, with the art of his colleague, the actor. The poet does not perceive the perturbations of his characters as the reader perceives the words of the drama, nor as the actor apprehends his rôle. Character, scene, every force, is presented to him in the mighty rapture of creation, in such a way that the significance of each for the whole is perfectly clear; while all that has gone before, all that comes after, vibrate as if in a gentle harmony in his mind. What reveals the real life of his characters, what holds spellbound in the action, the effect of the scenes,— he perceives as alluring, and powerfully so, perhaps, long before they have found expression in words.

The expression which he creates for them, often gives back but imperfectly to his own apprehension, the beauty and might with which they were endowed in his mind. While he is concerned in embodying in words the spiritual essence of his persons, and in creating for them an outward form, the effect of the words which he writes being only imperfectly clear, he accustoms himself but gradually to their sound; moreover, the enclosed space of the stage, the external appearance of his persons, the effect of a gesture, of a tone of voice, he feels only incidentally, now more, now less distinctly. On the whole, he who creates through speech, stands nearer to the demands of the reader or the hearer, than to the demands of the actor, especially if he himself is not proficient in the actor's art. The effects which he produces, then, correspond now more to the requirements of the reader, now more to those of the actor.

But the poet of greater feeling and perception must give a full and strong impression through speech; and the effects which one soul produces on another are brought about thus: its internal power breaks forth in a number of speech-waves, which rise higher and mightier, and beat upon the receptive mind. This demands a certain time, and with briefer, or more powerful treatment, a certain breadth of elaboration. The actor, on the other hand, with his art, requires the stream of convincing, seductive speech. Indeed, he needs the strong expression of passion, not always through speech.

His aim is to attain something through other means, the effectiveness of which the poet does not apprehend so clearly. By means of a gesture of fright, of hatred, of contempt, he may often express more than the poet can with the most effective words. Impatient, he will always feel the temptation to make use of the best means of his own art. The laws of stage effects are for him and the audience sometimes different from those which are found in the soul of the creating poet. In the struggle of passion, a word, a glance, is often specially adapted to bring out the strongest pantomime effects for the actor; all the subsequent mental processes expressed in his speech, however poetically true in themselves, will appear to him and to his audience only as a lengthening. In this way, much is unnecessary in acting which is fully justified in writing and reading.

That the actor, for his part, has the task of carefully following the poet, and as much as possible working out the poet's purposed effects, even with self-renunciation, is a matter of course. But not seldom his right is greater than that of the poet's lines, for the reason that his equipment, voice, invention, technique, even his nerves, place restrictions upon him which the poet does not find cogent. But with this right which the actor has, in view of his labor, the poet will have the more difficulties to overcome the further he keeps aloof from the stage, and the less distinct to him in single moments of his creative activity is his stage-picture of the characters. He will also be obliged to make clear to himself through observation and reflection, how he may plan and present his characters rightly to the actor for the best stage effects. He must not, however, always conform to the actor's art. And since it is his duty, at his desk, to be as much as possible the guardian of the histrionic artist, he must study most earnestly the essential laws of histrionic art.

III.

MINOR RULES.

The same laws which have been enumerated for the action, apply also to the characters of the stage. These, too, must possess dramatic unity, probability, importance and magnitude, and be fitted for a strong and progressive expression of dramatic life.

The persons of the drama must exhibit only that side of human nature, by which the action is advanced and given motive. No miser, no hypocrite, is always miserly, always hypocritical; no scoundrel betrays his degraded soul in every act he performs; no one always acts consistently; the thoughts which contend with each other in the human mind, are of infinite variety; the directions in which spirit, mind, volition, express themselves, are infinitely different. But the drama, like every form of art, has no right to select with freedom from the sum of all the things which characterize a man's life, and combine them; only what serves the idea and the action belongs to art. But only such selected impulses in the character as belong together and are easily intelligible, will serve the action. Richard III. of England was a bloody and unscrupulous despot; but he was not such always nor toward everyone; he was, besides, a politic prince; and it is possible, according to history, that his reign appears, in some directions, a blessing to England. If a poet sets himself the task of showing the bloody rigor and falseness of a highly endowed, misanthropic hero-nature, embodied in this character, it is understood that the traits of moderation and perhaps of benevolence, which are found to some extent in the life of this prince, the poet dare accept, only so far as they support the fundamental trait of character needed for this idea. And as the number of characterizing moments which he can introduce at all, is, in proportion to the reality, exceedingly small, every individual trait bears an entirely different relation to the aggregate than it bears in reality. But whatever is necessary in the chief figures is of value in the accessory figures. It is understood that the texture of their souls must be so much the more easily understood, the less the space which the poet has left for them. The dramatic poet will scarcely commit great mistakes in this. Even to unskilled talent, the one side from which it has to illuminate its figures, is accustomed to be very distinct.

The first law, that of unity, admits of still another application to the characters: The drama must have only one chief hero, about whom all the persons, however great their number, arrange themselves in different gradations. The drama has a thoroughly monarchic arrangement; the unity of its action is essentially dependent on this, that the action is perfected about one dominant character. But also for a sure effect, the first condition is that the interest of the spectator must be directed mostly toward one person, and he must learn as early as possible who is to occupy his attention before all other characters. Since the highest dramatic processes of but few persons can be exhibited in broad elaboration, the number of great rôles is limited to a few; and it is a common experience that nothing is more painful to the hearer than the uncertainty as to what interest he should give to each of these important persons. It is also one practical advantage of the piece to direct its effects toward a single middle point.

Whoever deviates from this fundamental law must do so with the keen perception that he surrenders a great advantage; and if his subject matter makes this surrender necessary, he must, in doubt, ask himself whether the uncertainty thus arising in the effects, will be counterbalanced by other dramatic advantages.

Our drama has for a long time entertained one exception. Where the relations of two lovers form the essentials of an action, these persons, bound by spiritual ties, are looked upon as enjoying equal privileges, and are conceived as a unit. Thus in *Romeo and Juliet*, *Love and Intrigue*, *The Piccolomini*, also in

Troilus and Cressida. But even in this case, the poet will do well to accord to one of the two the chief part in the action; and where this is not possible, he should base the inner development of the two upon corresponding motives. In Shakespeare, Romeo is the leading character in the first half of the play; in the second half, Juliet leads. In *Antony and Cleopatra*, Antony is the leading character up to his death.

But while in Shakespeare, Lessing, Goethe, the chief hero is unmistakable, Schiller, not to the advantage of his construction, has a peculiar inclination toward double heroes; this appears as early as *The Robbers;* and in his later years, after his acquaintance with the ancient drama, they become still more striking,—Carlos and Posa; Mary and Elizabeth; the hostile brothers, Max and Wallenstein; Tell, the Swiss, and Rudenz. This inclination is easily explained. Schiller's pathetic strain had only been strengthened by his acquaintance with Greek tragedy; not seldom in his dramas, it comes into contradiction with a greater poetic quality, dramatic energy. So under his hand, there were disjoined two tendencies of his own nature, which were transferred to two separate persons, one of whom received the pathetic part, the other the leading part of the action, the second sometimes also receiving a share in the pathos. How this division rendered less prominent the first hero, who was the pathetic character, has already been explained.

Another error the poet finds it more difficult to

avoid. The share of the persons in the advancement of the action must be so arranged that what they do shall have its logical basis in an easily understood trait of character, and not in a subtlety of judgment, or in a peculiarity which seems accidental. Above all, a decided advancement of the action must not proceed from the marvellous in a character, which has no motive, or from such weaknesses as in the eyes of our observant audiences lessen the enrapturing impression. Thus the catastrophe in *Emilia Galotti*, is, according to our notion, no longer tragic in a high degree, because from Emilia and her father, we demand a more virile courage. That the daughter fears being debauched, and the father, instead of seeking an escape from the castle for himself and his daughter, dagger in hand, despairs because the reputation of the daughter is already injured by the abduction,—this wounds our sensibilities, however beautifully the character of Odoardo is fashioned for this catastrophe. In Lessing's time, the ideas of the public regarding the power and arbitrariness of royal rulers were so vivid, that the situation had a far different effect than it has now. And yet with such assumptions, he could have motived the murder of the daughter more powerfully. The spectator must be thoroughly convinced that any escape for the Galotti from the castle, is impossible. The father must seek it with the last accession of power, he must thwart the prince by violence. For there remains still the greater disadvantage, that it was much more to Odoardo's advantage to kill the rascally prince, than his own innocent daughter. That would have been more according to custom, and humanly truer. Of course this tragedy could not bear such an ending. And this is an evidence that what is worthy of consideration in the piece, lies deeper than the catastrophe. The German atmosphere in which the strong spirit of Lessing struggled, still renders the creation of great tragic effect difficult. The brave Germans, like noble Romans of the imperial time, thought, "Death makes free?"[73]

When it is unavoidable to represent the hero, in an essential respect shortsighted and limited in the face of his surroundings, the oppressive burden must be lightened by the complementary side of his personality, which turns toward him an increased degree of respect and sympathy. This is successfully done in *Goetz von Berlichingen* and *Wallenstein*; it was tried, but did not succeed in *Egmont*.

The Greek author of *The Poetics* prescribed that the characters of the heroes, in order to awaken interest must be composed of good and evil; the law is still valid to-day, and applicable to the changed conditions of our stage. The figures, and all the material from which the German stage makes, preferably, its poetical characters, are from real life. Where the poet deems figures from legend worthy of use, he attempts more or less successfully to endow them with a more liberal humanity and a richer life, which invites to the idealization of historical characters or persons in the real world. And the poet will be able to use every character for his drama, that makes the representation of strong dramatic processes possible. Absolute and unchangeable goodness or evil are hereby excluded for chief characters. Art, in itself, lays no further restriction upon him; for a character which allows the most powerfully dramatic processes to be richly represented in itself, will be an artistic picture, whatever may be its relation to the moral import, or to the social views of the hearer.

The choice of the poet is also limited, especially through his own manly character, taste, morality, habits, and also through his regard for the ideal listener,—the public. It must be of great consequence to him, to inspire his audience with admiration for his hero, and to change his audience to fellow players, following the variations and mental processes which he brings to view. In order to maintain this sympathy, he is compelled to choose personages which not only enrapture by the importance, magnitude, and power of their characters, but win to themselves the sentiment and taste of the audience.

The poet must also understand the secret of ennobling and beautifying for his contemporaries the frightful, horrible, the base and repulsive in a character, by means of the combination which he gives it. The question for the German stage, how much dare the poet venture, is no longer doubtful since Shakespeare's time. The magic of his creative power works, perhaps, on everyone who himself attempts to poetize, most powerfully through the completeness which he gave to his villains. Richard III. and Iago are models, showing how beautifully the poet can fashion malevolence and wickedness. The strong vital energy, and the ironical freedom in which they play with life, attaches to them a most significant element which compels an unwilling admiration. Both are scoundrels with no addition of a qualifying circumstance. But in the self-consciousness of superior natures, they control those about them with an almost superhuman power and security. On close inspection, they appear to be very differently constituted. Richard is the son of a wild time full of terror, where duty passed for naught, and ambition ventured everything. The incongruity between an iron spirit and a deformed body, became for him the foundation of a cold misanthropy. He is a practical man, and a prince, who does only such evil as is useful to him, and is merciless with a wild caprice. Iago is far more a devil. It is his joy to act wickedly; he perpetrates wickedness with most sincere delight. He gives to himself and to others as his motive for destroying the Moor, that Othello has preferred another officer to him, and has been intimate with his wife. All this is untrue; and so far as it contains any truth, it is not the ultimate ground of his treachery. His chief tendency is the ardent desire of a creative power to make attacks, to stir up quarrels, especially for his own use and advantage. He was more difficult, therefore, to be made worthy of the drama than was the prince, the general, to whom environment, and his great purpose gave a certain importance and greatness; and therefore Shakespeare endowed him more copiously with humor, the beautifying mood of the soul, which has the single advantage of throwing upon even the hateful and low a charming light.

The basis of humor is the unrestricted freedom of a well-endowed mind, which displays its superior power to those about it in sportive caprice. The epic poet who in his own breast, bears inclination and disposition for these effects, may exhibit them in a twofold manner in the creatures of his art: he can make these humorists, or he can exercise his own humor on them. The tragic poet, who speaks only through his heroes, may of course, do only the first, because he communicates his humor to them. This modern intellectual inclination continually produces on the hearer a mighty, at the same time an enchanting and a liberating influence. For the serious drama, its employment has a difficulty. The conditions of humor are intellectual liberty, quiet, deliberation; the condition of the dramatic hero is embarrassment, storm, strong excitement. The secure and comfortable playing with events is unfavorable to the advance of an excited action; it almost inevitably draws out into a situation the scene into which it intrudes. Where, therefore, humor enters with a chief character, in order that this character may be raised above others, it must have other characteristics which prevent it from quietly delaying. It must have strong impelling force, and beyond this, a powerfully forward-moving action.

Now, it is possible so to guide the humor of the drama that it does not exclude violent commotions of the soul, so that an unobstructed view of one's own and another's fate is enhanced, through a corresponding capability of the character to express greater passion. But this is not to be learned.

And the union of a profound intellect with the confidence of a secure power and with superior fancy, is a gift which has hardly been conferred upon an author of serious dramas in Germany. When one receives such a gift, he uses it without care, without pains, with certainty; he makes himself laws, and rules, and compels his admiring contemporaries to follow him. He who has not this gift strives for it in vain, and tries in vain to paint into his scenes something of that embellishing brilliancy with which genius floods everything.

It was explained above, how in our drama, the characters must give motive to the progress of the action, and how the fate which rules them must not be anything else than the course of events brought about by the personality of these characters,—a course which must be conceived every moment by the hearer as reasonable and probable, however surprising individual moments may come to him. Right here the poet evinces his power if he knows how to fashion his characters deep and great, and conduct his action with elevated thought, and if he does not offer as a beautiful invention what lies upon the beaten track of ordinary understanding, and what is next to a shallow judgment. And with a purpose, it may be emphatically repeated, that every drama must be a firmly connected structure in which the connection between cause and effect form the iron clasps, and that what is irrational can, as such, have no important place at all in the modern drama.

But now mention must be made of an accessory motive for the advancement of the action, a motive which was not mentioned in the former section. In individual cases, the characters may receive as a fellow-player, a shadow, which is not gladly welcomed on our stage—the mischance. When what is being developed has been, in its essentials, grounded in the impelling personality of the characters, then it may become comprehensible that in the action, a single man is not able to guide with certainty the connection of events. When in *King Lear*, the villain, Edmund; when in *Antigone*, the despot, Creon, recall the death sentences which they have pronounced, it appears as an accident that these same sentences have been executed so quickly and in such an unexpected manner. When in *Wallenstein*, the hero will abrogate the treaty which he has concluded with Wrangel, it is strongly emphasized with what incomprehensible suddenness the Swede has disappeared. When in *Romeo and Juliet*, the news of Juliet's death reaches Romeo before the message of Friar Laurence, the accident appears of decisive importance in the course of the piece. But this intrusion of a circumstance not counted upon, however striking it may be, is at bottom no motive forcing itself in from without; it is only the result of a characteristic deed of the hero.

The characters have caused a portentous decision to depend on a course of events which they can no longer govern. The trap had already fallen, which Edmund had set for the death of Cordelia; Creon had caused Antigone to be locked up in the burial vault; whether the defiant woman awaited starvation or chose a death for herself—of this he had no longer the direction; Wallenstein has given his fate into the hands of an enemy; that Wrangel had good grounds to make the resolve of the waverer irrevocable, was evident. Romeo and Juliet have come into the condition, that the possibility of their saving their lives depends on a frightful, criminal, and extremely venturesome measure, which the priest had thought of in his anguish. In this and similar cases, the accident enters only because the characters under overpowering pressure have already lost the power of choice. For the poet and his piece, it is no longer accident, that is, not something extraneous which bursts asunder the joints of the action; but it is a motive like every other, deduced from the peculiarities of the characters; in its ultimate analysis, it is a necessary consequence of preceding events. This not ineffective means is to be used with prudence, and is to be grounded in the nature of the characters and in the actual situation.

For guiding the characters through individual acts, a few technical rules are to be observed, as has already been said. They will be brought forward, in this place, briefly, once more. Every single person of the drama is to show the fundamental traits of his character, as distinctly, as quickly, and as attractively as possible; and where an artistic effect lies in a concealed play of single rôles, the audience must be, to a certain extent, the confidant of the poet. The later a new characteristic trait enters the action, the more carefully must the motive for it be laid in the beginning, in order that the spectator may enjoy to the full extent the pleasure of the surprise, and perceive that it corresponds exactly to the constitution of the character.

Brief touches are the rule, where the chief characters have to present themselves at the beginning of the play. As a matter of course, the significant single characteristics are not to be introduced in an anecdotal manner, but to be interwoven with the action,— except that little episodes, or a modest painting of a situation, are thus allowed. The scenes at the beginning, which give color to the piece, which prepare the moods, must also at the same time present the ground texture of the hero. Shakespeare manages this with wonderful skill. Before his heroes are entangled in the difficulties of a tragic action, he likes to let them, while still unembarrassed in the introduction scenes, express the trend of their character most distinctly and characteristically; Hamlet, Othello, Romeo, Brutus, Richard III., illustrate.

It is not an accident that Goethe's heroes,—Faust, both parts, Iphigenia, even Götz,—are introduced in soliloquy, or in quiet conversation like Tasso, Clavigo. Egmont enters first in the second act. Lessing follows the old custom of his stage, of introducing his heroes by means of their intimates; but Schiller again lays great stress on the characteristic representation of unembarrassed heroes. In the trilogy of *Wallenstein*, the nature of the hero is first presented in rich mirrorings in *The Camp*, and in the first act of *The Piccolomini;* but Wallenstein himself appears, introduced by the astrologer, in the circle of his family and friends, out of which during the entire play, he is seldom removed.

It has already been said that new rôles in the second half of the drama, the return action, require a peculiar treatment. The spectator is inclined to consider with mistrust the leading of the rôles through new persons. The poet must take care not to distract or make impatient. Therefore the characters of the second part require a richer endowment, attractive presentation, most effective detailed delineation, in compact treatment. Excellent examples of elaboration are, besides those already named, Deveroux and Macdonald in *Wallenstein*, while Buttler, in the same piece, serves as model of a character whose active participation is saved for the last part,—not towed as a dead weight through the first, but interwoven with its internal changes.

Finally, the unpracticed playwright must take care, when it is necessary to have another person talk about his hero, to attach no great value to such exposition of the character; and will only, when it is entirely to the purpose, allow the hero to express a judgment concerning himself; but all that others say of a person, or what he says of himself, has little weight in comparison with what is seen coming into being, growing in counter-play with others, in the connections of the action. Indeed, the effect may be fatal if the zealous poet commends his heroes as sublime, as joyous, as shrewd, while in the piece, in spite of the poet's wish, it is not accorded them to show these qualities.

The conducting of characters through the scenes must occur with strict regard to the tableaux, or grouping, and the demands of scenic representation. For even in the conducting of a scene, the actor, as opposed to the poet, makes his demands prevail, and the poet does well to heed them. He stands in a delicate relation with his actor, which places obligations on both sides. In the essential thing, the aim of both is the same. Both exercise their creative power upon the same material; the poet as a silent guide, the actor as an executive power. And the poet will soon learn that the German actor, on the whole, adapts himself with a ready fervor and zeal to the effects of the poet, and seldom burdens him with claims, through which he thinks to place his own art in the foreground to the disadvantage of the poetry. Since, indeed, the individual actor has in his eye the effects of his rôle, and the poet thinks of the aggregate effect, in many cases there may be in the rehearsal of the piece, a division of interests. The poet will not always accord to his associate the better right,— if it is necessary to temper an effect, or to suppress a single character in single moments of an action. Experience teaches that the actor, in such a contradiction of the conceptions on either side, readily falls into line as soon as he receives the notion that the poet understands his own art. For the artist is accustomed to labor as a participant in a greater whole, and when he will give attention, right well perceives the highest demands of the piece. The claims which he puts forward with right,— good rôles, strong effects, economy of his strength, a convenient arrangement of scenes,— must be as much a matter of concern to the poet as to him.

These requirements may be traced back to two great principles, to the proposition which may be stated: The stage effect must be clear to the poet while he is composing; and to the short but very imperative proposition: The poet must know how to create great dramatic effects for his characters. In every individual scene, specially in scenes where groups appear, the poet must keep well in mind the general appearance of the stage; he must perceive with distinctness the positions of the persons, their movements toward and away from each other as they occur gradually on the stage. If more frequently than the character and the dignity of the rôle allow, he compels the actor to turn toward this or the other person, in order to facilitate subordinate rôles, or correct them; if he delays the motive, the transitions from one arrangement into another, from one side of the stage to another, as he presumes it to come at a later moment of the scene; if he forces the actor into a position which does not allow him to complete his movements unrestrained and effectively, or to come into the proposed combination with a fellow actor; if he does not remember which of his rôles every time begins the play, and which continues it; further, if he leaves one of the chief characters unoccupied for a long time on the stage, or if he attributes too much to the power of the actor,—the final result of this and similar difficulties is a representation too weak and fragmentary of the course on the stage, of the dramatic action which the poet may have perceived clear and effective in its course through his mind. In all such cases, the claims of the actor must be respected. And the poet will also, on this ground, give special attention to the claims of stage custom. For this, there is no better means of learning than to go with an actor through a new rôle which is to be practiced, and carefully watch the rehearsal under a competent stage director.

The old requirement that a poet must adapt his characters to the special line of work of the actors, appears more awkward than it really is. Well established principles once current for the government of chief rôles, have been abandoned by our stage; having once received an artist into the circle of prescriptions and prohibitions, they made it impossible for an "intriguer" to play a rôle outside of the first rank; and they separated the *bon-vivant* from the "youthful hero," by a wide chasm, almost impassable. Meantime, there remains so much of the custom as is useful for the actor and the stage director, in order to draw individual talent towards its special province, and to facilitate the setting of new rôles. Every actor rejoices in a certain stock of dramatic means which he has developed within his branch: the quality of his voice, accent of speech, physical bearing, postures, control of facial muscles. Within his accustomed limits, he moves with comparative security; beyond them, he is uncertain. If now the poet lays claim to the accustomed readiness of different specialties in the same rôle, the setting will be difficult, and the result, perhaps, doubtful. There is, for instance, an Italian party-leader of the fifteenth century, as to outsiders, sharp, sly, concealed, an unscrupulous scoundrel; in his family, warm in feeling, dignified, honored and honorable,—no improbable mixture;—his image on the stage would strike one very differently, when the character player or the older and dignified hero father represented him; probably in any setting, the one side of his nature would fall short.

This is no infrequent case. The advantage of

correct setting according to special capability of actors, the dangers of an inappropriate setting, can be observed in witnessing any new piece. The poet will never allow himself to be guided by such a prudent respect for the greater sureness of his results, when the formation of an unusual stage character is of importance to him. He is only to know what is most convenient for himself and his actors.

And when at last it is required of the poet that he fashion his characters effectively for the actor, this claim contains the highest requirement which can be placed upon the dramatic poet. To create effectively for the actor, means, indeed, nothing else than to create dramatically, in the best sense of the word. Body and soul, the actor is prepared to transform himself into conscious, creative activity, in order to body forth the most secret thought, feeling, sentiment, of will and deed. Let the poet see to it that he knows how to use worthily and perfectly this mighty stock of means for his artistic effects. And the secret of his art, — the first thing given a place in these pages and the last, — is only this: Let him delineate exactly and truly, even to details, however strongly feeling breaks forth from the private life as desire and deed, and however strong impressions are made from without upon the soul of the hero. Let him describe this with poetic fulness, from a soul which sees exactly, sharply, comprehensively, each single moment of the process, and finds special joy in portraying it in beautiful single traits. Let him thus labor, and he will set his actors the greatest tasks, and will worthily and completely make use of their noblest powers.

Again it must be said, no technique teaches how one must begin, in order to write in this way.

CHAPTER V.

VERSE AND COLOR.

The century in which the romance has become the prevailing species of poetry, will no longer consider verse an indispensable element of poetics. There are many dramas of a high order, favorite pieces upon our stage, composed in prose. At least in dramatic subjects from modern times, it is claimed, prose is the most appropriate expression of such thoughts and sentiments as can be placed on the stage, from a well-known real life. But the serious drama hardly concludes to abandon the advantages which verse affords, in order to win those of prose.

It is true, prose flows along more rapidly, more easily, indeed, in many respects more dramatically. It is easier in it, to discriminate the different characters; it offers, from the construction of the sentence to the qualities of voice and tones, the greatest wealth of colors and shades; everything is less constrained; it adapts itself quickly to every frame of mind; it can give to light prattle or to humorous delight a spirit which is very difficult to verse; it admits of greater disquiet, stronger contrasts, more violent movement. But these advantages are fully counterbalanced by the exalted mood of the hearer which verse produces and maintains. While prose easily incurs the risk of reducing the work of art to copies of ordinary reality, speech in verse elevates the nature of the characters into the noble. Every moment the perception and feeling of the hearer are kept alive to the fact that he is in the presence of a work of art which bears him away from reality, and sets him in another world, the relations of which the human mind has ordered with perfect freedom. Moreover, the limitation which is placed on logical discussion, and sometimes on the brevity and incisiveness of expression, is no very perceptible loss. To poetical representation, the sharpness and fineness of proof-processes are not so important as the operation on the mind, as the brilliance of imaginative expression, of simile and antithesis, which verse favors. In the rhythmic ring of the verse, feeling and vision raised above reality, float as if transfigured, in the hearer's soul; and it must be said that these advantages can be very serviceable, specially to subjects from modern times; for in these, the exaltation above the common frame of mind of every-day life, is most necessary. How this can be done, not only *The Prince of Homburg* shows, but the treatment which Goethe gave the undramatic material of *The Natural Daughter*, though the verse of this drama is not written conveniently for the actor.

The iambic pentameter has been our established verse since Goethe and Schiller. A preponderating trochaic accent of German words makes this verse peculiarly convenient. Of course, it is rather brief in relation to the little logical units of the sentence, the coupling of which in pairs makes up the essence of the verse-line. In its ten or eleven syllables, we cannot compress the fulness of meaning which it has, for example, in the terse English speech; and the poet thus inclined toward a rich, sonorous expression, falls easily into the temptation of extending part of a sentence into a line and a half or two lines, which it would be better to extend in an uninterrupted, and thus finer flow of words. But the pentameter has the advantage of the greatest possible fluency and flexibility; it can adapt itself more than any other kind of verse to changing moods, and follow every variation of the soul in time and movement.

The remaining kinds of verse which have been used in the drama, suffer the disadvantage of having too marked a peculiarity of sound, and more than a little limit characterization by speech, which is necessary to the drama.

The German trochaic tetrameter, which among many other measures for instance, Immermann used effectively in the catastrophe of his *Alexis*, flows like all trochaic verse, too uniformly with the natural accent of our language. The sharp time-beats which its feet make in the speech, and the long elevated course, give to it in the German language, a restlessness, a surging, a dark tone-color which would be appropriate only for high tragic moods. The iambic hexameter, the cæsura of which stands in the middle of the third foot, the tragic measure of the Greeks, has, so far, been used but little in Germany. From its translations from the Greek, it acquired the reputation of stiffness and rigidity which do not essentially belong to it; it has a vigorous movement and is capable of many variations. Its sonorousness is majestic, and full for rich expression which moves forward in long undulations, and is splendidly adapted to its use. It has only this disadvantage, that its chief division, which even in the drama must be made after the fifth syllable, gives to the parts of the verse very uneven length. Against five syllables stand seven, or eight if there is a feminine ending. A second cæsura intrudes so easily into the second half verse, that the line is divided into three parts. This aftertone of the longer half makes a masculine ending of the verse desirable; and the foretone of the masculine ending contributes to give weight, sometimes, hardness. The Alexandrine, an iambic hexameter, the cæsura of which lies after the third arsis, and divides the line into two equal parts, cuts the discourse too markedly in the German drama. In French, its effect is entirely different, because in this language the verse accent is much more covered and broken up in a greater number of ways, not only through the capricious and movable word accent, but through the free rhythmic swing of spoken discourse through a mingling and prolongation of words, which we cannot imitate; and this rests on a greater prominence of the element of sound, sonorousness, with which the creative power of the speaker knows how to play in an original manner. Finally, there is another iambic verse in the German, specially adapted to a vigorous movement, yet little used,—the hexameter of *The Nibelungen*, in the new language an iambic hexameter, the fourth foot of which may be not only an iambus, but an anapest, and always has the cæsura of the verse after the first thesis. What is characteristic and specially adapted to the German language, is the position of the cæsura so far along in the verse, which, deviating from all ancient measures, as a rule, shows a greater number of syllables in the first half. If the verses of this measure are not joined in strophes, but are used with slight variations in construction as continuous long verses, with a line frequently passing over into the next as a single sentence, then this measure is excellent and effective for the expression even of impassioned progress. It is possible that its nature, which, perhaps, corresponds best to the rhythmic relations of the German language, avails for animated narrative, and wins some significance for one species of comedy. To the elevated drama, rhyme, which in this measure, two long verses cannot dispense with as a connecting element, will always seem too harmonious and sportive, however well it may be modified through a rapid transition of voice, from one line to another.

For the modern drama, further, likeness of tone-color and uniformity of measure is indispensable. Our speech, and the receptivity of the hearer are, so far as the relations of sound are concerned, little developed. The differences in the sounds of the verses are conceived more as disturbing interruptions than as stimulating aids. But further, interest in the intellectual import of the discourse and in the dramatic movement of the characters, has come to the front to such an extent, that even for this reason, every verse unit which, in its contrast with what has preceded, calls attention to itself, will be counted a distraction.

This is also the ground that should easily exclude prose passages from between poetic passages in our drama; for by means of them, the contrast in color becomes still stronger. Inserted prose always gives to scenes something of the barren imitation of reality; and this disadvantage is increased, because prose serves the poet as a means of expressing moods for which the dignified sonorousness of verse appears too excellent.

The iambic pentameter has a fluency for the German poet, whose soul has accustomed itself in its soarings, to think and feel most easily during the process of composition. But its being made the vehicle of dramatic expression is still difficult for the German poet, and the poets are not numerous who have perfectly succeeded in it. And so distinctly this verse expresses the poet's quality, which is here called dramatic, that the reader of a new piece is able to perceive from a few verses of animated dialogue, whether this dramatic power of the poet is developed or not. Of course, it is always much easier for the Germans to feel the possibly dramatic than to express this inner life in a becoming manner in verse.

Before iambic verse is available for the stage, the poet must be in a position to make it correct, euphonious, and without too great effort; chief cæsura and secondary cæsura, arsis, thesis, masculine endings, feminine endings, must come out according to well-known laws, regularly and in pleasing variations.

If the poet has gained the technique of versification and succeeded in writing musical verse with pleasing flow and pithy substance, his verse is certainly not right undramatic; and the more difficult labor begins. Now the poet must acquire another art of rhythmic feeling, which shall occasion, in place of regularity, to place apparent irregularities, to disturb the uniform flow in manifold ways, which means, to imbue with strong dramatic life.

Previously it was said, that in French, the Alexandrine was animated and varied by the introduction of irregular modulations and cadences. The dramatic speech of the Germans does not allow the actors, like the French, unlimited play with words, through a rapidly changing rate of utterance, sharp accent, through a prolongation or tossing of the sounds, which proceed almost independently of their meaning, when representing single words. On the other hand, there is given to the German in an unusual degree, the capability of expressing the movements of his mind, in the structure of his verse, through the connecting and separating of sentences, through bringing into relief, or transposing single words. The rhythmic movement of the excited soul comes more into relief among the Germans, in the logical connection and division of sentences, than among the Latin races in the sonorous swing of their recitation.

In the iambus of the drama, this life enters by interrupting the symmetrical structure of the verse, checking it, turning it this way and that into the infinite shadings which are produced by the movements of the characters. The verse must accommodate itself obediently to every mood of the soul; it must seek to correspond to each, not only through its rhythm but through the logical connection of sentences which it combines. For quiet feeling and fine mental action, which move forward in repose and dignity or with vivid animation, he must use his purest form, his most beautiful euphony, and even flow of eloquence. In Goethe, the dramatic iambus glides thus in quiet beauty. If feeling rises higher, if the more excited mood flows out in more adorned, long-breathed lines, then the verse must rush in long waves, now dying out in preponderating feminine endings, now terminating more frequently in powerful masculine endings. This is, as a rule, Schiller's verse. The excitement becomes stronger; single waves of speech break over one verse, and fill a part of the next; then short impulses of passion throng and break up the form of single verses; but above all this eddying, the rhythmic current of a longer passage is quietly and steadily moving. So in Lessing. But the expression of excitement becomes stormier and wilder; the rhythmic course of the verse seems wholly disordered; now and again a sentence from the end of one verse rings over into the beginning of the next; here and there a part of a verse is torn from its connections, and attached to what has preceded or what follows; speech and counter-speech break the grammatical connections; the first word of a sentence, and the last,—two important places,—are separated from others and become independent members of a sentence; the verse remains imperfect; instead of the quiet restful alternations of strong and weak endings, there is a long series of verses with the masculine ending; the cæsura is hardly to be recognized; even in those unaccented syllables or groups, over which, in the regular course, the rhythm would flow swiftly, massive, heavy words throng together, and the parts of the verse tumble against each other as in chaos. This is the dramatic verse, as it produces the most powerful effects in the best passages of Kleist, in spite of all the poet's mannerisms; thus it whirls and eddies away more magnificently, more finished, in the passionate scenes of Shakespeare.

As soon as the poet has learned to use his verse in such a manner, he has imbued it with a dramatic life. But he must always keep in mind one dramatic rule: Dramatic verse is not to be read or recited quietly, but to be pronounced in character. For this purpose, it is necessary that the logical connection of sentences be made perfectly clear, through conjunctions and prepositions; and further, that the expression of sentiment correspond to the character of the speaker, not break off in unintelligible brevity, nor be prolonged to prolixity; finally, that uneuphonious combinations of sounds and indistinct words are to be carefully avoided. Spoken speech yields its thought, sometimes with more ease, sometimes with more difficulty. A dissonance which the reader hardly notices, when pronounced, distracts and offends in a marked degree. Every obscurity in the connection of sentences makes the actor and the hearer uncertain, and leads to false conceptions. But even for accurate expression in fine and spirited explication, the reader is more penetrating and receptive than the easily distracted and more busily occupied spectator. On the other hand, the actor may make many things clearer. The reader in a comparatively more quiet mood, follows the short sentences of a broken speech, the inner relations of which are not made plain by the usual particles of logical sentence sequences; but he follows with an effort which easily becomes exhaustion. To the actor, on the contrary, such passages are the most welcome as the foundation of his creative work. By means of an accent, a glance, a gesture, he knows how to render quickly intelligible to the hearer, the last connection, the omitted ideas necessary to completeness; and the soul which he puts into the words, the passion which streams forth from him, become a guide which fills out and completes for the hearer the import of the suppressed and fragmentary speech, and produces perhaps a powerful unity. It happens that in reading, long passages of verse give the impression of the artificial, of something vainly sought for; but this on the stage changes into a picture of intense passion. Now, it is possible that the actor has done his best with it; for his art is specially powerful where the poet has left a blank in the thought. But just so often the poetic art has the best right; and the fault is in the reader, because his power of following and thinking along with the poet, is not so active as it should be. It is easy to recognize this peculiarity of style in Lessing. The frequent interruptions in the discourse, the short sentences, the questions and chance remarks, the animated dialectic processes which his persons pass through, appear in reading as artificial unrest. But, with a few exceptions, they are so accurate, so profoundly conceived, that this poet, just on this account, is the favorite with actors. Still more striking is the same peculiarity in Kleist, but not always sound, and not always true. In the restlessness, feverishness, excitement of his language, the inner life of his characters, which struggles violently, sometimes helplessly for expression, finds its corresponding reflection.

But a useless interruption of the discourse is not

infrequent,—unnecessarily invented animation, purposeless questions, a misunderstanding that requires no explanation. For the most part, he has a practical purpose in this; he wishes to make very prominent individual ideas which appear of importance to him. But that seems to him important sometimes, which can really claim no significance; and the frequent recurrence of little leaps aside from the direct line of the action, disturb not only the reader but the hearer.

The effect of verse can be increased, in the German drama, by parallelisms, as well of single verses as of groups, especially in dialogue scenes; where proposition and denial come into sharp opposition, such a rotation of verses is an excellent means of indicating the contrast.

The expansion which the rhythmic sweep of the Greek drama had, the Germans cannot imitate. Owing to the character of our speech, we are in a position to set over against one another in our dramatic composition, every four verses as a unit, so that the hearer will distinctly perceive coincidence and contrast of accent. In a recitation, which makes the logical side less prominent, and brings out the euphony which allows the voice stronger variations, one may set a longer series of verses effectively over against another. If the Greeks, by means of their art in recitation, could combine ten trimeters into a unit, and in the reply to this, could repeat the same accent and cadence, there is nothing incomprehensible to us in it.

Possibly, in the older times of Greek tragedy, there were a number of recitation melodies, or refrains, which were specially invented for each piece, or were already known to the hearers, and which without elevating the speaking tones of the recitation to a song, bound a longer group of verses into a unit.

This method of delivery is not to be used by us. Even in using the customary rotation verses, which beat, one against one, two against two, three against three, a limit is set. For our kind of dramatic composition rebels against any artifice which restrains the movements of characters and their sentiments. The pleasure from the rhetoric of such counter-speeches is less than the danger that the truth of representation may be lessened by artistic limitation. The poet will, therefore, do well to modify this little effect, and take from it the severity and appearance of artificiality; this may be done by interspersing parallel propositions in verse, with irregularly placed verses.

In the soul of the poet, at the same time with the foundation of the characters and the beginnings of the action, the color begins to flash. This peculiar adjunct of every subject matter is more developed among us moderns than in earlier times; for historical culture has greatly enhanced our sense for, and interest in what deviates from our own life. Character and action are conceived by the poet in the peculiar circumstances which the time, the place, the relations of the civilization in the time of the real hero, his manner of speech and of dealing, his costume, and the forms of intercoürse,—have in contrast with our own time and life. Whatever of the original clings to the material of a play carries the poet back in his artistic work, to the speech of his hero, to his surroundings, even down to his costume, the scenery and stage properties. These peculiarities the poet idealizes. He perceives them as determined by the idea of the piece. A good color is an important matter. It works at the beginning of the piece, at once stimulating and enchanting to the hearer; it remains to the end a charming ingredient, which may sometimes serve to cover weaknesses in the action.

These embellishing colors do not develop in every poet with equal vividness; they do not come to light with the same energy in every subject. But they never entirely fail where characters and human circumstances are depicted. They are indispensable to the epic and the romance, as they are to the drama. Color is of the most importance in historical themes; it helps here to characterize the heroes. The dramatic character itself, must, in its feeling and its volition, have an import which brings it much nearer a cultured man of the present, than its original in reality corresponds to our conception of it. But it is the color which gracefully covers for the hearer the inner contradiction between the man in history and the hero in the drama; the hero and his action it clothes with the beautiful appearance of a strange being, alluring to the imagination.

The newer stage rightly takes pains, therefore,

to express in the costume which it gives to the actors, the time in which the piece is laid, the social position, and many peculiarities of the characters presented. We are now separated by about a century from the time when Cæsar came upon the German stage with dagger and wig, and Semiramis adorned her riding coat with much strange tinsel, and her hair with many jewels and striking trimmings, in order to give herself a foreign appearance. Now, on many prominent stages, imitation of historical costume has gone very far; but in the majority of cases, it remains far behind the demands which the audience, in its average historical knowledge, is justified in demanding with respect to scenic equipment. It is clear that it is not the duty of the stage to imitate antiquarian peculiarities; but it is just as clear that it must avoid shocking a multitude of its patrons by forcing its heroes into a costume which, perhaps, nowhere and never, certainly not in this century, was possible. If the poet must keep aloof the antiquarian enthusiasm of the over-zealous from the clothing of his heroes, because the unusual, the unaccustomed in accessory does not advance, but rather disorders his piece, he will oftener have occasion, in for instance, a Hohenstaufen drama, to forbid a Spanish mantle, and to refuse to put upon a Saxon emperor a glittering lead armor, which changes his Ottos and Henrys into gold-beetles, and proves by their intolerable brilliancy that they were never struck by a blow from a sword.

The same holds true with the scenery and stage properties. A rococo table in a scene from the fifteenth century, or a Greek pillared hall where King Romulus walks, have already been long painful to the spectator. In order to make such remissnesses difficult for individual directors and actors, the poet will do well, in pieces from ancient or remote times, to prescribe exactly upon a page devoted to that purpose, not only the scenic apparatus but the costumes.

But the most important means for his use in giving color to his piece, is the language. It is true, the iambus has a certain tone color and modifies the characteristic expression more than prose. But it admits of a great wealth of light and shade; it allows even to words a slight tint in dialect.

In subjects from remote times, a language must be invented, possessing a color corresponding to the period. This is a beautiful, delightful labor, which the creating poet must undertake right joyfully. This work will be most advanced by a careful reading of the written monuments received from the hero's time. This strange speech works suggestively on the mind of the poet, by its peculiar accents, its syntactical structure, its popular forms of expression. And with pen in hand, the poet arranges what appears useful to him for powerful expression,—striking imagery, telling comparison, proverbial dialect. Among every foreign people whose literature is accessible, such work is beneficial, and most advantageous with respect to any nation's own earlier times. Our language had in former periods, as the Sclavonic has still, a far greater proportion of figurative expressions, suggestive to the power of imagination. The sense of the words had not been evaporated through a long scientific labor; everywhere there attached to them something of the first mental expression, from the popular mind where they originated. The number of proverbs is large, as also is the number of terse forms and Biblical phrases, which the reflections of our time replace. Such ingredients the creating artist may hold firmly in mind; upon their melody his talent amplifies almost involuntarily, the ground tone and moods of the speech of the drama.

With such an inspection of the written works of old times, there remain connected with the poet, still others,—little traits of character, anecdotes, many striking things which may complete and illuminate his pictures.

What he has thus found, he must not use pedantically nor insert in his speeches like arabesques; each item may signify something to him; but the suggestion which he receives from it, is of highest value.

This mood which he has given his soul does not forsake him; even while he is conducting his hero through the scenes, it will suggest to him, not only the right kind of language, but the coöperation of persons, the way they behave toward each other, forms of intercourse, customs and usages of the time.

All this is true of the characters and their movements in the scenes. For at every point in the drama, in every sentiment, in every act, that which in the material of the play struck us as characteristic, clings to what is humanly exalted in the ideal figures as embellishing additions. It is seldom necessary to warn the poet that he is not to do too much with these colors toward scenic effects; for his highest task is, of course, to have his heroes speak our language of passion, and exhibit what is characteristic in them, in such vital expressions as are intelligible to every period, because, in every time they are possible and conceivable.

Thus the color of the piece is visible in the endowment of language, in the characters, in the details of the action. What the poet communicates to his play by color, is as little an imitation of reality, as his heroes are,—it is free creation. But this accessory helps so much the more to conjure up a picture in the imagination of the hearer, which has the beautiful appearance of historic truth, the more earnestly the poet has taken it upon himself to master the real circumstances of that old time, if he does not lack the power of reproducing what he perceived to be attractive.

CHAPTER VI.

THE POET AND HIS WORK.

Great is the wealth of beauty in the poetry of past peoples and times, specially in the century of our great poets who form the judgment and excite the imagination of the poet of the present. This immeasurable wealth of the products of art is perhaps the greatest blessing for a future in which the popular energy works most powerfully, taking up what has affinity for it and casting off what resists it. But during a time of weak rest of the national spirit, this inheritance was a disadvantage for the creative activity of the poets, because it favored a lack of distinctive style. Only a few years ago, in Germany, it was almost an accident whether an Athenian or a Roman, Calderon or Shakespeare, whether Goethe or Schiller, Scribe or Dumas, attracted the soul of the young poet into the magic circle of their style and their forms.

The poet of the present begins, furthermore, as a beneficiary who richly receives, and is thereby incited to his own creative activity. He has, usually, no life occupation which binds him to a particular, definite field of poetry. It is again almost by chance, what species of poetical composition attracts him. He may let his sentiments ring out in lyrics; he may write a romance; at last the theater entices him,—the brilliance of the author's evening, the applause of the audience, the power of the received tragic impressions. There are few German poets who have not first commended themselves to the public, in a volume of lyrics, then tried their luck on the stage, and finally contented themselves with the more quiet success of a romance. Without any doubt, their poetic talent showed greatest capability in one of these directions. But as external relations laid no restrictions on them, and now one, now another field attracted more strongly, the circle in which their power moved with greatest freedom, did not come into fullest completion. The great secret of a rich creative activity is limitation to a single branch of the beautiful art. This the Hellenes knew very well. Whoever wrote tragedies, let comedy alone. Whoever used hexameter, avoided the iambus.

But the poet, also, to whom the creation of dramatic figures is a necessity, lives, if he does not stride upon the boards as an actor or director, apart from the theater. He may write or not. External pressure, a mighty lever to move talent, is almost entirely wanting. The theater has become the daily pleasure of the peaceful citizen, and collects not the worst, but not the most pretentious social element. In this large expansion, it has lost some of the dignity and loftiness which the poet might wish for the drama of serious style. There are brought on the stage, buffoonery, opera, comedy, forms and theories of life of different centuries. All is sought which can please, the newest, the most singular; and, again, what affords the great multitude most pleasure, thrusts all else aside.

The resources of material for the poet have become almost boundless,—the Greek and the Roman worlds, the Middle Ages. Sacred writings and poetry of the Jews and Christians, even the people of the Orient, history, legends of the present, open their treasures to the searcher. But this offers the disadvantage, that with such infinite material, a choice becomes difficult, and is almost an accident, and that none of these sources is in a condition to attract the German exclusively, or preferably. Finally, for the German, as it appears, the time has not yet come when the dramatic life of the people, itself, flows out richly and unimpeded. Gladly would we see in the appearances of the newest present the beginnings of a new development of national character, beginnings which do not yet contribute to art. That it is still so difficult for the dramatic poet to raise himself from the epic and lyric conception of character and of situations, is no accident.

But the poet must labor for the stage. Only in connection with the actor's art does he produce the best results which are possible to his poetry. The reading drama is fundamentally only a makeshift of a time in which the full power of dramatic creation has not yet appeared among a people, or has disappeared again. The species is an old one. Already among the Greeks pieces were written for recitation, and still more of the Latin recitation pieces have been transmitted to us. Among the Germans, the reading drama, from the early comedies of nun Hroswith, through the stylistic attempts of the first humanists, even to the greatest poem of our language, has a long history. Infinitely varied is the poetical worth of these works. But the employment of poetic form for dramatic effects, which renounce the claim of being the highest of their species, is considered, on the whole, a limitation, against which art itself and the interested reader protests.

In the pages of this book, the attempt has been made to show that the technical work of the dramatic composer is not entirely easy and free from pains. This kind of poetry demands more from the poet than any other. It demands a peculiar, but rarely found capability for representing the mental processes of men of significant and unusual power of action; a nature well tempered with passion and clearness of vision; a developed and certain poetic endowment, and a knowledge of men, as well as what in real life, is called character; an accurate knowledge of the stage and its needs must be added. And yet it is striking, that of the many who make incursions into this field of creative work, the most are only dilettanti friends of the beautiful; but just these choose the most exacting labor, and such a one as promises them the very least success. It is indeed serious work to write a romance which merits the name of work of art; but every educated person with constructive skill and knowledge of men, who has not attempted anything as a poet, may offer something readable, wherein single significant impressions of real life, what he has seen, what he has felt, are spiritedly interwoven. Why does the most capricious muse of all muses, so unapproachable, so ill-mannered toward everybody who does not wholly belong to her, — why does she attract cultured men, very capable men? What enemy of their life guides just such warm-hearted friends, who busy themselves with poetry during their hours of leisure from active duties, into a poetical field, in which the closest combination of an always rare constructive energy, with an unusual, firm, secure mastery of the forms of art, is the assumed condition of lasting success? Does a secret longing of man for what is most lacking in him, possibly, lead him astray? And does the dilettanti, just for this reason, seek to develop the drama in himself, because it is denied him, with all his poetic visions, to animate creatively his restless fluttering feelings in the body of any other form of art? Undeniably, the attempts of such persons to labor for the stage, are vain and hopeless. But for the poet who has been equipped for all his life with dramatic power, we wish, before all other possessions, a firm and patient heart. He must, however, bring to his employment still another means of advancement; he must feel quickly and joyfully what is charming in a subject, and yet have the deliberation to carry it within his breast till it is natural. Before he ascends the stage as creative genius, he must for a long time make himself intimate with the chief laws of creation; for he must understand how to prove whether a subject is useful, in the essentials. Even in this, judgment must from the first moment watch over his warm heart, where the charm of composition arises; a play which has failed, means to him, on the average, a year of his life lost.

The imagination of different poets does not seize upon material with equal rapidity; the beginner's seeking soul hovers lightly about any summit which offers itself, and the nest is built beneath the first budding branch. He who is warned by experience, becomes critical and tests too long. Often it is not an accident that suggests a subject to the soul, but the mood and impressions of the soul's own life, which attract the fancy in a definite direction. For the soul works secretly upon a piece before it finds hero and chief scenes; and what it demands from the material is that this may offer the possibility of certain scenic effects.

The difficulties which the various subjects and materials offer, have been made sufficiently prominent. But he who finds it difficult to decide, may consider that it depends on the power of his talents whether, in most events, they are changed into a useful action. A positive poetic power needs only a few moments out of legend, history, narrative, only *one* strong and momentous contrast, out of which to form an action.

If the dramatic poet of old times found these traits in the legend shortly before the destruction of the hero of the epic, it may yet be asked whether, in historical dramas, it is just as necessary to make the chief heroes of this sort the central figures in an action, that this may have its movements about them, their adventures, and their overthrow. How difficult and perilous it is to make use artistically of an historical life, has already been discussed. Let it not be objected that the greater historical interest which the heroes awaken, and the patriotic enthusiasm which the poet and the spectator alike bring to them, make them specially adapted to the drama. The old German history offers comparatively few heroic figures whose remembrance is dear through a great interest, in the present time. What to our people are the emperors of the Saxon, Frankish, Staufen, or Hapsburg houses? The purposes for which they conquered and died are perhaps condemned by the convictions of the present time; the struggles of their life have remained with no occurrences easily understood by us; for the popular mind, they are dead and buried. But further, the conscientious poet, before the not numerous historical heroes who still live in the memory of the people, will recognize new restrictions which narrow the freshness of his creative power. Just this patriotic sympathy which he brings with him, and expects from the hearer, lessens the superior freedom with which, as poet, he must hover over every character, and misleads him into special kinds of presentation or a sort of portrait sketching. If once, to one German poet, the dramatic figure of the great Elector has been successful, Luther, Maria Theresa, "Old Fritz," have only so much the more frequently failed.

But it is not at all necessary to make historical kings and generals, the heroes of an historical drama, which can be constructed advantageously on only a little period of their historical life. Much more agreeably and profitably may be exhibited the reaction which their lives have had upon the lives of others. How well has Schiller done this in *Don Carlos*, in *Mary Stuart!* The Phillip of the former play is a brilliant example, showing how an historical character is to be used as a partner in a play.

With the life of well-known historical heroes a multitude of figures is connected, of whom single characteristic traits have been reported; and these successfully incite free invention. These accessory figures of history, whose life and its events the poet has at his free disposal, are specially convenient. One treasonous act and its punishment, one passionate deed of hatred and its consequences, one scene from a great family quarrel, one defiant struggle or sly play against a superior power, give him an abundant material. And such traits and such incidents are found on every page of our history, as in the history of all civilized nations.

Whoever is conscious of his own power chooses his pictures confidently, rather from the materials not yet arranged for art, but found in the real life of the past, and of modern times, than from such stock as is offered him from the other species of poetry. For the serious drama, material taken from romances and modern novels is not of much account. If Shakespeare used material from novels, his sources were, in our sense of the word, only short anecdotes, in which, of course, an artistic consistency and a powerful conclusion are already present. In the elaborated epic narrative of the present, the fancy of the poet shows its power frequently, just in effects which are intrinsically hostile to the dramatist; and the embellished and agreeable elaboration of the men and the situations in the romance, may rather dull than sharpen the imagination of the dramatist. He will hardly do wrong to the property of another if he draws his material from this circle of invention. For if he is an artist, very little will pass from the creation of another over into his drama.

The tragic poet is able, of course, to invent his action without using any material already at hand. But indeed, this happens less often, and with more difficulty than one would suppose. Among the great dramas of our stage, just as it once was in ancient times, there are few which are not constructed from already used material. For it is a characteristic of the power of imagination, that it perceives more vividly and exactly the movements in the life of men, if it can attach itself to a particular figure and its adventures. The image which imagination discovers for itself is not so easily made firm and powerful, that there is inclination to put upon it steady and assiduous labor.

And yet one conviction the poet may keep in his quiet soul, that no material is entirely good, little wholly bad. From this side also, there is no perfect work of art. Every subject has its inherent difficulties and disadvantages which the art of the poet is so far able to overcome, that the whole gives the impression of beauty and greatness. These weaknesses are to be recognized, but only by the practiced eye; and every work of art gives the critic, from this point of view, occasion for the exercise of his functions. He who judges must be on the lookout, that in the face of this deficiency, he understands whether the poet has done his duty, whether he has used all the means of his art, to master or to conceal.

In the joyful consciousness that he is beginning a gallant work, the poet must sternly take his position over against what has become dear to him, and test it, so soon as his soul begins to move about the accumulated material to beautify it. He will have to make the idea distinct, and eliminate everything accidental that clings to it from reality.

To the first charm that becomes ardent in his soul, belong characteristic utterances of the hero in single moments of his inner agitation or powerful activity. In order to increase the number of the pictures of such moments, and in order to intensify the characters, he will earnestly seek to understand the real life and surroundings of his hero. He will, therefore, contemplating a historical drama, make good studies, and this labor will have rich reward; for from it appear to him a great number of visions and pictures which may be readily joined in imagination to the growing work. The grateful soul of the German has, for just such characterizing details, a very sensitive feeling; and the poet will therefore have need to be on his guard that historic costume, the historic marvellous and infrequent do not assume too much importance.

If he has in this way extended, as much as possible, the world of his artistic vision, then let him throw aside his books, and wrestle for the freedom which is necessary to him, in order to have free play upon the accumulated material. But let him hold fast in his mind, as a restraint upon his directing power, four rules: a short course to the action, few persons, few changes, and even in the first plan, strong relief to the important parts of the action.

He may write out his plans or not; on the whole, this is not of much account. Elaborate written explanations have this advantage, that they make single purposes distinct through reflection; but they have the disadvantage, that they easily clog the imagination, and render more difficult the necessary transformation and elimination. One sheet is enough to contain a perfect outline.

Before the poet begins his elaboration, the characters of his heroes and their positions relative to one another, must be clearly fixed in mind, in all essentials; and so the results of each single scene. Then during the labor, the scenes take shape easily, as does their dramatic course.

Of course, this serious labor before beginning to write does not exclude minor changes in the characters; for the creative skill of the poet does not stand still. He intends to direct his characters, and they impel him. It is a joyful process which he notices in himself as the conceived characters, through his creative power and under the logical force of events, become living beings. A new invention attaches to one already expressed—and suddenly there flames up a beautiful and great effect. And while the goal and resting-place by the way are fixed in his clear gaze, the surging feeling labors over the effects, exciting and exalting the poet himself. It is a strong inner excitement, cheering and strengthening the favorably endowed poet; for above the most violent agitation, through the fancy which in the most passionate parts of his action excites his nerves almost to convulsion and reddens his cheeks, the spirit hovers in perfect clearness, ruling, choosing freely, and ordering and arranging systematically

The labor of the same poet is different at different moments. Many of these appear to him brilliant; their previously perceived effects move his spirit animatedly; what has been written down appears only as a weak copy of a glowing inner picture, whose magic color has vanished; other moments develop perhaps, slowly, not without effort; the fancy is sluggish, the nerve-tension not strong enough; and sometimes it seems as if the creative power rebels against the situation. Such scenes, however, are not always, the worst.

The force of creative energy, too, is quite varying. One is rapid in the labor of writing down what is composed; to another, forms take shape slowly, and do not express themselves fluently on paper. The more rapid workers do not always have the advantage. Their danger is that they often fix the images too soon, before the work of fancy has reached the needed maturity. It is often possible for the poet to say to himself, that the inner unconscious labor is done, and to recognize the moment when the details of the effects have been rightly completed. The maturing of the pictures, however, is an important matter; and it is a peculiarity of creative power, that, as we might say, it is in operation at hours in which the poet is not consciously at his work.

Not unimportant is the order of sequence in which the poet writes out his piece. For one, the well trained imagination works out scenes and acts in regular succession; for another, it seizes on, now this, now that part of a great effect. What has been written comes to exercise a controlling influence on what is to be written. As soon as conception and vision and feeling are recorded in words, they stand face to face with the poet as an outsider giving direction; they suggest the new, and their color and their effects change what may come later. Whoever works in the regular order will have the advantage that mood develops from mood, situation from situation, in regular course. He will not always avoid making the way over which he would guide his characters, deviate a little and gradually, under his hands. It appears that Schiller has so worked. Whoever, on the other hand, sets before himself what the sportive fancy has vividly illuminated, will probably supervise more securely the aggregate effect and movement of his masterpiece; he will, however, now here, now there, during his labor, have to make changes in motives and in individual traits. This was, at least in single cases, the work of Goethe.

When the piece has been completed beyond the catastrophe, and the heart is exalted with gladness on account of the finished work, then the reaction which prevails everywhere after a highly excited frame of mind, begins. The soul of the poet is still very warm, the aggregate of beauty which he has created, and enjoyed while creating, the inner image which he has of its effects, he embodies still unconfused in the written work. It appears to him, according to the mood of the hour, either a failure or a vast success; on the whole, if in a normal state of mind, he will feel an inclination to trust to the power which his work attests. But his work is not yet finished, at least if he is a German. If the poet writes to have his work put on the boards, he does not, as has been said, yet feel, every moment, the impressions which the forces of his piece produce on the stage. Dramatic power works unequally also in this direction; and it is pleasant to notice the oscillations, in themselves. They may be perceived in the works of even great poets. One scene is distinguished by a vivid conception of the scenic action, the discourse is broken, the effects more exactly harmonized by transitions; at another time, it flows more agreeably for the reader than for the actor. And however rightly the poet may have perceived the sum of scenic effects, in detail, the sense of the words and the effect which, from the writing-table, they produce on the receptive mind, have had more of his attention than their sound, and their mediation with the spectator through the actor. But not only does the actor's right prevail touching a piece, requiring here greater prominence of one effect, there a modification; but the audience is, to the poet, an ideal body demanding a definite treatment. As the power of imagination was greater in the hearer in the time of Shakespeare, the enjoyment of spoken words greater, but the comprehension of connections slower, so the audience of to-day has a soul with definite qualities. It has already taken up much, its comprehension of the connections is quick, its demands for powerful movement are great, its preference for definite kinds of situations is inordinately developed.

The poet will therefore be compelled to adapt his work to the actor's art and the demands of the public. This business, the stage term of which is "adapting" (*aptiren*), the poet is able only in rare cases to achieve alone.

In the land of dramatic poetry, the cutting out of passages is wrongly in bad repute; it is rather (since for a time, the creative work of the German poet is accustomed to begin with a weak development of the sense of form) the greatest benefit which can be conferred upon his piece, an indispensable prerequisite to presentation on the stage, the one means of insuring success. Further, it is frequently a right which the actor's art must enforce against the poet; omissions are the invisible helpers which adjust the demands of the spectator and the claims of the poet; whoever with quiet enjoyment perceives clearly, at his work-table, the poetical beauty of a piece, thinks, not willingly, how the effects will be changed in the light of the stage. Even worthy authors who have chosen the most serviceable calling of explaining to their contemporaries the beauties of the greatest poets, look down with contempt on a tradesman's custom of the stage, which unmercifully mangles the most beautiful poetry. Only from the brush of a careful manager do the beautiful forms in the masterpieces of Schiller and Shakespeare come forward in the right proportion for the stage. Of course, every theater does not have a technical director, who with delicacy and understanding arranges the pieces so as to adapt them to the stage. Very adverse is the rude hand that cuts into the dramatic beauty, because it may present an inconvenience or does not conform to the taste of an exacting audience. But the misuse of an indispensable means should not bring that means into ill-repute; and if one would depreciate the complaints of the poets, over the misuse of their works, according to their justification, one would in most cases do them wrong.

Now in this adapting of a piece, much is merely of personal opinion; the justification of many single omissions is sometimes doubtful. The direction of a theater, which has, as a matter of course, the effect on a particular stage in mind, will have greater regard to the personality of its actors than will be welcome to the poet before the presentation. To an able actor who is specially esteemed by the audience, the director will sometimes allow to remain what is unnecessary; when he expects some good result from it, he may take an accessory effect from a rôle whose setting must be imperfect, if he is convinced that the actor is unable to bring it out.

The author of a work must not, therefore, leave the cutting down of his play entirely to strangers. He can accomplish it himself if he has had long experience with the stage; but otherwise he will need the aid of other hands. He must reserve to himself the last judgment in the matter; and he will not usually allow the management to abridge his piece without his approval. But he will, with self-denial, listen to the opinions of men who have had greater experience, and have an inclination to yield to them where his artistic conscience does not make concessions impossible for him. But since his judgment is hardly unembarrassed, he must, at the first intrusion of a benevolent criticism into his soul, wind about through uncertainty and inner struggles, to the great exercise of his judgment. The first disturbance in the pleasant peace of a poetic mind, which is just rejoicing in a completed work, is perhaps painful for a weak soul; but it is as wholesome as a draft of fresh air in the sultry summer. The poet is to respect and love his work so long as he bears it about as an ideal, and works upon it; the completed work must be dismissed. It must be as if strange to him, in order that he may gain freedom for new work.

And yet the poet must attempt the first adaptation, while his work is still on his desk. It is an unfriendly business, but it is necessary. Perhaps while he has been writing, he has perceived that some parts are necessary. Many moods which have been dear to him, he has more broadly elaborated than a slight warning of his conscience now approves. Nay, it is possible that his work, after the completion of his labor, in the moment when he considers it done, is still a quite chaotic mass of correct and artistic effects, and of episodical or injuriously uneven finish.

Now the time has come when he may repair what he slighted in his former labor. He must go through scene by scene, testing; in each he must investigate the course of individual rôles, the posing, the proposed movements of the persons; he must try to make the picture of the scene vivid at each moment on the stage; he must hit upon the exact position of the entrances and exits through which his persons come upon the stage and leave; he must consider, also, the scenery and the properties, whether they hinder or whether they aid as much as possible.

Not less carefully let him examine the current of the scene itself. Perhaps in this process he will discover prolixities; for to one writing, an accessory trait of character may easily seem too important; or the rôle of a favorite has come to the front in a way to disturb the aggregate effect; or the presentations of speeches and responses are too frequent. Let him inexorably expunge what does not conduce to the worth of the scenic structure, however beautiful it may be in itself. Let him go further and test the connection of the scenes of an act, the one aggregate effect. Let him exert his whole art to avoid the change of scenery within acts, and fully, when by such a change the act will be twice broken. At the first glance, the probable seems impossible to him, but it must be possible.

And if he considers the acts concluded, their combination of scenes satisfactory, then let him compare the climax of effects in the single acts, and see that the power of the second part corresponds also to the first. Let him raise the climax by an effort of his best poetic power, and let him have a sharp eye upon the act of the return. For if the hearers should not be satisfied with the catastrophe, the fault lies frequently in the previous act.

The time within which the action must complete itself will be determined for the modern poet by the custom of his contemporaries. We read with astonishment of the capacity of the Athenians to endure for almost an entire day, the greatest and most thrilling tragic effects. Even Shakespeare's pieces are not much longer than our audience might be accustomed to, were they given unabridged, in a small auditorium where more rapid speaking is possible; they would not require, on the average, more than four hours. The German unwillingly tolerates now in a closed theater, a play which takes much longer than three hours. This is a circumstance in no way to be disregarded; for in the time which extends beyond this, however exciting the action may be, there are disturbances by the withdrawal of single spectators; and it is not possible to hinder the restlessness of the remaining ones. But such a limitation is for this reason a disadvantage, that in view of a great subject and great elaboration, three hours is a very short time; especially on our stage, where from the time of a five-act play, during the four intervals between acts, fully a half hour is lost. Of all the German poets, it was notoriously most difficult for Schiller to complete his play within the stage time; and although his verses flow rapidly, his plays, unabridged, would take more time on the whole than the audience would be willing to give.

A five act play, which after its arrangement for the stage contains an average of five hundred lines to the act, exceeds the allotted time. As a rule, not more than two thousand lines should be considered the regular length of a stage piece, a limit which is conditioned by the character of the piece, the average rate of utterance, compactness, or lighter flow of the verse; also through this, whether the action of the piece itself demands many divisions, pauses, movements of masses, pantomimic activity; lastly, through the stage upon which it is played; for the size and acoustics of the house and habits of the place exercise an essential influence.

Of course, most of the stage pieces of our great poets are considerably longer;[28] but the poet would now vainly appeal to their example. For their works all hail from a time in which the present stage usage was not yet adopted, or was less compulsory. And finally, in our time, patrons take the liberty of old friends, to chose the time of their departure, with no respect to the convenience of others. He who would now be at home on the stage, must submit to a usage which cannot at once be changed. The poet will then estimate his piece according to the number of verses; and if this, as may be feared, extends beyond the stage time, he must once more examine it with reference to what may be omitted.

When he has ended this severe labor of self-criticism, improving his piece as much as possible, then he may begin to think of preparing it for the public eye. For this work, an experienced theater friend is indispensable. The poet will seek such a one in the director or manager of a great stage. To him he will send his work in manuscript. Now begins a new examination, discussion, abridgement, till the wording is satisfactory for the presentation on the stage. If the poet has accepted the changes necessary to make his piece conform to its purpose, it is usually put at an early date on the boards, in the theater in connection with which he has confidently ventured his fortune. If it is possible for him to witness this performance, it will be very advantageous to him, not so much, however, because he at once perceives the disadvantages and defects of his work (for to young poets, self-knowledge comes seldom so quickly), as because, to the experienced director of a stage, many weaknesses and redundancies of a piece first become apparent on its being performed.

It is true that a poet's first connection with the stage is not free from discomfort. His anxiety about the reception of the piece creeps close about his brave heart. The abbreviated parts always cause pain; and the striding on the half-dark stage becomes painful on account of the secret uncertainty, and his consideration of the imperfect rendering of the actor. But this connection has also something that is refreshing and instructive: the trials, the apprehension of the real stage pictures, the acquaintance with the customs and arrangements of the theater. And with a tolerable success of the play, the remembrance of the occasion remains, perhaps, a worthy possession of the poet in his later life.

Here a warning. The young poet is to take part for a few times in the rehearsal and in the presentation. He is to make himself acquainted with the details of the arrangement, the control of the entire combination, the wishes of the actors. But he is not to make a hobby of his pieces. He is not to persist in these too warmly ; he is not to seek the applause of new men too zealously. And, further, he is not to play the director, and is to mingle in the rehearsal only where it is positively urged. He is no actor, and he may scarcely, in the rush of rehearsal, correct what an actor is failing in. Let him notice what strikes him ; and let him discuss this later with the actor. The place of the poet is in the test of reading. Let him so arrange his work that if he has voice and practice, he himself may first read it aloud, and in a second rehearsal hear the actors read their rôles. The good influence which he may exercise, will be best assured in this way.

The great independence of different provinces has hindered in Germany the success of a piece on the stage in a capital city, from being a criterion of its success on the other stages of the country. A German play must have the good fortune of meeting success in eight or ten of the great theaters in different parts of Germany, before its course upon the rest may be assured. While the reputation of a piece which comes from the stronghold of Vienna determines, to a certain degree, its fate at the other theaters of the empire, the Berlin court theater has a still smaller circle in which it gives prestige. What pleases in Dresden displeases perhaps in Leipsic, and a success in Hanover insures no success in Brunswick. Meantime, the connection of the German theaters reaches so far, that the success of a piece on one or two respectable stages calls the attention of the others to it. Lack of attention to what is available everywhere is, in general, not the greatest reproach which at present can be cast upon the German stage.

If a piece stood the test of a first appearance, there were formerly two ways of making its use more extensive. The first was to print the piece and send copies to different theaters ; the other was to commit the manuscript to an agent to be pushed.

Now, the Society of Dramatic Authors and Composition at Leipsic, by its director, represents the rights and interests of its members among the different theaters ; it takes charge of the business of getting a piece on the stage, supervises its appearance on the boards, attends to the collection of the compensation (*honoraria*) and percentages. Whoever has to do with theaters, as a young writer, cannot now dispense with the support of this society; and it is to his interest to become a member.

But besides this, it is desirable for a young

author to come into close relations with the theaters themselves, their distinguished managers, leaders, and professors. In this way he becomes acquainted with theatrical life, its demands and its needs. Therefore, with his first piece let him take a middle course. If his manuscript is printed (let him not use too small type and make the prompter weep over it), let him give it for the majority of theaters to the director of the Society; let him reserve to himself, however, the transmission to and intercourse with some theaters from which he can expect particular demands. Besides, it is desirable to send copies of his work to individual prominent actors at famous theaters. He needs the warm devotion and generous sympathy of the actors; it will be friendly, too, for him to facilitate the study of their rôles. A connection thus begun with the highly esteemed talent of the stage will not only be useful to the author; it can win to him men of prominence, ardent admirers of the beautiful, perhaps helpful and faithful friends. To the German poet there is greater need of fresh suggestions, stimulating intercourse with cultivated actors, than any thing else; for, in this way he attains most easily what too generally is lacking, an accurate knowledge of what is effective on the stage. Even Lessing learned this by experience.

If the poet has done all this, on the reasonable success of his piece, he will soon, through a somewhat extensive correspondence, be initiated into the secrets of stage life.

And finally, when the young dramatist has in this way sent the child of his dreams out into the world, he will have sufficient opportunity to develop within himself something besides knowledge of the stage. It will be his duty to endure brilliant successes without haughtiness and conceit, and to accept sorrowful defeats without losing courage. He will have plenty of occasion to test and fashion his self-consciousness; and in the airy realm of the stage, in face of the actors, the authors of the day, and the spectators, to make something of himself worth more than being a technically educated poet —a steadfast man, who not only perceives the beautiful in his dreams, but who shall be honestly determined unceasingly to represent it in his own life.

INDEX.

A

Abasement of hero....... 71
Accessories, essential..... 71
Accessory figures.....11, 32, 44
Achilles...........62, 179, 283
Accidents............311, 314
Acropolis................ 148
Act defined.............. 192
  divisions of............ 210
  of ascent.............. 198
  of catastrophe.......... 201
  of climax.............. 199
  of introduction.......... 196
  of return.............. 201
Acting, Greek........149, 152
Action.........9, 19, 22, 27, 36
  about one person...... 305
  beginning of........... 29
  characters in...266, 272, 275, 276, 278
  chief thing............ 89
  double................ 44
  importance of.......... 61
  influence of character.. 42
  length of..........360, 361
  magnitude of.......... 61
  movement in.......... 66
  probability of.......... 49
  progress of........... 29
  qualities of........... 27
  rising............... 66
  reflex............... 74
  subordinate............ 44
  time of............... 360
  construction of......... 196
Acts, five...........192, 210
Actor and poet...300, 317, 319, 321
  and verse............. 331
Actors, number.......145, 148
  personality.........149, 257
  special rôles........... 330
  three................ 162
Adapting to stage....356, 358
Ægisthos.............76, 174
Æschylus..25, 42, 75, 77, 112, 115, 141, 143, 146, 148, 157, 162, 173
  Agamemnon.......... 77
  Furies............... 160
  Libation Pourers...... 173
  Persians............. 141
  Suppliants.........42, 141
After-creation........... 246
Agamemnon...42, 62, 177, 283
Aggregate effect......... 94
Ajax-57, 107, 112, 153, 154, 156, 158, 161, 162, 176, 177
Ajax..42, 45, 153, 161, 162, 164, 176
Alba.................. 225
Alcestis............... 112
Alexandrine........326, 329
Alphonso...........197, 201

Andromache ... 112
Anne ... 256
Antigone, 107, 137, 153, 154, 155, 158, 170, 311
  plot of ... 170
Antigone, 42, 75, 137, 152, 153, 154, 155, 158, 164, 170, 171, 175, 314
Antonio ... 197, 199, 200, 201
Antony and Cleopatra, 41, 71, 186, 245, 306
Antony .. 71, 72, 95, 100, 132, 256, 306
Apollo ... 173
Aphrodite ... 116
Aristotle, 5, 6, 26, 36, 86, 88, 89, 93, 98, 100, 103, 308
  Poetics of ... 6, 101, 247
Appiani ... 198
Arrangement of parts ... 210
Art and nature ... 299, 300
Artist as hero ... 68
Ase-god ... 292
Athene ... 57, 161, 162
Athenian ... 341
  play, length of ... 146
  poets ... 141
  stage ... 36, 69, 101, 112, 140
  tragedy ... 141, 171
Athenians ... 6, 7, 153, 158, 160, 163, 164, 202, 360
Attic criticism ... 3, 158
  market ... 144
  orations ... 148
  poet ... 91, 157
  stage, 112, 143, 147, 151, 152, 154, 181
  tragedy ... 282
Audience and poet ... 354
Auditor ... 50, 51
Auerbach ... 241
Aufidius .. 76, 131, 136, 184, 187, 258
Augustus Cæsar ... 216

B

Banquo ... 59, 186
Baumgarten ... 123, 197
Beaumarchais ... 120, 122
Benvolio ... 126
Berlin ... 364
Bertha ... 200
Black Knight ... 60
Blasius von Böller ... 10
Bohemia ... 50
Bohemian cup ... 221, 237
Bride of Messina ... 228, 242
Brunhild ... 285
Brutus, 82, 95, 118, 121, 123, 124, 132, 135, 136, 186, 229, 254, 255, 256, 316
Burleigh ... 212, 213
Burlesque play ... 146
Burnam Wood ... 136
Buttler ... 78, 204, 207, 237, 316

C

Cæsar Julius 59, 77, 95, 100, 121, 123, 135, 224, 254, 255 265, 337
Cæsura ... 325, 326, 327
Calderon ... 341
Camp ... 209
Canossa ... 39, 293, 294, 295
Capulets ... 32, 34, 122, 123, 126, 182
Casca ... 256
Cassandra ... 77

Cassius..119, 121, 124, 186, 224, 254, 256
Catastrophe 35, 114
act of 201
defined 137
difficulties in 138
double 206
in *Antigone* 171
law of 139
Sophocles 169
Cause and effect 311
Chance 35
Character of poet.....134, 366
Characterization—
methods of 250, 251
German..........250, 251
Romances 250, 251
in different poets 252
Shakespeare's 258
Characters 21, 246
action influenced by 42, 266, 272, 275, 276, 278
chief 249
prominence of........23, 231
defining 247
dramatic life of 22
female 262
humorous 310
in Æschylus 162
in Euripides 252
in Goethe 262
in *Hamlet*....190, 192, 193
in *Iliad* 290
in Lessing 259
in *Nibelungen* 290
in *Odyssey* 290
in Shakespeare 253
in Schiller 264
in Sophocles 165
impelling force of.......... 258
last century 262
laws concerning 303, 314
material and 266
minor changes in 332
motive not marvelous. 307
must be good and evil 308
must show one side .. 303
must guide action 310, 314
must be true 274
on stage 262, 297
personality of 310
subordinate 256, 259
unity of 304
weakness of 65
with portraiture 273
Charlemagne 50
Charles V............267, 268
Chief effect 71
hero conquered.....106, 107
reaction on..........106, 306
triumphant 106
Christian 343
Christianity 293, 294
Chorus 140, 142
Chrysomethis.......48, 173, 174
Clara 139
Claudia 199
Clavigo,...43, 49, 107, 119, 120, 122, 130, 223
Clavigo 120, 130, 262, 314
Cleopatra...........71, 72, 239
Climax 105, 114, 130, 131
act of 199
defined 128
scene 199
Sophocles 161
Clytemnestra,...42, 62, 77, 152, 166, 173, 283
Closed stage 195
Colloquy scenes 145

Color—
a creation 340
and language 339
and verse 323
in poet's soul 336
Comparisons 298
Complication 121
Concert speech 243
Conradin 97
Construction of drama 104
of scenes 210
in Sophocles 140
Contest on Attic stage 143, 147
Conti 120
Contrast—
in character 163, 164 171
in scenes 81
necessary 44, 223
Sophocles 161
Cordelia 135, 257, 310, 314
Coriolanus 27, 131, 187, 258
Coriolanus 76, 131, 135, 136, 187, 246, 258
Costume, changes of 214
Greek 147
historical 337
Counterplay 45, 104, 122, 128, 130, 185, 186
in introduction 120, 220
Counterplayers 125, 162, 180, 200, 235, 253, 272
Craftsman's rules 3
Creation and after-creation 249
Creon 45, 137, 152, 158, 165, 170, 171, 172, 211, 314
Crises three 114
Cromwell 96
Curtain, effects of 193, 215
Custom, national 69
Cutting out 356, 357

D

Daja 118
Danger in hero's leading 109
Davison 213
Deed concealed 77
Deianeira 101, 153, 166, 176
Delivery, methods of 336
Demetrius 238, 239, 263
Desdemona 121
Deveroux 316
Devil 55, 57
Dialogue scenes 170, 221, 223, 225
Dionysus 94
Dionysian festivals 141, 147
Director's help 362, 365
Director Scenes 212
Distributed voices 244
Don Carlos 101, 223, 306, 348
Drama—
acts in 195
Attic 18, 45, 112, 143, 147, 306, 334, 343
beginning of 25
construction of 104
double 206
five parts of 114
Germanic 181, 184, 193, 334
in two halves 105
modern 195
music and 88
reading 344
three crises in 114
Dramatic—
action 9
art 19
characters 246
characterization 249
composition 344

effects 21
sociable 52
expression 19
forces or moments 18, 115, 211
recitation 330
unity 43
verse 330
what is 19
Dramatis personæ 21
Dramatist and spectator 52
Double action 44
danger in 46
Double drama 206
Double tragedy 202
Dumas 341
Duncan 77, 119

E

Edgar 129
Edipus, see Œdipus
Edmund 135, 136, 311
Effect and cause 311
Effects, great only 134
heightened 79, 153
in supreme moment 76
of old drama 90
on Attic stage 151
opera-like 283
Eger 204
Egmont 41, 139, 240, 308, 316, 324
Egmont 225
Egyptians 54
Electra 48, 76, 152, 172
Electra 76, 77, 164, 167, 174, 176, 283
Elizabeth 55, 111, 132, 199, 202, 212, 306
Emilia Galotti 49, 109, 120, 122, 130, 197, 198, 199, 201, 259, 307
Emilia Galotti 76, 120, 130, 197, 198, 199, 207
Enobarbus 236
Epic 18
heroes 278-282
material 278, 279
narrative 36
tradition 279, 284
Episodes 47, 134
in Goethe 49
in Lessing 48
in Shakespeare 48
in Schiller 49
in Sophocles 48
Eschylus, see Æschylus
Euripides, 25, 26, 42, 43, 62, 89, 112, 115, 142, 143, 157, 158, 166, 173, 282, 284, 296
Alcestis 112
Andromache 112
Hecuba 26, 116
Helena 112
Hippolytus 116, 157
Iphigenia in Aulis 62, 283
Medea 157
Eurydice 171
Events behind scenes 73
on stage 74, 75
Exciting force or moment 52, 114, 115, 121, 123, 127, 172-5, 197
convenient arrangement 125
diverse forms 123
double 205, 206
no elaboration 124
Exposition 21

F

Fall of action............ 115
False unity 38
Falstaff 46
Faust. 57, 61, 116, 122, 189, 241, 263
Faust...122, 165, 227, 241, 263
Ferdinand.......100, 111, 127
Field of poet now........ 342
Figures of Sophocles..... 166
Final suspense........... 135
First player..149, 154, 158, 178
Five acts............192, 196
Force—
final suspense......135, 137
irrational 98
tragic 95
Formula 12, 13
Francis 267
Franconian............ 275
Frederick the Great...... 273
French.......28, 196, 326, 329
Friedland 204

G

Galotti............198, 307
German—
actor 317
hero.......110, 255, 290, 291
life 254
method 265
poets..110, 200, 226, 259, 281, 328, 342, 343, 350, 353, 356, 365
stage ..111, 116, 263, 285, 308, 337, 363, 364
Germanic drama.7, 81, 155, 181, 184, 193, 254, 334
Germans.... 24, 25, 28, 41, 42, 43, 45, 48, 54, 57, 75, 77, 80, 84, 110, 114, 120, 127, 128, 195, 199, 200, 223, 226, 246, 247, 265, 279, 284, 285, 289, 293, 308, 360
Germany..96, 98, 245, 253, 325, 341, 363
Ghost 186
Gloucester............ 45
Goethe..1, 2, 8, 43, 49, 61, 153, 227, 228, 240, 259, 262, 263, 278, 306, 329, 343, 359
Clavigo..43, 49, 107, 119, 122, 130, 233
Egmont.41, 139, 240, 308, 316, 324
Faust...57, 61, 116, 122, 189, 246, 263
Goetz von B.....40, 240, 308
Iphigenia........43, 49, 120
Natural Daughter..... 324
Tasso....43, 49, 112, 118, 197, 198, 199, 201
Goetz von Berlichingen, 40, 240, 314
Great poets compared, 110, 222
Great strokes............ 134
Greeks...28, 42, 43, 45, 47, 54, 70, 74, 75, 81, 86, 88, 90, 91, 92, 94, 98, 101, 102, 103, 113, 137, 144, 149, 153, 158, 246, 279, 281, 284, 289, 325, 335
Greek acting.........149, 152
actors 75
drama...3, 7, 18, 45, 306, 334, 343
costume 75
heroes.102, 158, 290, 291, 316

subjects 143
tragedy.... 100, 140, 222, 282, 335, 336
development. 141, 142, 143
Gretchen.... 122, 123, 226, 227, 262, 278
Ground mood............ 80
Gustavus Adolphus 268

H

Hades.................. 153
Haemon.. 45, 152, 158, 170, 171
Halle 269
Hamburgische Dramaturgie 6
Hamlet.. 118, 119, 186, 188, 190, 191, 192, 258
analysis of 190, 191, 192, 193
Hamlet.... 48, 59, 123, 124, 136, 165, 180, 186, 190–3, 218, 219, 220, 253, 314, 273, 287, 288, 289, 293, 295, 347
Hapsburg 347
Hebrews 54
Hecuba............. 26, 116
Helena 112
Hellenes.......... 24, 192, 342
Henry IV 45
Henry IV.......... 39, 293–5
Henry V 26
Henry VI 27
Henry VIII 273
Hercules 154, 176, 179, 181
Hero abasement of 71
and audience 308
and color 336
character 62
chief 306
classes unavailable for. 64, 65
double.......... 128, 305, 306
end of................. 128
German and Greek..... 290
Greek.......... 102, 158, 248
historical.... 273, 287–9, 293–5, 347
single 304
talked about........... 317
Heroic accounts......... 71
Hesse 267
Hexameter 326, 327, 342
Hindoos 54
Heightened effects 79
Hippolytus............ 116, 157
Historic idea 37
Historian and poet . 16, 39, 67, 266, 274, 349
Historical material. 15, 37, 41, 296, 336, 346, 347
heroes in....... 273, 347, 364
Hohenstaufen.... 275, 337, 347
Hohenzollern 70
Holy One............... 292
Homer 284
Hovel scene 188
Hroswith 344
Humor 129
basis of............... 310
in chief character...... 310
Hyllos.............. 101, 176

I

Iago.......... 83, 121, 253, 368
Iambic hexameter.... 326, 327
Iambic pentameter ... 324, 328, 329
in German and English 325

Iambus—
in Goethe 329
in Lessing 330
in Schiller 329
Idea of drama 9, 11
Idea of *Wallenstein* 205
Ideal figures 340
Idealization of history 40, 267, 296, 308
Iffland 111
Iliad 290
Immermann 325
Inheritance of poet 341
Intensification of soul 24
Introduction 114, 115, 118, 123, 196
structure of 120
Invention 11
Inventor as hero 68
Involution 121
Ion 112
Ion 103
Iphigenia 43, 49, 120
Iphigenia 45, 49, 50, 62, 103, 283
Iphigenia in Aulis 62, 283
Iphigenia in Tauris 112
Irrational forces 98
Ismene 45, 48, 165, 170

J

Japanese 54
Jews 343
Jocasta 101, 153, 172
Juliet 34, 35, 36, 95, 99, 100, 122, 126, 127, 135, 183, 187, 306, 311, 314
Julius Cæsar 27, 80, 82, 119, 120, 121, 126, 132, 153, 186, 244, 256
Julius Cæsar 59, 77, 95, 100, 121, 123, 135, 224, 253, 254, 255, 265, 337
Justice on either side 105

K

Kolb 127
Kätchen of Heilbronn 116
Keeping things silent 78
Kennedy 118 119, 167
Keynote 119
Kleist 280
Kriemhild 280
Kritz 10

L

Lady Macbeth 135, 188
Laertes 136
Laius 51, 171, 172
Language and color 339
and poet 338
Last suspense 115
Latins 24, 114, 250, 279
Laws, minor of characters 303
Lear 27, 45, 129, 135, 136, 186, 187, 188, 258, 311
Leicester 199, 202, 212
Length of play 360, 361
Leipsic 364
Leonora 199, 200, 201
Lessing 2, 6, 8, 43, 48, 84, 193, 198, 200, 201, 223, 259, 260, 262, 306, 307, 317, 365
Emilia Galotti 49, 107, 120, 122, 130, 198, 200, 201, 223, 254, 260, 262, 306, 307, 317, 365
Hamburgische Dramaturgie 6

Minna Von Barnhelm 49, 261
Nathan The Wise---49, 118, 261
Sara Sampson-120, 260, 261
Lepidus ---------------- 236
Libation Pourers--------- 173
Lichas ---------------- 154
Limits of poet ---------- 51
Laurence 33, 34, 35, 126, 127, 136, 313
Louise--------10, 100, 110, 128
Love and Intrigue--13, 28, 43, 76, 100, 107, 127, 264, 305
Love scenes-226, 228, 229, 278, 288, 298
Lucius ---------------- 82
Luther------------96, 273, 348

M

Macbeth-27, 60, 77, 83, 118, 119, 186, 258, 276
Macbeth-59, 123, 127, 136, 158, 186, 244
Macbeth, Lady-------135, 188
Macdonald ------------- 216
Macduff ------------188, 244
Maid of Orleans ---49, 60, 107, 116, 241, 265
Manager's help--------- 365
Manuel --------------- 265
Margaret -------------- 229
Maria Theresa---------- 348
Marie ----------------- 130
Marinelli-120, 197, 198, 199, 201
Martha ---------------- 227
Marvelous-------------- 53
Mary----120, 132, 197, 199, 200, 202, 306
Mary Stuart---13, 99, 111, 118, 119, 120, 122, 124, 125, 132, 197, 199, 200, 201, 202, 207, 208, 212, 348
Mary Stuart-----------95, 119
Material---------------- 14
from epic------------- 43
historical-----15, 296, 344-49
modern --------------- 157
novel----------------- 43
old ------------------ 344
onesidedness in-------- 44
Max----204, 205, 206, 207, 235, 237, 265, 271, 272, 306
Medea ---------------- 157
Melfort -------------260, 262
Melchthal------------198, 338
Menas ----------------- 236
Menelaus---------62, 161, 177
Merchant of Venice----- 83
Mercutio-----32 33, 48, 96, 126
Mephistopheles-57, 58, 122, 227
Merovingians----------- 286
Messenger scenes-72 116, 145, 170, 220
Middle ages-285, 286, 292, 293, 295, 343
Middle class life--------- 113
Milford --------------47, 128
Minna von Barnhelm--49, 261
Minna ----------------- 259
Minor rules------------- 303
Modern theater---------- 342
Molière ---------------- 250
Moments or forces------- 196
Moment of last suspense- 115
Monologue-----------219, 220
Moods unexpressed------ 70
Moor ------------------ 121
Moritz ----------------- 267

Mortimer....122, 123, 197, 199, 200, 212
Motive, broad.....82, 110, 123
  repeated............29, 42
Movement of action..... 66
Murder scenes........... 132
Mysteries on stage....... 58

N

Narrative remodeled..... 30
Nathan The Wise-49, 118, 260
Nathan................. 118
National custom......... 69
Nature and art.......299, 300
Natural Daughter....... 324
Neoptolemus-101, 158, 177, 178, 179, 180
Nessos.................. 101
New persons............. 187
New rôles............... 200
Nibelungen - 279, 284, 290, 327
Number of persons....... 216

O

Octavianus.............. 71
Octavio--204, 206, 237, 238, 271
Odoardo..............201, 307
Odysseus-42, 103, 161, 162, 165, 177, 178, 179, 180, 181, 280
Odyssey............281, 290
Œdipus at Colonos--7, 48, 51, 112, 150, 156, 160, 167, 174
Œdipus, King---107, 155, 171, 178
Œdipus....7, 167, 168, 171, 172, 175
Old Fritz............... 348
Old material.........350, 351
One hero................ 304
Opening scene........... 117
Opera like effects...... 283
Ophelia................. 189
Opposing characters..... 107
Orange.................. 225
Oration scenes.......... 132
Orestes....42, 76, 152, 165, 173, 174
Orsina.................49, 201
Othello, 14, 27, 83, 100, 107, 121, 122, 123, 130, 258
Othello.......45, 130, 310, 314
Otto.................285, 337

P

Parallelisms in verse..... 332
  in scenes.............. 82
  in German and Greek.. 334
Paris 34, 35, 36, 76, 99, 122, 135
Parody, Greek........... 92
Parricida..........49, 81, 202
Parts of drama.......... 114
  summary of............ 140
  women's............... 184
  arrangements.......... 210
Pathos scenes, 132, 142, 145, 170, 174, 177, 178
Paulet.................. 118
Pauses.................. 214
Penelope................ 280
People and poets........ 246
Percy................... 76
Peripeteia............ 101
Persians.............. 141
Personality of poet..... 17
Personification......... 248
Persons in Greek drama.. 42
Phillip................. 348

Philoctetes---101, 112, 138, 153, 174, 178
Philoctetes---164, 165, 167, 178, 179, 180
Piccolomini--118, 202, 205, 206, 207, 236, 305
Piccolomini-------237, 238, 270
Pilsen ---------------- 203
Play and counter play---- 114
order of parts-------- 169
Shakespeare's---------- 182
Sophocles' and Teutonic 155
spectacle ------------- 111
symmetry of ----------- 182
time of acting--167, 360, 361
Player, first--149, 154, 158, 178
second-----150, 154, 158, 178
third---150, 154, 180, 228, 229
Players, number limited-- 234
of Shakespeare's time - 182
Players and poets-300, 317, 319, 321, 355
Plot of *Ajax*------------- 176
Antigone -------------- 170
Electra ---------------- 172
Œdipus King----------- 171
Œdipus at Colonos----- 174
Philoctetes------------ 177
Trachinian Women---- 176
and poet--------------- 351
Poet as actor and director 342
and audience ---------- 354
books ----------------- 351
character ---------86, 134
field ------------------ 342
hero------------350, 351
historian--67, 266, 274, 347
limit ------------------ 51
material ---------346, 347
people----------------- 246
plan-------------------- 351
resources -------------- 340
stage ---------343, 362, 363
task ------------------- 31
tragedy---------------- 86
work ----------341, 344, 354
Poetic energy ----------- 253
truth ------------------ 50
Poetics, Aristotle's ---5, 6, 101
Poetics, Greek ---------- 247
Political history--------- 66
Polydorus --------------- 116
Polymnestor------------- 26
Polynices -----------170, 175
Pompey-------------235, 236
Posa -------------------- 306
Premises, monstrous of Sophocles ----------- 309
Presuppositions---------- 117
in Sophocles---155, 168, 309
in Teutonic drama----- 159
Prince of Homburg, 38, 70, 112, 139, 324
Probability of action----- 49
Prolixity---------------- 359
Prologue-------------115, 168
Prometheus -----------57, 166
Properties --------------- 338
Prose and drama-----323, 328
Protagonist-------------- 154
Public, influence of------ 309
Purification---- -------87, 93
Pylades------------------ 76
Pyramidal structure, 114, 153, 218, 225

Q

Qualities of action------- 27
Queen Mab-------------- 48
Questenberg, 118, 203, 207, 269

R

Raumer ... 275
Reaction, beginning of ... 99
Reaction in poet's mind ... 354
Reading drama ... 344
Recognition scenes ... 101, 145, 169
Recha ... 259
Reflex action ... 74
Reformation ... 288
Relief before catastrophe ... 136
Religious changes ... 292
Repetition of motive ... 82
Return action ... 115, 133, 166, 177, 186, 187, 188, 200
Revolution ... 101, 145, 169
Riccault ... 49
Richard III ... 27, 41, 118, 121, 122, 186, 229, 244, 256, 276
Richard III ... 59, 83, 136, 148, 186, 253, 304, 308, 316
Richmond ... 37
Rise of action ... 69, 115
  scenes of ... 128
Rising movement ... 125, 126
  rules for ... 125
Roderigo ... 83, 121
Rôles, celebrated ... 223
  chief ... 306
  collective ... 162, 341
  distribution of ... 149, 156, 162
  great, limited ... 304
  kinds of ... 143
  length of ... 148
  not interchangeable ... 320
  number of ... 133
  of Euripides ... 283
  of second half of play ... 316
  subordinate ... 256
Romans ... 24, 28, 95, 279, 289, 290, 308
Roman stage ... 195, 343
Romeo and Juliet ... 27, 30, 76, 82, 99, 118, 122, 123, 124, 187, 258, 305, 311
Romeo ... 32, 33, 34, 36, 95, 100, 123, 124, 127, 135, 136, 165, 182, 183, 187, 226, 306, 311, 316
Romulus ... 338
Rosalind ... 32
Rudenz ... 200, 306
Rules, craftsmen's ... 3
  minor ... 303
Rütli ... 198, 199

S

Sapieha ... 240
Sara Sampson ... 120, 260, 261
Sara ... 259, 260
Saxon ... 347
Scenes ... 210, 211
  balcony ... 227
  changed relation ... 224
  devices for ... 241
  dialogue ... 221, 223, 225
  director ... 212
  double ... 212
  ensemble ... 229-245
    battle ... 244
    camp ... 244
    devices ... 241
    difficulties ... 232, 233, 241
    galley ... 235
    mass ... 242
    pageant ... 241
    parliament ... 239, 240
    populace ... 240, 241
    rules for ... 231, 232

Rütli 238, 239
signature 237
time of 234
five parts of........... 217
in *Mary Stuart*........ 212
jumble in.............. 217
love....... 226–229, 278, 298
danger in............ 228
monologue 219
number of persons 216
order of parts........... 213
parallel 82
poets' 212
pyramidal form......... 225
sequence of........133, 353
structure 210
technique 223
third person in.......... 228
Scenery 338
shifting................ 215
Scenic contrasts.......... 81
Scythians............... 282
Schiller..2, 4, 8, 14, 17, 40, 43, 46, 49, 60, 61, 69, 78, 81, 107, 110, 132, 195, 208, 220, 227, 236, 240, 242, 259, 262, 263, 265, 268, 269, 271, 272, 298, 306, 316, 324, 341, 348, 354, 356, 360
Bride of Messina...228, 242
Demetrius..43, 238, 239, 240, 263
Don Carlos......43, 46, 348
Love and Intrigue...13, 28, 76, 100, 107, 110, 127, 264, 305
Maid of Orleans..49, 60, 107, 116, 241
Mary Stuart..13, 43, 46, 100, 111, 118, 119, 120, 122, 124, 125, 130, 197, 199, 200, 201, 202, 204, 207, 208, 212, 348
Piccolomini, 118, 202, 205, 206, 207, 236, 305
Robbers 263, 306
Tell...43, 46, 49, 81, 123, 197, 199, 200, 201, 202, 228, 238
Wallenstein...40, 43, 46, 72, 78, 107, 116, 119, 120, 202, 206, 207, 208, 220, 223, 228, 308, 311, 316
Camp 209
Death 206, 217
Scribe 341
Semiramis 337
Sequence of scenes....... 133
Serious drama 111
Sesina.................. 206
Shakespeare...7, 8, 25, 27, 29, 34, 40, 41, 43, 45, 46, 48, 58, 59, 62, 69, 71, 81, 82, 83, 107, 110, 113, 116, 118, 119, 120, 123, 128, 181, 182, 183, 184, 185, 186, 187, 189, 193, 196, 200, 227, 228, 235, 237, 241, 244, 245, 252, 255, 256, 258, 259, 273, 298, 306, 310, 314, 330, 341, 349, 354, 356, 360
Anthony and Cleopatra 41, 71, 189, 245, 306
Coriolanus..27, 130, 131, 135, 187, 258
Hamlet....118, 119, 186, 188, 190, 191, 192, 193, 258
Henry IV............. 45

Henry V. 26
Henry VI. 27
Henry VIII. 273
Julius Cæsar-27, 80, 82, 119, 120, 126, 132, 186, 244, 256
Lear-27, 45, 107, 129, 186, 188, 258, 311
Macbeth--27, 77, 83, 118, 119, 186, 258, 276
Merchant of Venice 83
Othello--14, 27, 83, 100, 107, 121, 122, 123, 130, 258
Richard III.-27, 41, 118, 121, 122, 186, 229, 244, 256, 276
Romeo and Juliet-27, 30, 76, 82, 99, 118, 122, 126, 133, 187, 258, 305, 311
Timon of Athens 62
Shakespeare's
actors 184
audiences 183
ardor for heroes 187
change of scenes 185
characters 253
characteristics 186
drama 189
heroes and action--185, 252, 258
method 185, 189, 258
spirits 58
stage 181
technique 184-193
times 184-194
Shylock 50, 253
Society of Dramatic Authors 364
Sophocles--7, 8, 25, 42, 43, 47, 75, 81, 91, 92, 98, 110, 112, 115, 137, 140, 141, 146, 147, 148, 149, 150, 153, 155, 157, 158, 160, 163, 166, 168, 169, 173, 174, 176, 178, 179
Ajax--112, 153, 154, 156, 158, 161, 162, 176, 177
Antigone--107, 137, 153, 154, 155, 158, 170, 311
Electra 48, 76, 152, 172
Œdipus at Colonos- 7, 48, 112, 156, 160, 167, 174
Œdipus, King--101, 107, 155, 171, 178
Philoctetes-101, 112, 133, 153, 177, 178
Trachinian Women-101, 153, 154, 176
episodes in 47
Soul processes 39, 104
Spanish 29, 222
Speech and reply 222, 229
Spectacle play 111
on modern stage 112
tragedy and 113
Spectator and dramatist 32
Spirits not dramatic 56
in comedy 57
in Shakespeare 58
Stauffacher 197, 238, 239
Stenzel 275
Stimulation 97
Structure of drama 104
of scenes 210
Struggle, tragic 85
of Greek hero 159
of Teutonic hero 159
Superhuman 55
Supernatural 55
Suppliants 42, 141

Suspense final............ 133
  force of............135, 137
Swedes......204, 206, 221, 311
Swiss....197, 198, 199, 201, 306

T

Tableaux................ 317
Tasso..43, 49, 113, 118, 197, 198, 199, 201, 359
Tasso........197, 201, 202, 314
Tecmessa.........45, 162, 177
Technique 4, 8
  not absolute 1
  not enough 322
  of versification......... 329
Tell....43, 49, 80, 197, 199, 200, 201, 202, 228, 238
Tell......... 197, 198, 201, 265, 306
Tellheim.............260, 262
Templer 260
Terzky 228, 237, 273
Testing 359
Teucros 153, 162, 177
Teutonic.......91, 94, 226, 254
Theatre, modern.......... 342
Thebes 103, 171, 175
Thekla..205, 206, 221, 228, 265
Theseus 158, 165, 175
Thoas.................. 50
Time of action........... 360
Timon of Athens........ 62
Tiresias 152, 158, 171
Tone color.............. 328
Trachinian Women..153, 154, 176
Tragedy 81, 87
  Athenian 140
  double 202
  Greek 222, 282
  influence of........... 87
  kind of second......... 111
Tragic, what is.........7, 84
  aggregate effect........ 94
  causal connection...... 97
  force or moment..95, 111, 115, 130, 131, 132
  in Greek drama........ 100
  in real life............ 99
  narrower sense......... 94
  place of 100
  scene of 99
  two meanings.......... 86
Trilogy..........147, 157, 173
Tristan 285
Trochaic tetrameter...... 325
Two arrangements....... 105
Two heroes............. 128
Tybalt ...33, 34, 76, 98, 99, 126, 127, 136

U

Unit, logical............ 213
Unity of action......9, 27, 36
  place 29
  time.................. 29
Unity, false............. 38
Unusual, the............ 54
Urians 238

V

Verona................. 30
Verse and color......... 323
  and drama 324
  dramatic recital........ 330
Vienna 364
Virgin Mary 56, 60, 61
Voices distributed....... 244
Volscians.............76, 185

W

Wallenstein-40, 43, 72, 78, 107, 116, 119, 120, 165, 202, 206, 207, 220, 223, 228, 308, 311, 316
Camp 209
Death 206, 207
five acts of 203
Wallenstein -16, 17, 40, 45, 203, 204, 205, 206, 207, 220, 265, 268, 269, 270, 271, 272, 306, 316
Walter Fürst............ 198
Weislingen 262
Will and deed 188
Witches in *Macbeth* ...60, 188
Women's parts 184
Work, poet and his....... 341
not easy 344
Worms.................. 267
Wrangel-204, 206, 207, 223, 269, 272, 311, 314
Wuoton 292
Wurm 127

NOTES.

NOTE 1, page 18.—Even Aristotle comprehended most thoroughly this first part of the poet's work, the fashioning and developing of the poetic idea. If, in comparison with history, he makes poetry the more significant and philosophical, because poetry represents what is common to all men, while history gives an account of the incidental, or special detail; and because history presents what has happened, while poetry shows how it could have happened,—yet we moderns, impressed with the weight and grandeur of historical ideas, must reject his comparative estimate of the two fundamentally different kinds of composition; we shall, however, concede the fine distinction in his definition. He indicates, in a sentence immediately following this and often misunderstood, the process of idealization. He says, IX., 4: "That which in poetry is common to humanity, is produced in this way,—the speeches and actions of the characters are made to appear probable and necessary; and that which is humanly universal poetry works out from the raw material and then gives to the characters appropriate names," —whether using those already at hand in the raw material or inventing new ones. (Buckley's translation is as follows: But *universal* consists indeed in relating or performing certain things which happen to a man of a certain description, either probably or necessarily, to which the aim of poetry is directed in giving names.) Aristotle was of the opinion, too, that a poet would do well at the beginning of his work to place before himself the material which had attracted him, in a formula stripped of all incidentals, or non-essentials; and he develops this idea more fully in another place, XVII., 6, 7: "The Iphigenia and the Orestes of the drama are not at all the same as those in the material which came to the poet. For the poet who composed the play it is almost an accident that they bear these names.

Only when the poet has raised his actions and his characters above the incidental, the real, that which has actually happened, and in place of this has put a meaning, a significance which will be generally received, which appears to us probable and necessary,—only then is he again to make use of color and tone, names and circumstances, from the raw material." Therefore it is also possible that dramas which have been taken from very different realms of material, express, fundamentally, the same meaning, or, as we put it, represent the same poetical idea. This is the thought in the passages cited.

NOTE 2, page 22.—The few technical terms used in this book must be received by the reader without prejudice and without confusion. In their common use for the last century several of them have passed through many changes of meaning. What is here called *action*, the material already arranged for the drama (in Aristotle, *myth*; in the Latin writers, *fable*), Lessing sometimes still calls *fable*, while the raw material, the *praxis* or the *pragma* of Aristotle, he calls *action*. But Lessing also sometimes uses the word *action* more correctly, giving it the meaning which it has here.

NOTE 3, page 28.—As is well known, unity of place is not demanded by Aristotle; and concerning the uninterrupted continuity of time he says only that tragedy should try as far as possible to limit its action to one course of the sun. Among the Greeks, as may be shown, it was only Sophocles and his school who, in the practice of their art, adhered to what we call the unity of place and of time. And with good reason. The rapid, condensed action of Sophocles, with its regular structure, needed so very short a part of the story or tradition that the events underlying it could frequently occur in the same brief space of a few hours which the representation on the stage required. If Sophocles avoided such a change of scene, as, for example, occurs in Æschylus's *Eumenides*, he had a peculiar reason. We know that he thought much of scenic decoration; he had introduced a more artistic decoration of the background; and for his theatrical day he positively needed for the four pieces four great curtains, which with the gigantic proportions of the scene at the Acropolis occasioned an immense outlay. A change of the entire background during the representation was not allowable; and the mere transposition of the *periakte*, if these had been introduced at all in the time of Sophocles, would be to the taste of an ancient stage director as imperfect an arrangement as the change of side curtains, without the change of background, would be to us. It may not be so well known that Shakespeare, who treats time and space with so much freedom, because the fixed architecture of his stage spared him from indicating, or made it easy for him to indicate the change of scenes, presented his pieces on a stage which was the unornamented successor of the Attic proscenium. This proscenium had been gradually transformed by slight changes into the Roman theater, the mystery-platform of the middle ages, and the scaffold of Hans Sachs. On the other hand, the same classical period of the French theater, which so rigidly and anxiously sought to revive the Greek traditions, has bequeathed us the deep, camera-like structure of our stage, which had its origin in the needs of the ballet and the opera.

NOTE 4, page 31.—The details of the novel, and what Shakespeare changed in it, may be here passed over.

NOTE 5, page 46.—It is a poor expedient of our stage directors to neutralize or render harmless the weakest of these groups, the Attinghausen family, by cutting their rôles as much as possible, and then depreciating them still more by committing them to weak actors. The injury is by this means all the more striking. This play of Schiller's should either be so presented as to produce most completely the effects intended by the author, in which case the three barren rôles, Freiherr, Rudenz, Bertha, must be endowed with sufficient force,—our actors can thus express their gratitude to the poet who has done so much for them; or else, the Tell action only should be presented as it may be most easily made effective on our stage, and the three rôles should be entirely stricken out,—a thing that is possible with very slight changes.

NOTE 6, page 47.—Even in the time of the Greeks the word, episode, had a little history. In the earliest period of the drama it denoted the transition from one choral song to the following: then, after the introduction of actors, first, the short speeches, messenger-scenes, dialogues, and so forth, which comprised the transitions and motives for the new moods of the chorus. After the extension of these recited parts the word remained, in the developed drama, as an old designation of any part of the drama which stood between two choral songs. In this meaning it nearly corresponds to our act, or more accurately, to our elaborated scene. In the workshop of the Greek poet it became a designation of that part of the action which the poet with free invention inserted as a richer furnishing, as a means of animating his old mythological material; for instance, in *Antigone*, that scene between Antigone, Ismene, and Creon, in which the innocent Ismene declares herself an accomplice of her sister. In this signification, an episode might fill the entire interval between two choral songs; but as a rule it was shorter. Its places were generally in the rising action, only occasionally in the return action—our second, and fourth act. Because with this meaning it denoted little portions of the action, which might indeed have originated in the most vital necessities of the drama, but which were not indispensable for the connection of the events; and because since Euripides, poets have sought more and more frequently for effect-scenes which stood in very loose connection with the idea and the action,—there came to be attached to the word this secondary meaning of an unmotived and arbitrary insertion. In *The Poetics* the word is used in all of the three meanings: in XII., 5, it is a stage-manager's term; in XVII., 8-10, it is a technical expression of the poet; in X., 3, it has its secondary significance.

NOTE 7, page 72.—The structure of the drama is disturbed by this irregularity in the ordering of the action, which appears like a relapse into the old customs of the English popular theater. The action offered in the material and the idea was as follows: Act I. Antony at Cleopatra's, and his separation from her. Act II. Reconciliation with Cæsar, and restoration to power. Act III. Return to the Egyptian woman, with climax. Act IV. Sacrifice of principle, flight, and last struggle. Act V. Catastrophe of Antony and of Cleopatra. But the deviation of Shakespeare's play from the regular structure is for a more profound reason. The inner life of the debauched Antony possessed no great wealth, and in its new infatuation offered the poet little that was attractive. But his darling dramatic figure, Cleopatra, in the development of which he had evinced his consummate, masterly art, was not a character adapted to great dramatic emotion and excitement; the various scenes in which she appears full of passionate demeanor without passion, resemble brilliant variations of the same theme. In her relations with Antony she is portrayed just often enough and from the most diverse points of view to present a rich picture of the vixenish coquette. The return of Antony gave the poet no new task with respect to her. On the other hand, the exaltation of this character in a desperate situation, under the fear of death, was a fascinating subject for him, and to a certain extent rightly so; for herein was an opportunity for a most peculiar, gradual intensification. Shakespeare, then, sacrificed to these scenes a part of the action. He threw together the climax and the return action, indicating them in little scenes, and accorded to the catastrophe two acts. For the aggregate effect of the play, this is a disadvantage. We are indebted to him, however, for the scene of Cleopatra's death in the monument,—of all that is extraordinary in Shakespeare, perhaps the most astonishing. That the accessory persons, Octavianus and his sister, just at the summit of the action, were more important to the poet than his chief person, is perhaps due to the fact that to the poet in advanced life, any single person with his joy and his sorrow must seem small and insignificant, while the poet was contemplating, prophetically and reverentially, the historical and established order of things.

NOTE 8, page 83.—The scene is, however, by no means to be omitted,—as indeed happens. Moreover, an abbreviation must make prominent the contrast with the first, the imperial hardness of the tyrant, the lurking hostility of the mother, and Richard's deception by a woman whom he despises. If our stage directors would not endure more, they might tolerate the following: Of the lines in the passage beginning,

Stay, madam, I must speak a word with you,

and extending to the end of the scene, to Richard's words,

Bear her my true-love's kiss; and so farewell,

numbered consecutively from 198 to 436, Globe Edition, the following lines might remain: 198–201; 203–206; 251–256; 257;

293–298; 300; 301; 310, 311; 320–325; 328; 330; 340–357; 407–418; 420; 422–424; 433–436.

NOTE 9, page 101.—Both of these expressions of the craft are still occasionally misunderstood. *Peripeteia* does not always denote the last part of the action from the climax downward, which in Aristotle is called *Katabasis*; but it is only what is here called "tragic force,"—a single scene-effect, sometimes only a part of a scene. The chapter on the *Anangorisis*, however, one of the most instructive in the *Poetics*, because it affords a glimpse into the craftsman's method of poetic work, once appeared to the publishers as not authentic.

NOTE 10, page 147.—That the choruses did not, as a rule, rush in and off again, but claimed a good share of the time, may be inferred from the fact that in Sophocles sometimes a brief chorus fills up the time which the player needs to go behind the scenes to change his costume, or to pass from his door to the side-entrance, through which he must enter in a new rôle. Thirteen lines and two strophes of a little chorus suffice for the *deuteragonist* whose exit, as Jocasta, has been made through the back-door, to change costume and reappear upon the stage as shepherd from the field side. Upon the stage of the Acropolis this was no little distance.

NOTE 11, page 147.—That a favorite order of presentation was from the gloomy, the horrible, to the brighter and more cheerful, we may infer from the circumstance that *Antigone* and *Electra* were first pieces of the day. This is known from *Antigone* not only by the first choral-song, the first beautiful strophe of which is a morning song, but also from the character of the action which gives to the great rôle of the pathos actor only the first half of the piece, and thus lays the center of gravity toward the beginning. In the most beautiful poem it would not have been advisable to entrust to the so-little-esteemed third actor (who, nevertheless, is sometimes shown a preference by Sophocles) the closing effects of the last piece, so important in securing the decision of the judges. In the prologue of *Electra*, also, the rising sun and the festal Bacchic costume are mentioned. The beautiful, broadly elaborated situation in the prologue of *King Œdipus* and the structure of

Ajax, the center of gravity of which lies in the first half, and which distinctly reveals the early morning, seem to point to these as first pieces. The *Trachinian Women* probably entered the contest as a middle piece; *Œdipus at Colonos*, with its magnificent conclusion, and *Philoctetes* with its splendid pathos rôle and reconciling conclusion, as closing pieces. The conjectures which are based upon the technical character of the pieces, have at least more probability than conjectures which are drawn from a comparison or collation of dramas which have been preserved, with such as have not been.

NOTE 12, page 148.—Six pieces of Sophocles contain an average of about 1,118 verses, exclusive of the speeches and songs of the chorus. Only *Œdipus at Colonos* is longer. If, again, the number of verses of each of the three players is on the average about equal, the tragedies of a day, together with a burlesque of the length of *The Cyclops* (about 500 verses for three players) would give to each player a total of about 1,300 verses. But the task of the first player was already, on account of the affecting pathos scenes and on account of the songs, disproportionately greater. Besides, much more must be expected from him. If in the three pieces of Sophocles in which the hero suffers from a disease inflicted by the gods (*Ajax, The Trachinian Women, Philoctetes*) the parts of the first player are summed up, (Ajax, Teucros, Heracles, Lichas, Philoctetes) there will be about 1,440 verses; and with the burlesque, there will be about 1,600 verses: and there is the effort required to carry through six rôles and sing about six songs. There is no doubt that, in the composition of his tetralogies, Sophocles gave attention to the pauses for rest for his three players. Each last tragedy demanded the most powerful effort; and it must also, as a rule, have demanded most from the first actor. That *The Trachinian Women* was not a third piece may be inferred from the fact that in it the second actor had the chief rôle.

NOTE 13, page 153.—In the extant plays of Sophocles, the assignment of rôles among the three actors is as follows, Protagonist, Deuteragonist, Tritagonist, being indicated by the numbers 1, 2, 3, respectively:—

King Œdipus: 1, Œdipus. 2, Priest, Jocasta, Shepherd, Messenger of the catastrophe. 3, Creon, Tiresias, Messenger.

Œdipus at Colonos: 1, Œdipus, Messenger of the catastrophe. 2, Antigone, *Theseus (in the climax scene). 3, Colonians, Ismene, Theseus (in the other scenes), Creon, Polynices.

Antigone: 1, Antigone, Tiresias, Messenger of the catastrophe. 2, Ismene, Watchman, Hæmon, *Eurydice, Servant. 3, Creon.

The Trachinian Women: 1, *Maid-servant, Lichas, Heracles. 2, Deianeira, Nurse (as messenger of the catastrophe), Old man. 3, Hyllos, Messenger.

Ajax: 1. Ajax, Teucros. 2, Odysseus, Tecmessa. 3, Athene, Messenger, Menelaus, Agamemnon.

Philoctetes: 1, Philoctetes. 2, Neoptolemos. 3, Odysseus, Merchant, Heracles.

Electra: 1, Electra. 2, Warden, Chrysothemis, Ægisthos. 3, Orestes, Clytemnestra.

The rôles marked * are uncertain. Besides the three actors, the Attic stage always had several accessory players for dumb-show rôles: thus in *Electra*, Pylades; in *The Trachinian Women*, the especially distinguished rôle of Iole in which perhaps Sophocles would present to the public a young actor whom he esteemed. It is probable that these accessory players sometimes relieved the actors of less important subordinate rôles,—for example, in *Antigone*, Eurydice, which is treated very briefly; and in *The Trachinian Women*, the maid-servant of the prologue. How else could they test their voices and their powers? Such aid as was rendered by characters disguised from the audience by masks, was not reckoned playing. The accessory actors were also needed as representatives of the three players upon the stage, if the presence of a mask was desirable in a scene, and the player of this scene must at the same time assume another rôle; then the accessory player figured in like costume and the required mask, as a rule without saying any lines; but sometimes single lines must be given him. Thus Ismene, in the second half of *Œdipus at Colonos*, is represented by an accessory player, while the player himself represents Theseus and Polynices. This piece has the peculiarity that at least at the climax, one scene of Theseus is presented by the second actor, the player of Antigone, while the remaining scenes of this rôle are presented by the third actor. If the player had practiced the voice, and so forth, this substitution for a single scene did not offer special difficulty. It is possible, however, that the player of the rôle of Antigone, also gave the first Theseus scene. Antigone has gone into the grove in the background, in order to watch her father; she may very conveniently appear again as Theseus, while a stage-walker goes up and down in her mask. If even in this play, a fourth actor had taken part, in any rôle of importance, some account would have come to us of what even at that time would have been a striking innovation.

NOTE 14, page 155.—Upon our stage every play has one first hero, but more chief rôles; not frequently is one of these more ample and of deeper interest than that of the first hero, as, for example, the rôle of Falstaff in *Henry IV.*

NOTE 15, page 156.—The presuppositions of *The Trachinian Women* are, so far as Deianeira is concerned, very simple; but Heracles is the first hero, and his preparation for being received among the gods was the master-stroke of the play.

NOTE 16, page 156.—It is impossible just in Sophocles, from the extant names of lost plays and from scattered verses, to come to any conclusion as to the contents of the plays. What one might think from the tradition to be the contents of the play, could often prove to be only the contents of the prologue.

NOTE 17, page 178.—Prologue: Neoptolemos, Odysseus.
Chorus and Neoptolemos in Antiphone—

Ascent of Action,	1. Messenger scene with recognition,	Philoctetes, Neoptolemos.
	2. Messenger scene,	The same, and Merchant.
	3. Recognition scene (of the bow),	Philoctetes, Neoptolemos.

Choral song—

Climax,	1. Double pathos scene,	Philoctetes, Neoptolemos.
Tragic Force,	2. Dialogue scene,	The same, Odysseus.

Chorus and Philoctetes in Antiphone—

Falling Action and Catastrophe,
1. Dialogue scene, Neoptolemos, Odysseus.
2. Dialogue scene, Philoctetes, Neoptolemos; afterward Odysseus.
3. Announcement and conclusion, Philoctetes, Neoptolemos, Heracles.

NOTE 18, page 183.—The "balcony scene" belongs, on our stage, at the end of the first act, not in the second; but this makes the first act disproportionately long. It is a disadvantage that our (German) division of plays often makes a break in the action where a rapid movement is demanded, or only a very short interruption is allowed.

NOTE 19, page 208.—Let this structure be represented by means of lines. (See page 115.)

1. A DRAMA, such as did not lie in Schiller's plan. Idea: A perfidious general endeavors to make the army desert its commander, but is deserted by his soldiers and put to death.
   a. Exciting force: inciting to treason.
   b. Rising action: certain stipulations with the enemy.
   c. Climax: apparent success; the subtly sought signature of the generals.
   d. Return action: the conscience of the army is awakened.
   e. Catastrophe: death of the general.
2. SCHILLER'S *Wallenstein* without *The Piccolomini*. Idea: Through excessive power, intrigues of opponents, and his own proud heart, a general is betrayed into treason; he seeks to make the army desert its commander, etc.

   In this a, b, c, rising action to climax; inner struggles and temptations. 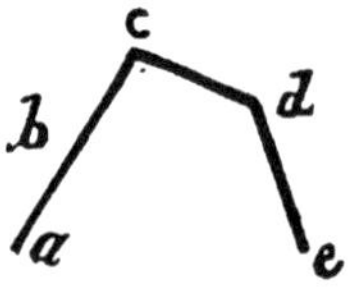
   a. Questenberg in camp, and separation from emperor.
   b. Testing the generals; banquet scene.
   c. Climax: the first act of treason; for example, the treating with Wrangel.
   cd. Attempts to mislead the army.
   d. Return action: the conscience of the soldiers is awakened.
   e. Catastrophe: death of Wallenstein.

THE DOUBLE DRAMA.

A. *The Piccolomini*, indicated by the dotted lines.

B. *Wallenstein's Death*, indicated by plain lines.

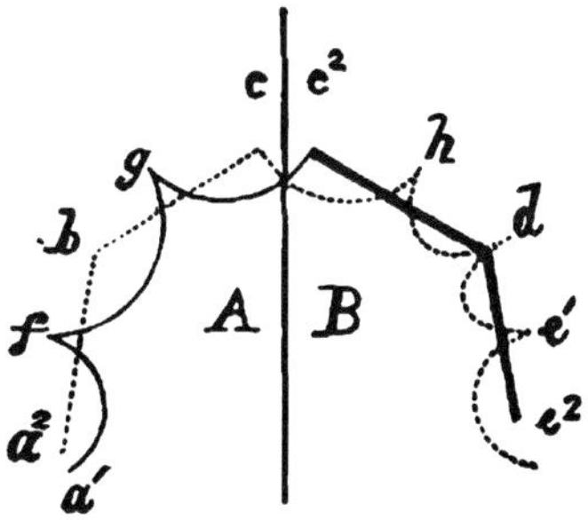

aa. The two exciting forces, a′, the generals and Questenberg, for the combined action; a^2, Max's and Thekla's arrival for *The Piccolomini*.

cc. The two climaxes, c, release of Max from Octavio, at the same time, catastrophe of *The Piccolomini*; c^2, Wallenstein and Wrangel, at the same time the exciting force of *Wallenstein's Death*.

ee. The two concluding catastrophes, e′, of the lovers, and e^2, of Wallenstein. Further, b, the love scene between Max and Thekla is the climax of *The Piccolomini*; f and g are the scenes interwoven from *Wallenstein's Death*: audience of Questenberg, and banquet, the second and fourth acts of *The Piccolomini*; h, d, and e′ are scenes interwoven from *The Piccolomini* and *Wallenstein's Death*: Octavio's intrigue, the departure of Max, the announcement of his death, together with Thekla's flight,—the second, third, and fourth acts, d, is the scene of the cuirassiers, at the same time the climax of the second drama.

NOTE 20, page 212.—In printing our plays, it frequently ippens that within acts, only those scenes are set off and num-:red which demand a shifting of scenery. The correct method, ›wever, would be to count and number the scenes within an :t according to their order of succession; and where a change scenery is necessary, and must be indicated, add to the current scene number the word "change," and indicate the charac-r of the new stage setting.

NOTE 21, page 237.—The act is in two parts. The first preparatory part contains three short dramatic components: the entrance of Max, the submitting of the forged documents by the intriguers, Buttler's connection with them. At this point the great conclusion begins, introduced by the conversation of the servants. The carousing generals must not be seen during the entire act in the middle and back ground: the stage presents to better advantage an ante-room of the banquet hall, separated from this by pillars and a rear wall, so that the company, previous to its entrance at the close, is seen only indistinctly and only an occasional convenient call and movement of groups are noticed. In *Wallenstein*, Schiller was still a careless stage director; but from the date of that play he became more careful in stage arrangement. Among the peculiarities of clear portrayal in this scene, belongs the unfeeling degradation of Max. It is wonderfully repeated by Kleist in *The Prince of Homburg*. Shakespeare does not characterize dreamers by their silence, but by their distracted and yet profound speeches.

NOTE 22, page 308.—Of course *Emilia Galotti* must be represented in the costume of the time, 1772. The piece demands another consideration in acting. From the third act, the curtain must not be dropped for pauses between acts; and these should be very short.

NOTE 23, page 361.—Twenty of our great dramas have the following lengths in verses:

Don Carlos - -	5,471	*Othello* - - -	3,133
Maria Stuart -	3,927	*Coriolanus* - -	3,124
Wallenstein's Death -	3,865	*Romeo and Juliet* -	2,979
Nathan the Wise -	3,847	*Bride of Messina* -	2,845
Hamlet - - -	3,715	*The Piccolomini* -	2,669
Richard III. - -	3,603	*Merchant of Venice*	2,600
Torquato Tasso -	3,453	*Julius Cæsar* - -	2,590
Maid of Orleans -	3,394	*Iphigenia* - -	2,174
William Tell - -	3,286	*Macbeth* - - -	2,116
King Lear - -	3,255	*Prince of Homburg*	1,854

These figures do not pretend to absolute correctness, since the incomplete verses are to be deducted; and the prose passages, in which Shakespeare is especially rich, admit of only a rough estimate. The prose plays, *Emilia Galotti, Clavigo, Egmont, Love and Intrigue,* correspond more nearly to the length of the plays of our own time. Of the dramas in verse, enumerated above, only the last three can be presented entire, without that abbreviation which is necessary on other grounds. It would require six hours to play all of *Don Carlos,* which in length exceeds all bounds.

Since *Wallenstein's Camp*—together with the lyric lines—has 1,105 rapid verses, the three parts of the dramatic poem, *Wallenstein,* contain 7,639 verses; and their representation on the stage, the same day, would require about the same time as the *Oberammergau Passion Play.* No single chief rôle is so comprehensive that it would place an excessive burden upon an actor to carry it through in a single day.

CPSIA information can be obtained at www.ICGtesting.com
Printed in the USA
BVOW030609140312

284915BV00006B/11/P